Drug Abuse Bibliography

for 1970

Drug Abuse Bibliography
for 1970

compiled by
Jean Cameron Advena

The Whitston Publishing Company
Incorporated
1971

PREFACE

This is the first supplement to DRUGS OF ADDICTION
AND NON-ADDICTION, THEIR USE AND ABUSE, A COMPREHENSIVE
BIBLIOGRAPHY, 1960-1969, compiled by Joseph Menditto
(Whitston, 1970). It will be succeeded by annual sup-
plements which will be cumulated each five years.

The arrangement is slightly different from that of
the original volume. Although it is basically, like
that volume, a title bibliography with an author index;
interfiled in this basic arrangement are entries under
as logical as possible subject heads. That is, since
subject heads inclusions are essentially a matter of
intent of the indexer, the user is free to ignore what
may appear to him to be defective intent. The following general considerations were used in arranging matter by subject. Articles dealing with diagnosis, which
is not used as a subject head here, were filed with
those dealing with detection under "Detection;" in general, articles filed under "Treatment" deal with inpatient activity, those under "Rehabilitation and Therapy" with outpatient activity; articles dealing with
hashish are found under "Hashish," and not "Cannabis,"
although both subject heads are used--that is, the
more generic subject heads deal in general with more
inclusive subjects.

In general, even trivia has been included in this
annual index on the grounds that it is of some, if
only minor, immediate interest. On the same grounds,
however, it will be deleted from cumulations. All
articles in foreign languages are translated with no
comment.

SUBJECT HEADINGS USED IN THIS BIBLIOGRAPHY

Aerosol Abuse
Amine Abuse
Amphetamines
Amyl Nitrate Abuse
Analgesic Abuse
Analgesics
Antagonists
Anticoagulants Abuse
Architecture
Arthur Kill Rehabilitation
    Center
Awareness House Project
Barbiturates
Behavior
Benzedrex Abuse
Bibliography
Blue Velvet Abuse
Business and Drugs
Business and Industry and
    Drugs
California Civil Addict
    Program
Cannabis
Catecholamine Abuse
Catha Edulis
Chloramphenicol Abuse
Chlordiazepoxide
Chromosomes and Drugs
Cirrhosis
Clinicians and Drugs
Cocaine
College Students and Drugs
Commissions on Drugs
Committee on Safety of Drugs
Complications
Cyclamates
Cyclazocine
Dagga
Dentistry and Drugs
Detection
Dextromorphan
Diazepam Abuse
Diet and Drugs
Diet Pill Abuse

Dimyril Abuse
Diphenoxylate
Diphenylhdantoin
Dopamine and Drugs
Drinamyl Abuse
Education
Endocarditis
Epidemiology
Ethanol Abuse
Etiology
Federal Drug Programs
Fenfluoramine
Films
Glossaries
Glue Sniffing
Glutethimide Abuse
Hallucinogens
Hashish
Heminevrin
Hepatitis and Drugs
Heroin
Hypnosis and Drugs
Industry and Drugs
Infants and Drugs
Ipecac
Isoprenaline Abuse
Jews and Drugs
Johns Hopkins Hospital Drug
    Abuse Center
Journalism and Drugs
LSD
Law Enforcement
Laws and Legislation
Lexington Hospital
Liver Diseases and Drugs
Lomotil
Marijuana
Mephentermine Abuse
Meprobamate Abuse
Methadone
Methadrine
Mexican-Americans and Drugs
Morphine
Mortality

ii

BOOKS

Aronoff, Leah S. DRUG ABUSE: A NEW CHALLENGE FOR THE PLANNER. 1970, Council of Planning Librarians. 21 p., $2.00.

Ball, John C. and Carl D. Chambers. EPIDEMIOLOGY OF OPIATE ADDICTION IN THE U.S. 1970, C. C. Thomas.

Becker, Howard S. OUTSIDERS: STUDIES IN THE SOCIOLOGY OF DEVIANCE. 1970, Free Press. $6.50.

Bejerot, Nils. ADDICTION AND SOCIETY. 1970, C. C. Thomas.

Bennett, James C. and George D. Demos, editors. DRUG ABUSE AND WHAT WE CAN DO ABOUT IT. 1970, C. C. Thomas.

Bergel, Franz and D. R. A. Davies. ALL ABOUT DRUGS. With the collaboration of Peter Ford. 1970, Nelson and Horizon. x+203 p., SBN 17-147401-5.

Birdwood, George. WILLING VICTIM: A PARENT'S GUIDE TO DRUG ABUSE. 1970, Humanities. $5.25, ISBN 0-391-00040-3.

Blachly, Paul H. SEDUCTION: A CONCEPTUAL MODEL IN DRUG DEPENDENCIES AND OTHER CONTAGIOUS SOCIAL ILLS. 1970, C. C. Thomas.

-- editor. DRUG ABUSE: DATA AND DEBATE. 1970, C. C. Thomas.

Blake, John B., editor. SAFEGUARDING THE PUBLIC: HISTORICAL ASPECTS OF MEDICINAL DRUG CONTROL. 1970, Johns Hopkins. $7.50, ISBN 0-8018-1054-X.

Byrd, Oliver E. MEDICAL READINGS ON DRUG ABUSE. 1970, A-W. $3.95, ISBN 0-201-00748-7.

California Department of the Youth Authority. Division of Research. A FINAL EVALUATION OF THE NARCOTIC CONTROL PROGRAM FOR YOUTH AUTHORITY PAROLEES by Chester F. Roberts, Jr. 1970, The Department. Research Department No. 58. State Office Building 1. Sacramento, California 95814.

Cassel, Russell N. DRUG ABUSE EDUCATION. 1970, Chris Mass. $5.95, ISBN 0-8158-024-5.

Cassens, James. CHRISTIAN ENCOUNTERS: DRUGS AND DRUG ABUSE. 1970, Concordia. $1.50 paper.

Coles, Robert, et al. DRUGS AND YOUTH. 1970, Liveright. $4.95, ISBN 0-87140-501-6.

Conte, Anthony E. and Eugene R. Mason. DRUG ABUSE: A CHALLENGE FOR EDUCATION. 1970, New Jersey Urban Schools Development Council, 1000 Spruce Street, Trenton, New Jersey 08638. $2.50.

Council of State Governments. STATE DRUG ABUSE CONTROL. 1970, The Council. LC 77-147130.

Einstein, Stanley. USE AND MISUSE OF DRUGS: A SOCIAL DILEMMA. (Health Service). 1970, Wadsworth Publishing. $1.25 paper.

Erlich, Lillian and Child Study Association of America Staff. YOUR CHILD AND DRUGS. 1970, Child Study. $2.00, ISBN 0-87183-238-0.

Garmon, William S., and Phil Strickland. HOW TO FIGHT THE DRUG MENACE. 1970, Broadman. $1.50. (Inner Circle Book Service).

Governor's Conference on Drug Abuse. PROCEEDINGS, ATLANTA, GEORGIA, OCTOBER 2-3, 1970, Bureau of State Planning and Community Affairs, 270 Washington Street, SW, Atlanta 50334.

Great Britan. Home Office. Department of Health and Social Security. THE AMPHETAMINES AND LYSERGIC ACID DIETHYLAMIDE (LSD): THE REPORT BY THE ADVISORY COMMITTEE ON DRUG DEPENDENCE. 1970, The Department. H.M. Stationery Office, British Information Services.

Greenberg, Harvey R. WHAT YOU SHOULD KNOW ABOUT DRUGS AND DRUG ADDICTION. (Grades 5-11). 1970, Four Winds, School Book Service. $4.75.

Hart, Harold, editor. DRUGS; FOR AND AGAINST. Discussion by experts on how to handle one of the prime problems of our day. 1970, Hart.

-- WHAT SHOULD WE DO ABOUT DRUGS. 1970, Hart. $7.50.

Horman, Richard and Alan Fox. DRUG AWARENESS. 1970,

Avon. $1.45 paper.

Imlah, Norman. DRUGS AND MODERN SOCIETY. 1970, Chapman, Geoffrey. ISBN 0-2235-48929-5.

International Narcotic Enforcement Officers Association. 1971 DIRECTORY. 1971, The Association.

Jones, Kenneth L., etal. DRUGS, ALCHOL AND TOBACCO. 1970, Harper and Canfield. $2.50, ISBN 0-06-384330-7; 1970, Canfield. $2.75. Text edition.

-- DRUGS AND ALCOHOL 1969, Har-Row. $2.75, ISBN 0-06-043426-0.

Kaplan, John. MARIJUANA - THE NEW PROHIBITION. 1970, World, Nelson, Foster and Scott.

Kaplan, Robert. DRUG ABUSE: PERSPECTIVES ON DRUGS. (Contemporary Topics in Health Science Series). 1970, Wm. C. Brown. ISBN 0-697-07328-9.

Krystal, Henry and Herbert Raskin. DRUG DEPENDENCE AND ASPECTS OF EGO FUNCTIONS. 1970, Wayne State University Press. $5.95, ISBN 0-8143-1419-8.

Lecker, Sidney and William Pigott. COPING WITH DRUG ABUSE (Montreal, Quebec). (Canada's Mental Health Supplement No. 64). Mental Health Division. Department of National Health and Welfare, Ottawa, Ontario. 13 p.

Leech, Kenneth. PASTORAL CARE AND THE DRUG SCENE. 1970, Allenson. $4.25.

Leinwand, Gerald, editor. DRUGS. (Problems of American Society Series). 1970, WSP. $ .75, ISBN 0-671-47185-6.

Louria, Donald B. DRUG SCENE. 1970, Bantam. $ .95, N5760.

Lowrie, Donald. DRUG ABUSE: A GUIDE FOR PARENTS, EDUCATORS AND LEGISLATORS. 1970, McGraw. $5.95.

Marin, Peter and Allen Y. Cohen. PARENTS GUIDE TO ADOLESCENCE AND DRUGS. 1970, Har-Row. $5.95, ISBN 0-06-012818-6.

Marr, John S. GOOD DRUG AND THE BAD DRUG. (Grade 3 up). 1970, M. Evans. $3.95.

MEET THE PRESS: John E. Ingersol, Director of Bureau
of Narcotics and Dangerous Drugs. 1970, Merkle.
9p. (v.14:33), $.10 with sae. Television and radio
interview, August 16, 1970.

Menditto, Joseph. DRUGS OF ADDICTION AND NON-ADDICTION,
THEIR USE AND ABUSE; A COMPREHENSIVE BIBLIOGRAPHY 1960
1969. 1970, Whitston. iii+315 p.. $11.50.

Milbauer, Barbara. DRUG ABUSE AND ADDICTION: A MANUAL
FOR PARENTS AND TEENAGERS. 1970, Crown.

Moore, Robin. FRENCH CONNECTION: THE WORLD'S MOST CRU-
CIAL NARCOTICS INVESTIGATION. 1970, Bantam. $ .95,
N5369.

Moreau, J. HASHISH AND MENTAL ILLNESS. 1970, Harlequin-
Raven.

New Jersey Department of Education. Division of Curricu-
lum and Instruction. BIBLIOGRAPHY OF DRUG EDUCATION
MATERIALS. 1970, The Department. 225 West State
Street, Trenton, New Jersey. 08625.

New Jersey. Governor. DRUG ABUSE-PROBLEM OF THE DECADE!
Special message of William T. Cahill, governor of New
Jersey to the Legislature, April 27, 1970. 1970, The
Governor. 26 p. State House, Trenton, New Jersey
08625.

New Jersey. Legislature. Public hearing before Senate
committee on air, water pollution and public health,
and Assembly committee on law, public safety and defense, on pending narcotics legislation, held Trenton, New Jersey, September 9, 1970. 1970, The Legislature. 76+213 p. State House, Trenton, New Jersey
08625.

New York. New York Human Resources Administration.
Addiction Services Agency. SOMEONE CLOSE TO YOU IS
ON DRUGS: CAN NEW YORK CITY'S NEW PROGRAM HELP YOU
DO SOMETHING ABOUT IT? 1970, The Administration.
Unpaged. 71 Worth Street, New York, N. Y. 10013.

New York. New York Human Resources Administration.
Community Information Office. NARCOTIC SERVICES
DIRECTORY. 1970, The Administration. 42 p. 220
Church Street, New York, N. Y. 10013.

New York. New York Office of the Comptroller. Research and Liaison Unit. DRUG ADDICTION AND THE AD-

MINISTRATION OF JUSTICE. 1970, The Office. 28+22 p.,
Free. 625 Municipal Building, New York, N. Y. 10007.

99+FILMS ON DRUGS. 1970, New York Educational Film Li-
brary Association, 17 West 60th Street, New York,
N.Y. 10023. 68 p.

O'Callaghan, Sean. DAMAGED BAGGAGE: THE WHITE SLAVE
TRADE AND NARCOTICS TRAFFICKING IN THE AMERICAS.
1970, Roy. $4.75.

Peterson, Mark E. DRUGS, DRINKS AND MORALS. 1970, Des-
eret Book. $1.95 paper $ .35, ISBN 0-87747-345-5;
paper 0-87747-346-3.

Popham, Robert E. INTERACTION OF ALCOHOL AND OTHER DRUGS:
AN ANNOTATED BIBLIOGRAPHY. 1970, Toronto: Addiction
Research Foundation.

Schoenfeld, Eugene. DEAR DOCTOR HIP POCRATES. 1970,
B. C. Grove. $1.25 paper.

Shiller, Alice. DRUG ABUSE AND YOUR CHILD. (Public
Affairs pamphlet no. 448). May 1970, Public Affairs
Commission. 28 p. $ .25.

Sjoeqvist, Folke and Malcom Tottie, editors. ABUSE OF
CENTRAL STIMULANTS. 1970, Raven. ISBN 0-911216-17-0.

South Dakota. State Legislature. Research Council.
DRUG EDUCATION IN SOUTH DAKOTA. 1970, The Legislature. 37 p. State Capitol, Pierre, South Dakota
57501.

Stricker, George. T.O.P.I.C: TREATMENT OF PEOPLE IN
CRISIS, THE TOPIC HOUSE APPROACH TO DRUG ADDICTION.
1970, Lion. $5.95, ISBN 0-87460-237-8.

Taylor, Norman. NARCOTICS: NATURE'S GIFTS. 1970, Dell.
$ .75 paper.

Terry, Charles E. and Mildred Pellens. OPIUM PROBLEM.
1970, Patterson Smith.

United Nations. International Narcotics Control Board.
ESTIMATED WORLD REQUIREMENTS OF NARCOTIC DRUGS AND
ESTIMATES OF WORLD PRODUCTION OF OPIUM IN 1971. 1970,
The Board. (Sales No:E. 71. XI. 1) (E/INCB/10).

United Nations. International Narcotics Control Board.
REPORT OF THE INTERNATIONAL NARCOTICS CONTROL BOARD

ON ITS WORK IN 1970. 1970, The Board. (Sales No: E. 71. XI. 2) (E/INCB/9).

United Nations. International Narcotics Board. STATIS-TICS ON NARCOTIC DRUGS FOR 1969, Furnished by Govern-ments in accordance with the international treaties, and maximum levels of opium stocks. 1970, The Board. (Sales No:E. 70. XI. 7) (E/INCB/11).

United States. Bureau of Customs. NARCOTIC IDENTIFICA-TION MANUAL. 1970, Government Printing Office.

United States. Bureau of Narcotics and Dangerous Drugs. Office of Science and Drug Abuse Prevention. Drug Science Division. ILLICIT USE OF DANGEROUS DRUGS IN THE UNITED STATES: A COMPILATION OF STUDIES, SURVEYS, AND POLLS, by Dorothy F. Berg. 1970, Government Print ing Office. 38 p.

United States. Department of Defense. A FEDERAL SOURCE BOOK: ANSWERS TO THE MORE FREQUENTLY ASKED QUESTIONS ABOUT DRUGS. 1970, Government Printing Office. 42 p. Prepared jointly with the Departments of Health, Edu-cation and Welfare: Justice; Labor; and The Office of Economic Opportunity.

United States. Department of Justice. Bureau of Nar-cotics and Dangerous Drugs. PUBLIC SPEAKING ON DRUG ABUSE PREVENTION: A HANDBOOK FOR THE LAW ENFORCEMENT OFFICER. 1970, Government Printing Office. 40 p., $ .30.

United States. House of Representatives. Commission on Education and Labor. Select subcommittee on Edu-cation. DRUG ABUSE: HEARINGS. Parts 1-2. July 9-September 19, 1969. On H.R. 9312 and other bills. 91st Congress, First Session. 1970, Government Printing Office. 2 volumes, 1102p.

United States. House of Representatives. Commission on Government Operations. Intergovernmental Relations Subcommittee. DRUG EFFICACY: HEARINGS. Part 1. April 17-22, 1969. 91st Congress, First Session. 1970 Government Printing Office. iv+171 p.

United States. House of Representatives. Commission on Government Operation. Special Studies Subcommittee. FEDERAL INVOLVEMENT IN THE USE OF BEHAVIOR MODIFICA-TION DRUGS ON GRAMMAR SCHOOL CHILDREN OF THE RIGHT TO PRIVACY IN INQUIRY: HEARING, September 29, 1970. 91st Congress, First Session. 1970, Government Printing Office.

United States. House of Representatives. Commission on
Interstate and Foreign Commerce. Subcommittee on Public Health and Welfare. DRUG ABUSE CONTROL AMENDMENTS
-1970: HEARINGS. Parts 1-2, February 3 - March 3, 1970,
on H.R. 11701 and H.R. 13743, bills to provide for increased research and training of personnel to deal
with drug abuse problems; increased educational and in-
formational efforts to attempt to prevent drug abuse;
providing facilities for the care and rehabilitation
of drug abusers; and with revision of existing restrictions on distribution of drugs subject to abuse (and
related bills). 91st Congress, Second Session. 1970,
Government Printing Office. 857 p.

United States. House of Representatives. Commission on
the Judiciary Subcommittee. No. 3. COMMISSION ON
MARIJUANA: HEARINGS, October 15-16, 1969. On H.R.
10019 (and other bills) to provide for the establish-
ment of a commission on marijuana. 91st Congress,
First Session. 1970, Government Printing Office.
iv+125 p.

United States. House of Representatives. Commission on
Ways and Means. CONTROLLED DANGEROUS SUBSTANCES, NAR-
COTICS AND DRUG CONTROL LAWS: HEARINGS, July 20-27,
1970. On legislation to repute controlled dangerous
substances and amend narcotics and drug laws. 91st
Congress, Second Session. 1970, Government Printing
Office. vi+536.

United States. House of Representatives. Commission on
Ways and Means. Materials prepared by the administration relating to proposed legislation to regulate controlled dangerous substances and amend narcotics and
drug laws; including the President's message, proposed
bills, and other material prepared by the Department
of Justice. 91st Congress, Second Session. 1970,
Government Printing Office. iii+254 p.

United States. House of Representatives. Commission on
Ways and Means. Prepared statements presented by administration witnesses appearing before the Committee
on Ways and Means at hearings on legislation to regulate controlled dangerous substances and to amend
narcotics and drug laws, together with the administration's proposal, H.R. 17463 and other material prepared by the Department of Justice. 91st Congress,
Second Session. 1970, Government Printing Office.
iii+178 p.

United States. House of Representatives. Select Com-

mission on Crime. CRIME IN AMERICA - HEROIN IMPOR-
TATION, DISTRIBUTION, PACKAGING AND PARAPHERNALIA:
HEARINGS, June 25-30, 1970. Pursuant to H. Res. 17.
91st Congress, Second Session. 1970, Government
Printing Office. v+436 p.

United States. House of Representatives. Select Commission on Crime. CRIME IN AMERICA: THE HERION PARA-
PHERNALIA TRADE: HEARINGS, October 5-6, 1970. Pursuant to H. Res. 17. 91st Congress, Second Session.
1970, Government Printing Office.

United States. House of Representatives. Select Com-
mission on Crime. CRIME IN AMERICA: VIEWS ON MARI-
JUANA: HEARINGS, October 14-15, 1969. Pursuant to
H. Res. 17. 91st Congress, First Session. 1970,
Government Printing Office. iii+115 p.

United States. House of Representatives. Select Commission on Crime. CRIME IN AMERICA - WHY 8 BILLION
AMPHETAMINES? HEARINGS:, November 18, 1969. Pursuant to H. Res. 17. 91st Congress, First Session.
1970, Government Printing Office. iii+45 p.

United States. National Clearing House for Drug Abuse
Information. A FEDERAL SOURCE BOOK: ANSWERS TO THE
MOST FREQUENTLY ASKED QUESTIONS ABOUT DRUG ABUSE.
1970, Government Printing Office.

United States. Senate. Commission on the District of
Columbia. CRIME IN THE NATIONAL CAPITAL: HEARINGS,
Part 10. April 14-30, 1970. On drug abuse education and prevention. 91st Congress, Second Session.
1970, Government Printing Office. vi+2229-2447+
1746 p.

United States. Senate. Commission on the District of
Columbia. CRIME IN THE NATIONAL CAPITAL- HEARINGS,
Part 11. November 25, 1969 - March 2, 1970. On
S. 3071, Drug abuse and narcotics crime control act
for the District of Columbia. 91st Congress, First
and Second Sessions. 1970, Government Printing
Office. iii+2449-2654 p.

United States. Senate. Commission on the District of
Columbia. STAFF STUDY ON DRUG ABUSE IN THE WASHING-
TON AREA, 1970. 91st Congress, Second Session. 1970,
Government Printing Office. ii+40 p.

United States. Senate. Commission on Labor and Public
Welfare. Special Subcommittee on alcoholism and

8

narcotics. ALCOHOLISM AND NARCOTICS: HEARINGS, Part 1. September 26-27, 1969. 91st Congress, First and Second Session. 1970, Government Printing Office. iv+263 p.

United States. Senate. Commission on Labor and Public Welfare. Special Subcommittee on alcoholism and narcotics. REVIEW OF SUBSTITUTE AMENDMENT TO TITLE I of H.R. 18583: COMPREHENSIVE DRUG ABUSE PREVENTION AND CONTROL ACT OF 1970, INCLUDING SECTION-BY-SECTION ANALYSIS AND CHANGES IN EXISTING LAW. 91st Congress, Second Session. 1970, Government Printing Office. ii+37 p.

Washington (state). TASK FORCE ON DRUG ABUSE. Report to Governor Daniel J. Evans. 1970, Olympia. iii+ 36 p.

White, A. et al. PRESCRIPTION FOR DRUGS. 1970, Bow Group Pamphlet. ISBN 0-85070-459-6.

Whitney, Elizabeth D. WORLD DIALOGUE ON ALCOHOL AND DRUG DEPENDENCE. 1970, Beacon Press. $12.50, ISBN 0-8070-2776-6.

Wiener, F. S. DRUGS AND SCHOOLCHILDREN. 1970, Humanities. $7.50, ISBN 0-391-00038-1.

Wise, Francis H. YOUTH AND DRUGS: PREVENTION, DETECTION AND CURE. 1970, Association Press. $4.95, ISBN 0-8096-1781-1.

PERIODICAL LITERATURE

"Abandonment--Sign of the times." NURSING OUTLOOK. 18:23, July, 1970.

"Absence of major medical complications among chronic opiate addicts," by J. C. Ball,et al. BRITISH JOURNAL OF ADDICTION. 65:109-112, August, 1970.

"Abuse of amphetamine and amphetamine-like drugs," by W. R. Clement,et al. PSYCHOLOGICAL REPORTS. 26: 343-354, April, 1970.

"The abuse of drugs and its prevention. The pharmacist's role," by J. C. Bloomfield. ROYAL SOCIETY OF HEALTH JOURNAL. 90:193-195, July-August, 1970.

"Abuse of drugs by the public and by doctors," by D. Dunlop. BRITISH MEDICAL BULLETIN. 26:236-239, September, 1970.

"Abuse of hallucinogenic drugs: some observations of a college psychiatrist," by P. K. Munter. INTERNATIONAL PSYCHIATRY CLINICS. 7:153-168, 1970.

"The abuse of psychodelics: a social and medical problem," by S. Nowak, et al. POLSKI TYGODNIK LEKARSKI. 25: 698-701, May 11, 1970.

"Abusive prescriptions of vitamin D." PRESSE MEDICALE. 78:556, March 7, 1970.

"Acid by accident; case of mass hallucinogenic poisoning." TIME. 95:8, April 20, 1970.

"Acid report on acid." NATURE (London). 226:4-5, April 4, 1970.

"Action on amphetamines," by F. O. Wells. BRITISH MEDICAL JOURNAL. 1:361, May 9, 1970.

"The acute pulmonary edema of heroin intoxication," by W. J. Morrison, et al. RADIOLOGY. 97:347-351, November, 1970.

"The addict: criminal or cripple? hard drug dilemma,"
by Gertrude Samuels. NEW LEADER. 53:10-12, March
16, 1970.

"The addict today - 1970," by Kevin P. O'Brien and
Robert C. Sullivan. POLICE. 14:35-41, May-June,
1970.

"Addiction hazards for youths," by W. Schweisheimer.
AGNES KARLL-SCHWESTER. 24:312-313, August, 1970.

"Addiction, medicine and the law." SCIENTIFIC AMERICAN.
223:50, July, 1970.

"Addiction to pentazocine (Fortral)," by J. Geerling.
PHARMAZEUTISCHE WEEKBLAD VOOR NEDERLAND. 105:405,
March 27, 1970.

"Addiction to pentazocine: report of two cases," by
W. F. Weber, et al. JOURNAL OF THE AMERICAN MED-
ICAL ASSOCIATION. 212:1708, June 8, 1970.

"Addiction to propoxphene," by F. J. Kane, Jr., et al.
JOURNAL OF THE AMERICAN MEDICAL ASSOCIATION. 211:
300, January 12, 1970.

"Addicts and zealots; chaotic war against drug abuse
in New York City," by M. K. Sanders. HARPERS. 240:
71-73+, June, 1970; READER'S DIGEST. 97:95, December, 1970.

"Addicts in a therapeutic community," by C. Tarry and
R. Wilk. NURSING MIRROR. 131:32+, September 11,
1970.

"Adolescence and drug abuse," by J. H. McKeen. JOUR-
NAL OF THE ROYAL COLLEGE OF GENERAL PRACTITIONERS.
20:288-290, November, 1970.

"Adolescent drug abuse in a North London suburb," by
A. Anumonye, et al. BRITISH JOURNAL OF ADDICTION.
65:24-33, May, 1970.

"Adolescents and adults: the prism of drugs," by W.
J. Cook. ILLINOIS EDUCATION. 58:293-296, March,
1970.

"Adrenergic blockade and the corticosteroid and growth
hormone responses to methylamphetamine," by L. Rees,
et al. NATURE (London). 228:565-566, November 7,
1970.

AEROSOL ABUSE
"Aerosol inhalation for 'kicks'," by J. L. Chapel, et al. MISSOURI MEDICINE. 67:378-380, June, 1970.

"Aerosol inhalation for 'kicks'," by J. L. Chapel, et al. MISSOURI MEDICINE. 67:378-380, June, 1970.

"Alarm grows in U.S. as youth moves on to heroin," by F. Hechinger. TIMES (London) EDUCATIONAL SUPPLEMENT. 2859:9, March 6, 1970.

"Alcohol or Marijuana: A Follow up Survey at Ithaca College," by M. E. Rand, et al. JOURNAL OF THE AMERICAN COLLEGE HEALTH ASSOCIATION. 18,5:366-367, June, 1970.

"Alcoholism and drug dependence amongst Jews," by M. M. Glatt. BRITISH JOURNAL OF ADDICTION. 64:297-304, January, 1970.

"Alcoholism, drug addiction, and nutrition," by C. M. Leevy, et al. MEDICAL CLINICS OF NORTH AMERICA. 54:1567-1575, November, 1970.

"Alternative Strategies for Developing a Campus Drug Policy," by S. T. Rickard. NASPA, JOURNAL OF THE ASSOCIATION OF DEANS AND ADMINISTRATORS OF STUDENT AFFAIRS. 8,1:64-68, July, 1970.

"Amassed tablets." SOUTH AFRICAN MEDICAL JOURNAL. 44:910, August 15, 1970.

"America should not "go to pot," by Thomas F. Coon. POLICE. 14:65-68, March-April, 1970.

"Americans abroad; the jail scene." TIME. 95:36, April 13, 1970.

AMINE ABUSE
"Central-stimulating amines--international control," by N. Retterstol. TIDSSKRIFT FOR DEN NORSKE LAEGEFORENING. 90:2096, November 15, 1970.

"Amphetamine abuse amongst psychiatric in-patients. The use of gas chromatography," by A. E. Robinson, et al. BRITISH JOURNAL OF PSYCHIATRY. 116:643-644, June, 1970.

"Amphetamine addiction," by A. A. Bartholomew. MEDICAL JOURNAL OF AUSTRALIA. 1:1209-1214, June 13, 1970.

"Amphetamine dependence and misuse," by R. Gardner. NURSING MIRROR AND MIDWIVES JOURNAL. 130:22-25, March 6, 1970.

"Amphetamine: differentiation by d and l isomers of behavior involving brain norepinephrine or dopamine," by K. M. Taylor and S. H. Snyder. SCIENCE. 168:1487-1489, June 19, 1970.

"Amphetamine taking among young offenders," by B. Lancaster, et al. BRITISH JOURNAL OF PSYCHIATRY. 116:349-350, March, 1970.

"Amphetamine toxicity and endogenous noradrenaline concentrations in isolated and aggregated mice," by D. J. George, et al. JOURNAL OF PHARMACY AND PHARMACOLOGY. 22:947-949, December, 1970.

AMPHETAMINES
"Abuse of amphetamine and amphetamine-like drugs," by W. R. Clement, et al. PSYCHOLOGICAL REPORTS. 26:343-354, April, 1970.

"Action on amphetamines," by F. O. Wells. BRITISH MEDICAL JOURNAL. 1:361, May 9, 1970.

"Adrenergic blockade and the corticosteroid and growth hormone responses to methylamphetamine," by L. Rees, et al. NATURE (London). 228:565-566, November 7, 1970.

"Amphetamine abuse amongst pychiatric in-patients. The use of gas chromatography," by A. E. Robinson, et al. BRITISH JOURNAL OF PSYCHIATRY. 116: 643-644, June, 1970.

"Amphetamine addiction," by A. A. Bartholomew. MEDICAL JOURNAL OF AUSTRALIA. 1:1209-1214, June 13, 1970.

"Amphetamine dependence and misuse," by R. Gardner. NURSING MIRROR AND MIDWIVES JOURNAL. 130:22-25, March 6, 1970.

"Amphetamine: differentiation by d and l isomers of behavior involving brain norepinephrine or dopamine," by K. M. Taylor and S. H. Snyder. SCIENCE. 168:1487-1489, June 19, 1970.

"Amphetamine taking among young offenders," by B. Lancaster, et al. BRITISH JOURNAL OF PSYCHIATRY.

AMPHETAMINES (cont'd.)
116:349-350, March, 1970.

"Amphetamine toxicity and endogenous noradrenaline concentrations in isolated and aggregated mice," by D. J. George, et al. JOURNAL OF PHARMACY AND PHARMACOLOGY. 22:947-949, December, 1970.

"Amphetamines and their derivatives," by W. S. Haynes. MEDICAL JOURNAL OF AUSTRALIA. 1:566, March 14, 1970.

"Amphetamines in human urine: rapid estimation by gas-liquid chromatography," by J. W. Schweitzer, et al. CLINICAL CHEMISTRY. 16:786-788, September, 1970.

"Amphetamines outmoded," by E. Wayne. BRITISH MEDICAL JOURNAL. 4:801, December 26, 1970.

"Amphetamines, the teenagers' basic drug," by V. Brittain. LONDON TIMES. p.10, September 22, 1970.

"Another abusable amphetamine," by B. Jackson, et al. JOURNAL OF THE AMERICAN MEDICAL ASSOCIATION. 211:830, February 2, 1970.

"Ban on amphetamines and barbiturates," by H. Matthew. BRITISH MEDICAL JOURNAL. 4:801, December 26, 1970.

"Behavioural effects of some derivatives of amphetamines and LSD and their significance," by J. R. Smythies, et al. NATURE (London). 226:644-645, May 16, 1970.

"Comparative effects of amphetamine, scopolamine, chlordiazepoxide, and diphenylthydantoin on operant and extinction behavior with brain stimulation and food reward," by M. E. Olds. NEUROPHARMACOLOGY. 9:519-532, November, 1970.

"Control of amphetamines and LSD." LANCET. 1:708, April 4, 1970.

"Dangerous abuses of amphetamines." CANADIAN JOURNAL OF PSYCHIATRIC NURSING. 11:12, March, 1970.

"Death of a young athlete: possible role of doping. Apropos of 2 cases," by M. Yacoub, et al. MEDECINE LEGALE ET DOMMAGE CORPOREL (Paris). 3:275-

AMPHETAMINES (cont'd.)
277, July-September, 1970.

"Determination and identification of sympathomimetic amines in blood samples from drivers by a combination of gas chromatography and mass spectrometry," by R. Bonnichsen, et al. ZEITSCHRIFT FUER RECHTSMEDIZIN. 67:19-26, 1970.

"Distribution and metabolism of neuroleptic drugs, I. Pharmacokinetics of haloperidal," by P. J. Lewi, et al. ARZNEIMITTEL-FORSCHUNG. 20:943-948, July, 1970.

"Doing something about amphetamines," by B. Yellen. NEW ENGLAND JOURNAL OF MEDICINE. 283:1349-1350, December 10, 1970.

"Drug-induced changes of urinary catecholamines in the rat; role of the adrenal medulla," by P. Del Basso, et al. EUROPEAN JOURNAL OF PHARMACOLOGY. 13:83-89, 1970.

"Drug therapy today; use and abuse of the amphetamines," by M. J. Rodman. RN. 33:55+, August, 1970.

"EEG arousal reactions to amphetamine and 2,5-dimethoxy-4-methylamphetamine in reserpine-pretreated rabbits," by M. Fujimori, et al. BIOLOGICAL PSYCHIATRY. 2:241-250, July, 1970.

"The effect of nialamide, pargyline and tranylcypromine on the removal of amphetamine by the perfused liver," by F. R. Trinker, et al. JOURNAL OF PHARMACY AND PHARAMACOLOGY. 22:496-499, July, 1970.

"Effect of psychoton and dexfenmetrazin on maximum physical performance," by K. Barak, et al. PHYSIOLOGIA BOHEMOSLOVACA. 19:117-121, 1970.

"The effects of altered brain norepinephrine levels on continuous avoidance responding and the action of amphetamines," by F. P. Miller, et al. NEUROPHARMACOLOGY. 9:511-517, November, 1970.

"Effects of amphetamine upon relearning pattern and black-white discriminations following neocortical lesions in rats," by K. R. Jonason, et al. JOURNAL OF COMPARATIVE AND PHYSIOLOGICAL PSYCHOLOGY. 73:47-55, October, 1970.

AMPHETAMINES (cont'd.)
"Effects of cocaine and amphetamine on the metabolism of tryptophan and 5-hydroxytryptamine in
mouse brain in vivo," by J. Schubert, et al.
JOURNAL OF PHARMACY AND PHARMACOLOGY. 22:860-
862, November, 1970.

"Effects of lithium pretreatment on amphetamine
and DMI tetrabenazine produced psychomotor be-
habior," by P. S. D'Encarnacao, et al. DISEASES
OF THE NERVOUS SYSTEM. 31:494-496, July, 1970.

"Effects of systemically administered drugs on intraocular pressure in rabbits," by P. Burberi, et al.
ARZNEIMITTEL-FORSCHUNG. 20:1143-1147, August,
1970.

"Gas chromatographic determination of amphetamine
in blood, tissue, and urine," by E. Anggard, et al.
SCANDINAVIAN JOURNAL OF CLINICAL AND LABORATORY
INVESTIGATION. 26:137-143, September, 1970.

"Growing menace of pep pills," by B. Surface. SEVEN-
TEEN. 29:146-147+, May, 1970.

"Hepatitis associate with illicit use of intravenous
methamphetamine," by L. E. Davis, et al. PUBLIC
HEALTH REPORTS. 85:809-813, September, 1970.

"Identification of various amphetamines and amphetamine-like substances in urine using thin-layer
chromatography," by J. P. de Man. PHARMAZEUTISCHE
WEEKBLAD VOOR NEDERLAND. 105:1218-1228, October
16, 1970.

"Inhibition by p-chloroamphetamine of the conversion
of 5-hydroxytryptamine to 5-hydroxyindoleacetic
acid in rat brain," by R. W. Fuller, et al. JOUR-
NAL OF PHARMACY AND PHARMACOLOGY. 22:634-635,
August, 1970.

"The inhibitory effect of amphetamine on exploration
in mice," by J. G. Bainbridge. PSYCHOPHARMACOLOG-
IA. 18:314-319, 1970.

"Intracranial hemorrhage associated with amphetamine
abuse," by S. J. Goodman, et al. JOURNAL OF THE
AMERICAN MEDICAL ASSOCIATION. 212:480, April 20,
1970.

"Intravenous amphetamine poisoning. Report of three
cases," by R. H. Cravey, et al. JOURNAL OF THE

17

AMPHETAMINES (cont'd.)
FORENSIC SCIENCE SOCIETY. 10:109-112, April, 1970.

"Investigation into the possible influence of chlorinated amphetamine derivatives on 5-hydroxytryptamine synthesis in man," by H. M. van Praag, et al. PSYCHOPHARMACOLOGIA. 18:412-420, 1970.

"Lethal amphetamine intoxication. A report of three cases," by S. Orrenius, et al. ZIETSCHRIFT FUER RECHTSMEDIZIN. 67:184-189, 1970.

"Motivation for addiction to amphetamine and reducing drugs," by S. Robinson, et al. PSYCHIATRY DIGEST. 31:26 passim, July, 1970.

"P-chloroamphetamine; in vivo investigations on the mechanism of action of the selective depletion of cerebral serotonin," by E. Sanders-Bush, et al. JOURNAL OF PHARMACOLOGY AND EXPERIMENTAL THERAPEUTICS. 175:419-426, November, 1970.

"P-chloroamphetamine. Temporal relationship between psychomotor stimulation and metabolism of brain norepinephrine," by S. J. Strada, et al. BIOCHEMICAL PHARMACOLOGY. 19:2621-2629, September, 1970.

"Pep pills common in secondary schools," by C. Moorehead. TIMES (London) EDUCATIONAL SUPPLEMENT. 2895:6, November 13, 1970.

"Pep pills for youngsters: treatment of hyperactive children in Omaha." U. S. NEWS AND WORLD REPORT. 69:49, July 13, 1970.

"Pharmacological actions of 1-(o-methoxyphenoxy)3-isopropylamino-2-propanol hydrochloride (S-D-1601), a new beta-blocking agent," by R. Ferrini, et al. ARZNEIMITTEL-FORSCHUNG. 20:1074-1079, August, 1970.

"Pharmacology of a nicotinamido-methylaminopyrazolone (Ra 101)," by E. Tubaro, et al. ARZEIMITTELFORSCHUNG. 20:1019-1023, August, 1970.

"Preliminary report on the detection and quantitation of opiates and certain other drugs of abuse as trimethysilyl derivatives by gas-liquid chromatography," by K. D. Parker, et al. JOURNAL OF THE FORENSIC SCIENCE SOCIETY. 10:17-22, January, 1970.

AMPHETAMINES (cont'd.)
"A rating scale for evaluation of the clinical
course and symptomatology in amphetamine psychosis," by L. E. Jonsson, et al. BRITISH JOUR-
NAL OF PSYCHIATRY. 117:661-665, December, 1970.

"The relationship of amphetamine-induced anorexia
and freezing under a multiple CRF-EXT operant
schedule," by S. O. Cole. JOURNAL OF GENERAL
PSYCHOLOGY. 83:163-168, October, 1970.

"Relative acitivity of psychotoxic drugs on the
avian optic lobe," by N. W. Scholes, et al.
EUROPEAN JOURNAL OF PHARMACOLOGY. 12:289-296,
1970.

"The role of brain dopamine in behavioral regula-
tions and the actions of psychotropic drugs,"
by S. H. Snyder, et al. AMERICAN JOURNAL OF PSY-
CHIATRY. 127:199-209, August, 1970.

"The role of methylamphetamine on plasma hexocamine
level under stress," by A. K. Chatterjee, et al.
JAPANESE JOURNAL OF PHARMACOLOGY. 20:439-441,
September, 1970.

"Sensitivity changes to noradrenaline in the guinea-
pig vas deferens induced by amphetamines, cocaine
and denervation," by S. de Moraes, et al. JOUR-
NAL OF PHARMACY AND PHARMACOLOGY. 22:717-719,
September, 1970.

"Simultaneous measurement technics; urinary CO2
(C14-02) elimination and motor activity in mice
during metabolic experimentation with amphetamines," by A. Benakis. EXPERIENTIA. 26: 1163-
1164, October 15, 1970.

"Slowdown for pep pills; new restrictions." NEWS-
WEEK. 76:77, August 17, 1970.

"A spectrophotofluorometric method for the determination of amphetamine," by C. R. Nix, et al.
JOURNAL OF THE FORENSIC SCIENCE SOCIETY. 15:
595-600, October, 1970.

"Speed kills: the adolescent methadrine addict," by
R. R. Rodewald. PERSPECTIVES IN PSYCHIATRIC CARE.
8:160-167, July-August, 1970.

"Speed that kills, or worse," by J. Black. NEW YORK
TIMES MAGAZINE. pp. 14-15+, June 21, 1970;

AMPHETAMINES (cont'd.)
READER'S DIGEST. 97:153-157, October, 1970.

"Symposium--drug action and animal behavior. 3.
Comparison of the effects of amphetamines, pheno-
barbital, chlorpromazine and benzodiazepines on
conditioned suppressive behaviors in monkeys and
rats," by S. Tadokoro. FOLIA PHARMACOLOGICA JAP-
ONICA. 66:78-79, July 20, 1970.

"Thyroid as an adjuvant to amphetamine therapy of
obesity. A controlled double-blind study," by
N. M. Kaplan, et al. AMERICAN JOURNAL OF MEDICAL
SCIENCES. 260:105-111, August, 1970.

"Use of amphetamine by medical students," by C. Watkins. SOUTHERN MEDICAL JOURNAL. 63:923-929, August, 1970.

"Why speed kills." NEWSWEEK. 76:121, November 16,
1970.

"Amphetamines and their derivatives," by W. S. Haynes.
MEDICAL JOURNAL OF AUSTRALIA. 1:566, March 14,
1970.

"Amphetamines in human urine: rapid estimation by gas-
liquid chromatography," by J. W. Schweitzer, et al.
CLINICAL CHEMISTRY. 16:786-788, September, 1970.

"Amphetamines outmoded," by E. Wayne. BRITISH MED-
ICAL JOURNAL. 4:801, December 26, 1970.

"Amphetamines, the teenagers' basic drug," by V. Brittain. TIMES (London). p. 10, September 22, 1970.

AMYL NITRATE ABUSE
"Amyl nitrite inhalation fad," by J. T. Pearlman,
et al. JOURNAL OF THE AMERICAN MEDICAL ASSOCIA-
TION. 212:160, April 6, 1970.

"Amyl nitrite inhalation fad," by J. T. Pearlman, et al.
JOURNAL OF THE AMERICAN MEDICAL ASSOCIATION. 212:
160, April 6, 1970.

ANALGESIC ABUSE
"Analgesic abuse and tumours of the renal pelvis,"
by A. Kennedy, et al. LANCET. 1:42-43, January
3, 1970.

"Analgesic abuse and tumours of renal pelvis," by
U. Bentsson, et al. LANCET. 1:305, February 7,
1970.

ANALGESIC ABUSE (cont'd.)
"Analgesic abuse in psychiatric patients," by R. M.
Murray, et al. LANCET. 760: 1303-1305, June 20,
1970.

"Anaplastic transitional-cell carcinoma of the renal
pelvis in association with analgesic abuse," by
W. R. Adam, et al. MEDICAL JOURNAL OF AUSTRALIA.
1:1108-1109, May 30, 1970.

"Disease course observation in patients with kidney
diseases following abuse of analgesics," by T.
Nitzsche, et al. DEUTSCHE MEDIZINISCHE WOCHEN-
SCHRIFT. 95:927-934, April 24, 1970.

"Morphine dependent rats as a model for evaluating
potential addiction liability of analgesic compounds," by O. J. Lorenzetti, et al. ARCHIVES
INTERNATIONALES DE PHARMACODYNAMIE ET DE THERAPIE.
183:391-402, February, 1970.

"Obscure hemolytic anemia due to analgesic abuse.
Does enterogenous cyanosis exist?" by E. A.
Azen, et al. AMERICAN JOURNAL OF MEDICINE. 48:
724-727, June, 1970.

"Analgesic abuse and tumours of renal pelvis," by U.
Bentsson, et al. LANCET. 1:305, February 7, 1970.

"Analgesic abuse and tumours of the renal pelvis," by
A. Kennedy, et al. LANCET. 1:42-43, January 3,
1970.

"Analgesic abuse in psychiatric patients," by R. M.
Murray, et al. LANCET. 760:1303-1305, June 20,
1970.

ANALGESICS
"Compound analgetics with morphine content," by
P. Flatberg. TIDSSKRIFT FOR DEN NORSKE LAEGE-
FORENING. 90:1562, August 15, 1970.

"Anaplastic transitional-cell carcinoma of the renal
pelvis in association with analgesic abuse," by
W. R. Adam, et al. MEDICAL JOURNAL OF AUSTRALIA.
1:1108-1109, May 30, 1970.

"And pep in America." NEW ENGLAND JOURNAL OF MED-
ICINE. 283:761-762, October 1, 1970.

"Anonymous versus identifiable questionnaires in drug
usage surveys," by F. W. King. AMERICAN PSYCHOL-

OGIST. 25:982-985, October, 1970.

"Another abusable amphetamine," by B. Jackson, et al. JOURNAL OF THE AMERICAN MEDICAL ASSOCIATION. 211: 830, February 2, 1970.

"Another checkup on drug use by GI's." U.S. NEWS AND WORLD REPORT. 69:33, August 31, 1970.

"Antagonism of the behavioral effects of morphine and methadone by narcotic antagonists in the pigeon," by D. E. McMillan, et al. JOURNAL OF PHARMACOLOGY AND EXPERIMENTAL THERAPEUTICS. 175:443-458, November, 1970.

ANTAGONISTS

"Antagonism of the behavioral effects of morphine and methadone by narcotic antagonists in the pigeon," by D. E. McMillan, et al. JOURNAL OF PHARMACOLOGY AND EXPERIMENTAL THERAPEUTICS. 175: 443-458, November, 1970.

"Distribution and metabolism of neuroleptic drugs, I. Pharmacokinetics of haloperidal," by P. J. Lewi, et al. ARZNEIMITTEL-FORSCHUNG. 20:943-948, July, 1970.

"Narcotic antagonists in opiate dependence; report of meeting," by M. Fink. SCIENCE. 169:1005-1006, September 4, 1970.

"Pharmacological actions of 1-(o-methoxyphenoxy)3-isopropylamino-2-propanol hydrochloride (S-D-1601), a new beta-blocking agent," by R. Ferrini, et al. ARZNEIMITTEL-FORSCHUNG. 20:1074-1079, August, 1970.

"Subjective effects of narcotic antagonists cyclazocine and nalorphine on the Addiction Research Center Inventory (ARCI)," by C. A. Haertzen. PSYCHOPHARMACOLOGIA. 18:366-377, 1970.

"Treatment of heroin dependence with opiate antagonists," by M. Fink, et al. CURRENT PSYCHIATRIC THERAPIES. 10:161-170, 1970.

ANTICOAGULANTS ABUSE

"Surreptitious ingestion of oral anticoagulants," by T. H. Greidanus, et al. HENRY FORD HOSPITAL MEDICAL JOURNAL. 18:99-106, Summer, 1970.

"Anti-narcotics drive 40 years old," by A. C. Vaigo.
TIMES (London) EDUCATIONAL SUPPLEMENT. 2861:16,
March 20, 1970.

"Appraising marijuana: the new American pastime," by
J. Keats. HOLIDAY. 47:52-53+, April, 1970.

"An approach to the treatment of drug abuse," by R.
I. Wang, et al. WISCONSIN MEDICAL JOURNAL. 69:148-
150, May, 1970.

ARCHITECTURE
  "Eighteen narcotic-addiction buildings in eighteen
  months; Arthur Kill Rehabilitation Center, Staten
  Island." AMERICAN CITY. 85:152+, June, 1970.

"Architecture to help drug addicts calls for speed and
  inventiveness: Manhattan Rehabilitation Center."
  ARCHITECTURAL RECORD. 147:160-161, January, 1970.

ARTHUR KILL REHABILITATION CENTER
  "Eighteen narcotic-addiction buildings in eighteen
  months; Arthur Kill Rehabilitation Center, Staten
  Island." AMERICAN CITY. 85:152+, June 1970.

"At least a million people smoke pot." OBSERVER. p. 1-2,
  March 15, 1970.

"Atypical reasoning errors in sociopathic, paranoid and
  schizophrenic personality types," by J. Fracchia, et
  al. JOURNAL OF PSYCHOLOGY. 76:91-95, September, 1970.

"Australia-SH-antigen and diseases of the liver. Preliminary investigations of Danish drug addicts and patients with chronic liver diseases," by V. Reinicke,
  et al. SCANDINAVIAN JOURNAL OF GASTROENTEROLOGY SUP-
  PLEMENT. 7:85-88, 1970.

"Australian Patterns of Drug Abuse." MEDICAL JOURNAL
  OF AUSTRALIA. 2:1105-1106, December 12, 1970.

AWARENESS HOUSE PROJECT
  "Leaving the drug world behind; results from the
  Awareness House project," by R. Moskowitz. AMER-
  ICAN EDUCATION. 6:3-6, January, 1970; EDUCATION
  DIGEST. 35:5-7, May, 1970.

"Ban on amphetamines and barbiturates," by H. Matthew.
BRITISH MEDICAL JOURNAL. 4:801, December 26, 1970.

"Ban on barbiturates," by F. Wells. BRITISH MEDICAL
JOURNAL. 4:552, November 28, 1970.

"Banality of the new evil; games the survivors play,"
by W. Kloman. ESQUIRE. 73:115-117+, March, 1970.

BARBITURATES
   "Ban on amphetamines and barbiturates," by H. Mat-
      thew. BRITISH MEDICAL JOURNAL. 4:801, December
      26, 1970.

   "Ban on barbiturates," by F. Wells. BRITISH MED-
      ICAL JOURNAL. 4:552, November 28, 1970.

   "Dangers of barbiturates," by E. Tylden, et al.
      BRITISH MEDICAL JOURNAL. 2:49, April 4, 1970.

   "Development of tolerance to and physical depen-
      dence on barbiturates in rhesus monkeys," by
      T. Yanagita, et al. JOURNAL OF PHARMACOLOGY AND
      EXPERIMENTAL THERAPEUTICS. 173:163-169, March,
      1970.

   "Effect of intra-arterial injections of barbiturates,"
      by D. Albo, Jr, et al. AMERICAN JOURNAL OF SUR-
      GERY. 120:676-678, November 8, 1970.

   "Frequency--specific relation between hippocampal
      theta rhythm, behavior, and amobarbital action,"
      by J. A. Gray and G. G. Ball. SCIENCE. 168:
      1246-1248, June 8, 1970.

   "A new method for treatment of barbiturate depen-
      dence," by D. E. Smith, et al. JOURNAL OF THE
      AMERICAN MEDICAL SOCIETY. 213:294-295, July,
      13, 1970.

   "Personality factors and barbiturate dependence,"
      by A. Anumonye. BRITISH JOURNAL OF ADDICTION.
      64:365-370, January, 1970.

   "The pill head meanace. Barbiturates and tran-
      quilizers; non-hard core addicting drugs," by
      H. S. Feldman. PSYCHOSOMATICS. 11:99-103,
      March-April, 1970.

   "The sensitivity of the brain to barbiturate during
      chronic administration and withdrawal of barbitone

24

BARBITURATES (cont'd.)
sodium in the rat," by I. H. Stevenson, et al.
BRITISH JOURNAL OF PHARMACOLOGY AND CHEMOTHERAPY.
39:325-333, June, 1970.

"The syndrome of barbiturate dependence," by F. A.
Whitlock. MEDICAL JOURNAL OF AUSTRALIA. 2:391-
396, August 29, 1970.

"Treatment of barbiturate dependence," by D. Goldman, et al. JOURNAL OF THE AMERICAN MEDICAL AS-
SOCIATION. 213:2272-2273, September 28, 1970.

"Value of serum and urine barbiturate tests in monitoring barbiturate withdrawal," by M. S. Kleckner,
et al. JOURNAL OF THE AMERICAN MEDICAL ASSOCIA-
TION. 213:1909, September 14, 1970.

BEHAVIOR
"Behavior of some young men," by F. Horstein. PRESSE
MEDICALE. 78:387-388, February 14, 1970.

"Behavioral patterns in sex and drug use on the college campus," by S. Herz. JOURNAL OF THE MEDICAL
SOCIETY OF NEW JERSEY. 67:3-6, January, 1970.

"Behavioural effects of some derivatives of ampheta-
mines and LSD and their significance," by J. R.
Smythies, et al. NATURE (London). 226:644-645,
May 16, 1970.

"Do drugs lead to violence?" by D. M. Rorvik. LOOK.
34:58+, April 7, 1970.

"Effects of lithium pretreatment on amphetamines
and DMI tetrabenazine produced psychomotor behavior," by P. S. D'Encarnacao, et al. DISEASES
OF THE NERVOUS SYSTEM. 31:494-496, July, 1970.

"Frequency--specific relation between hippocampal
theta rhythm, behavior, and amobarbital action,"
by J. A. Gray and G. G. Ball. SCIENCE. 168:
1246-1248, June, 1970.

"Marijuana and behavior; the unfilled gaps," by L.
Massett. SCIENCE NEWS. 97:156-158, February 7,
1970.

"Marijuana and temporal disintegration," by F. T.
Melges, et al. SCIENCE. 168:1118-1120, May
29, 1970.

BEHAVIOR (cont'd.)
"Mood-altering substances: a behavior inventory,"
by M. B. Pollock. JOURNAL OF EDUCATIONAL MEASURE-
MENT. 7:211-212, Fall, 1970.

"Mood, behavior, and drugs," by C. D. Leake. AAAS
Symposium, December 27-28, 1970, Chicago. SCIENCE.
170,3957:559-560, October, 1970.

"Research study on behavioral patterns in sex and
drug use on college campus," by S. Herz. ADO-
LESCENCE. 5:1-16, Spring, 1970.

"The role of brain dopamine in behavioral regulation
and the actions of psychotropic drugs," by S. H.
Snyder, et al. AMERICAN JOURNAL OF PSYCHIATRY.
127:199-207, August, 1970.

"Users and nonusers of marijuana; some attitudinal
and behavioral correlates," by F. W. King. JOUR-
NAL OF THE AMERICAN COLLEGE HEALTH ASSOCIATION.
18:213-217, February, 1970.

"Behavior of some young men," by F. Horstein. PRESSE
MEDICALE. 78:387-388, February 14, 1970.

"Behavioral patterns in sex and drug use on the college
campus," by S. Herz. JOURNAL OF THE MEDICAL SO-
CIETY OF NEW JERSEY. 67:3-6, January, 1970.

"Behavioural effects of some derivatives or amphetamine
and LSD and their significance," by J. R. Smythies,
et al. NATURE (London). 226:644-645, May 16, 1970.

BENZEDREX ABUSE
"Propylhexedrine (Benzedrex) psychosis," by E. D.
Anderson. NEW ZEALAND MEDICAL JOURNAL. 71:302,
May, 1970.

BIBLIOGRAPHY
"On teaching about drugs; guide to books and audio-
visual aids," by S. J. Feinglass. MEDIA AND
METHODS. 7:36-39+, September, 1970.

"Biochemistry of addiction," by V. P. Dole. ANNUAL
REVIEW OF BIOCHEMISTRY. 39:821-840, 1970.

"Blacks declare war on dope; Mothers against drugs."
EBONY. 25:31-34+, June, 1970.

BLUE VELVET ABUSE
"Pulmonary angiothrombosis caused by 'blue velvet'

addiction," by J. J. Szwed. ANNALS OF INTERNAL MEDICINE. 73:771-774, November, 1970.

"Body image and defensiveness in an LSD-taking subculture," by J. R. Hartung, et al. JOURNAL OF PROJECTIVE TECHNIQUES AND PERSONALITY ASSESSMENT. 34: 316-323, August, 1970.

"Booming traffic in drugs: the government's dilemma." U.S. NEWS AND WORLD REPORT. 69:40-41, December 7, 1970.

"The brain acetylcholine system in barbitone-dependent and withdrawn rats," by A. McBride, et al. BRITISH JOURNAL OF PHARMACOLOGY AND CHEMOTHERAPY. 39:210P-211P, May, 1970.

"Bridge to the turned on," by K. H. Dansky. AMERICAN JOURNAL OF NURSING. 70:778-779, April, 1970.

"Brief to the commission of inquiry into non-medical use of drugs." MANITOBA MEDICAL REVIEW. 50:16, January-February, 1970.

"Broader attack on drug abuse, to dry up the flow of drugs." U.S. NEWS AND WORLD REPORT. 68:38, March 23, 1970.

BUSINESS AND DRUGS
"Drug abuse in business." NATURE (London). 227: 331-332, July 25, 1970.

"Drug abuse is your headache too; excerpts from Drug abuse as a business problem," by C. Kurtis. NATION'S BUSINESS. 58:38+, November, 1970.

"Drug culture; use of stimulants, sedatives, and tranquilizers by office workers." BUSINESS WEEK. pp. 83-84, August 15, 1970.

"Drug threat in business." NATION. 211:484, November 16, 1970.

"Pot-smoking young executives," by S. Margetts. DUNS. 95:42-43, February, 1970.

BUSINESS AND INDUSTRY AND DRUGS
"Rising problem of drugs on the job." TIME. 95: 70, June 29, 1970.

"Bust insurance; organization Free weed, dedicated to

the legalization of marijuana." TIME. 96:15, July 20, 1970.

"Busting the boys." NEWSWEEK. 76:32, August 17, 1970.

"$C_{21} H_{23} No_5$: a primer for parents and children," by L. Edson. NEW YORK TIMES MAGAZINE. pp. 92-93+, May 24, 1970.

CALIFORNIA CIVIL ADDICT PROGRAM
"The state versus the addict; uncivil commitment," by J. C. Kramer. BOSTON UNIVERSITY LAW REVIEW. 50:1-22, Winter, 1970.

"Callaghan hard line likely on soft drugs," by N. Fowler. TIMES. p. 6, February 7, 1970.

"The campaign against drug addiction." MEDECINE LEGALE ET DOMMAGE CORPOREL (Paris). 3:216-219, April-June, 1970.

"Can this marriage be saved?", by D.C. Disney. LADIES HOME JOURNAL. 87:12+, December, 1970.

CANNABIS
"The epidemiology of cannabism in France," by B. Defer, et al. ANNALES MEDICO-PSYCHOLOGIQUES (Paris). 2:113-120, June, 1970.

"Toxic derivitives of cannabis sativa," by G. Nanas, et al. PRESSE MEDICALE. 78:1679-1684, September 19, 1970.

"Unwanted effects of cannabis." LANCET. 2:1350, December 26, 1970.

"Caring for the "bad trip". A review of current status of LSD," by C. M. Martin. HAWAII MEDICAL JOURNAL. 29:555-560, September-October, 1970.

"A case of glutethimide and meprobamate dependance with delirium as a drug withdrawal sympton," by J. Svestka, et al. ACTIVITAS NERVOSA SUPERIOR (Praha). 12:70-71, January 12, 1970.

"The case of Heikki (voluntary application for treatment of drug addiction)." SAIRAANHOITAJA. 46:174-177,

March 10, 1970.

"A case of phenmetrazine addiction," by M. Slizewski. WIADOMOSCI LEKARSKI. 23:419-421, March 1, 1970.

"Case study on the attitudes of drug addicts to treatment," by A. M. Toll. BRITISH JOURNAL OF ADDICTION. 65:139-158, August, 1970.

CATECHOLAMINE ABUSE
"Catecholamine dependence. Pathogenesis and treatment," by F. Milazzotto, et al. CARDIOLOGIA PRATICA. 21:11-16, February, 1970.

"Catecholamine dependence. Pathogenesis and treatment," by F. Milazzotto, et al. CARDIOLOGIA PRATICA. 21: 11-16, February, 1970.

CATHA EDULIS
"The use of catha edulis among Yemenite Jews," by J. P. Hes. HAREFUAH. 78:283-284, March 15, 1970.

"Causes of death among institutionalized narcotic addicts," by J. D. Sapira, et al. JOURNAL OF CHRONIC DISEASES. 22:733-742, April, 1970.

"Central-stimulating amines--international control," by N. Retterstol. TIDSSKRIFT FOR DEN NORSKE LAGE-FORENING. 90:2096, November 15, 1970.

"Centrilobular hepatic necrosis and acute renal failure in "solvent sniffers"," by R. D. Baerg, et al. ANNALS OF INTERNAL MEDICINE. 73:713-720, November, 1970.

"Changes in brain RNA metabolism during audiogenic crisis in mice," by R. DiCarlo, et al. PHYSIOLOGIE (Paris). 62:Suppl. 2:271, 1970.

"Changes in the picture of drug addiction in adolescents," by R. Mader, et al. WIENER MEDIZINISCHE WOCHENSCHRIFT. 120:330-333, May 2, 1970.

"Changing British drug scene," by M. M. Glatt. LANCET. 1:143-144, January 17, 1970.

"The changing British drug scene," by C. P. Hallett. LANCET. 1:93, January 10, 1970.

"The changing British drug scene," by J. Merry. LANCET. 1:252, January 31, 1970.

"Checkpoints for fighting the drug menace in camp:
education program at Camp Narrin, Michigan," by
S. C. Huck and P. A. Denomme. CAMPING MAGAZINE.
42:19+, September, 1970.

"Chemical basis of hashish activity," by R. Mechoulam,
et al. SCIENCE. 169:611-612, August 7, 1970.

"Chemical intoxication and civilization crisis."
PRESSE MEDICALE. 78:763, March 28, 1970.

CHLORAMPHENICOL ABUSE
   "Chloramphenicol misuse," by E. P. Cronkite. NATURE
   (London). 227:533, August 1, 1970.

"Chloramphenicol misuse," by E. P. Cronkite. NATURE
(London). 227:533, August 1, 1970.

CHLORDIAZEPOXIDE
   "Comparative effects of amphetamine, scopolamine,
   chlordiazepoxide, and diphenylhydantoin on operant
   and extinction behavior with brain stimulation
   and food reward," by M. E. Olds. NEUROPHARMACOL-
   OGY. 9:519-532, November, 1970.

   "An oral method of the withdrawal treatment of heroin
   dependence; a five years' study of a combination
   of diphenoxylate (lomotil) and chlormethiazole
   (Heminevrin)," by M. M. Glatt, et al. BRITISH
   JOURNAL OF ADDICTION. 65:237-243, November, 1970.

"Chromosomal aberrations induced by barley by LSD,"
by M. P. Singh, et al. SCIENCE. 169:491-492, July
31, 1970.

"Chromosome abnormality in offspring of LSD user. D
trisomy with D-D translocation," by L. Y. Hsu, et al.
JOURNAL OF THE AMERICAN MEDICAL ASSOCIATION. 1:
987-990, February 9, 1970.

CHROMOSOMES AND DRUGS
   "Chromosome abnormality in offspring of LSD user. D
   trisomy with D-D translocation," by L. Y. Hsu,
   et al. JOURNAL OF THE AMERICAN MEDICAL ASSOCIA-
   TION. 1:987-990. February 9, 1970.

"Chronic non-psychiatric hazards of drugs of abuse,"
by S. S. Epstein and J. Lederberg. SCIENCE. 168:
507+, April 24, 1970.

"Chronic psychosis associated with long-term psycho-

tomimetic drug abuse," by G. S. Glass, et al.
ARCHIVES OF GENERAL PSYCHIATRY. 23:97-103, August,
1970.

CIRRHOSIS
"Hepatitis complicated by cirrhosis as a sequel of
occasional drug abuse," by H. A. Jensen. UGE-
SKRIFT FOR LAEGER. 132:880-881, May 7, 1970.

"Cladestine drug laboratories," by J. W. Gunn, Jr., et
al. JOURNAL OF FORENSIC SCIENCES. 15:51-64, January, 1970.

"Classroom drug scene; training sessions for educators,"
by M. V. Gelinas. AMERICAN EDUCATION. 6:3-5, November, 1970.

"Clinical evaluation of the drug user: current concepts,"
by G. G. Dimijian. TEXAS MEDICINE. 66:42-49, January, 1970.

"A clinical examination of chronic LSD use in the community," by S. P. Barron, et al. COMPREHENSIVE
PSYCHIATRY. 11:69-79, January, 1970.

CLINICIANS AND DRUGS
"Clinical evaluation of the drug user; current concepts," by G. G. Dimijian. TEXAS MEDICINE. 66:
42-49, January, 1970.

"A clinical examination of chronic LSD use in the
community," by S. P. Barron, et al. COMPREHEN-
SIVE PSYCHIATRY. 11:69-79, January, 1970.

"The clinician's role in the problem of drug usage
by young people," by D. H. Milman. AMERICAN
JOURNAL OF PSYCHIATRY. 126:1040, January, 1970.

"The clinician's role in the problem of drug usage by
young people," by D. H. Milman. AMERICAN JOURNAL
OF PSYCHIATRY. 126:1040, January, 1970.

COCAINE
"Sensitivity changes to noradrenaline in the guinea-
pig vas deference induced by amphetamine, cocaine
and denervation," by S. de Moraes, et al. JOUR-
NAL OF PHARMACY AND PHARMACOLOGY. 22:717-719,
September, 1970.

"College Student Attitudes Toward Marijuana," by M. F.
Amo and J. R. Bittner. COLLEGE STUDENT SURVEY.

4,2:52-54, February, 1970.

"College student drug use," by E. S. Robbins, et al. AMERICAN JOURNAL OF PSYCHIATRY. 126:1743-1751, June, 1970.

COLLEGE STUDENTS AND DRUGS
"Abuse of hallucinogenic drugs: some observations of a college psychiatrist," by P. K. Munter. INTERNATIONAL PSYCHIATRY CLINICS. 7:153-168, 1970.

"Alcohol or marijuana: a follow up survey at Ithaca College." JOURNAL OF THE AMERICAN COLLEGE HEALTH ASSOCIATION. 18,5:366-367, June, 1970.

"Alternative strategies for developing a campus drug policy," by S. T. Rickard. NASPA, JOURNAL OF THE ASSOCIATION OF DEANS AND ADMINISTRATORS OF STUDENT AFFAIRS. 8,1:64-68, July, 1970.

"Behavioral patterns in sex and drug use on the college campus," by S. Herz. JOURNAL OF THE MEDICAL SOCIETY OF NEW JERSEY. 67:3-6, January, 1970.

"College student attitudes toward marijuana," by M. F. Amo and J. R. Bittner. COLLEGE STUDENT SURVEY. 4,2:52-54, February, 1970.

"College student drug use," by E. S. Robbins, et al. AMERICAN JOURNAL OF PSYCHIATRY. 126:1743-1751, June, 1970.

"Consumption of psychoactive drugs and illegal drugs by the Zurich university students," by K. Battig. SCHWEIZERISCHE MEDIZINISCHE WOCHENSCHRIFT. 100: 1887-1893, October 31, 1970.

"Counseling the college student drug user," by J. L. Kuehn. BULLETIN OF THE MENNINGER CLINIC. 34: 205-214, July, 1970.

"Developing a new policy on campus drugs," by C. Stauth. COLLEGE MANAGEMENT. 5:15-16, November, 1970.

"Dimensions of marijuana usage in a land grant university," by L. B. DeFleur and G. R. Garrett. JOURNAL OF COUNSELING PSYCHOLOGY. 17,5:468-475, September, 1970.

COLLEGE STUDENTS AND DRUGS (cont'd.)

"Drug abuse prevention," by J. D. Swisher and R. E.
Horman. JOURNAL OF COLLEGE STUDENT PERSONNEL.
11:337-341, September, 1970.

"Drug offenses and the university." UNIVERSITIES
QUARTERLY. 24,3:243-257, Summer, 1970.

"Drug use by university freshmen," by K. R. Mitchell,
et al. JOURNAL OF COLLEGE STUDENT PERSONNEL. 11:
332-336, September, 1970.

"Drug use on a university campus," by B. C. Smith.
JOURNAL OF THE AMERICAN COLLEGE HEALTH ASSOCIATION.
18:360-364, June, 1970.

"Drugs and the college student," by C. Knipmeyer.
NEBRASKA NURSE. 3:8-9, July, 1970.

"Drugs and the small college," by C. S. Olton. NA-
TIONAL ASSOCIATION OF STUDENT PERSONNEL ADMINIS-
TRATORS BULLETIN. 8,2:83-89, October, 1970.

"Drugs on the college campus," by H. B. Bruyn. JOUR-
NAL OF SCHOOL HEALTH. 40:91-98, February, 1970.

"A graduate student looks at the drug problem," by
R. R. Shibuya. JOURNAL OF SCHOOL HEALTH. 40:4335-
437, October, 1970.

"Law'n order in Dallas; case of four black students
from the University of California." NATION.
211:582, December 7, 1970.

"Marihauna," by D. Perna. JOURNAL OF THE AMERICAN
MEDICAL ASSOCIATION. 214:760, October 26, 1970.

"Moderation in drug use at Michigan; survey of University of Michigan students." SCHOOL AND SOCIETY.
98:134-135, March, 1970.

"Nonmedical drug use among college student psychiatric patients," by R. G. Hinckley. JOURNAL OF
THE AMERICAN COLLEGE HEALTH ASSOCIATION. 18:333-
341, June, 1970.

"On campus; drugs vs. drinking." MADEMOISELLE. 70:
230, March, 1970.

"Patterns of drug use among college students; a preliminary report," by G. L. Mizner, et al. AMERI-
CAN JOURNAL OF PSYCHIATRY. 127:15-24, July, 1970.

COLLEGE STUDENTS AND DRUGS (cont'd.)
"Patterns of drug use in a provincial university,"
by I. Hindmarch. BRITISH JOURNAL OF ADDICTION.
64:395-402, January, 1970.

"Personality correlates of undergraduate marijuana
use," by R. Hogan, et al. JOURNAL OF CONSULTING
AND CLINICAL PSYCHOLOGY. 35:58-63, August, 1970.

"Purposes, patterns, and protection in a campus
drug using community," by E. Schaps, et al.
JOURNAL OF HEALTH AND SOCIAL BEHAVIOR. 11:135-
145, June, 1970.

"Research study on behavioral patterns in sex and
drug use on college campus," by S. Herz. ADOLES-
CENCE. 5:1-16, Spring, 1970.

"The student drug user and his family," by J. L.
Kuehn. JOURNAL OF COLLEGE STUDENT PERSONNEL.
11,6:409-413, November, 1970.

"Use of a 'Freak Out' Control Center." JOURNAL OF
COLLEGE STUDENT PERSONNEL. 11,6:403-408, November, 1970.

COMMISSIONS ON DRUGS
"Brief to the commission of inquiry into non-medical
use of drugs." MANITOBA MEDICAL REVIEW. 50:16,
January-February, 1970.

"The Committee and the pill," by P. Diggory. LANCET.
1:86, January 10, 1970.

COMMITTEE ON SAFETY OF DRUGS
"The role of the Committee on Safety of Drugs," by
D. Mansel-Jones. BRITISH MEDICAL BULLETIN. 26:
257-259, September, 1970.

"A Community Approach to Drug Abuse Education," by L.
B. Donner. JOURNAL OF SCHOOL HEALTH. 40,8:417-419,
October, 1970.

"Community control of addiction." BRITISH MEDICAL JOUR-
NAL. 1:313, May 9, 1970.

"Community Programs and the Underlying Problem," by O.
H. Entwistle. COMPACT. 4,3:41-43, June, 1970.

"Community where drug addicts grow up; Phoenix houses
in New York City," by A. W. Birch. PTA MAGAZINE.
65:2-5, November, 1970. Same abr. with title "Where

addicts become adults." READER'S DIGEST. 97:92-96,
December, 1970.

"Comparative effects of amphetamine, scopolamine, chlordiazepoxide, and diphenylhydantoin on operant and
extinction behavior with brain stimulation and food
reward," by M. E. Olds. NEUROPHARMACOLOGY. 9:519-
532, November, 1970.

COMPLICATIONS
"Absence of major medical complications among chronic
opiate addicts," by J. C. Ball, et al. BRITISH
JOURNAL OF ADDICTION. 65:109-112, August, 1970.

"The acute pulmonary edema of heroin intoxication,"
by W. J. Morrison, et al. RADIOLOGY. 97:347-
351, November, 1970.

"Centrilobular hepatic necrosis and acute renal
failure in 'solvent sniffers'," by R. D. Baerg,
et al. ANNALS OF INTERNAL MEDICINE. 73:713-720,
November, 1970.

"Chronic non-psychiatric hazards of drugs of abuse,"
by S. S. Epstein and J. Lederberg. SCIENCE. 168:
507+, April 24, 1970.

"Chronic psychosis associated with long-term psycho-
tomimetic drug abuse," by G. S. Glass, et al.
ARCHIVES OF GENERAL PSYCHIATRY (Chicago). 23:
97-103, August, 1970.

"Complications caused by anonymous preclinical medication," by A. Voelkel. ARZNEIMITTEL-FORSCHUNG.
20:873-875, July, 1970.

"Complications of narcotic addiction," by R. S. Kurtzman. RADIOLOGY. 96:23-30, July, 1970.

"Cor pulmonale secondary to talc granulomata in the
lungs of a drug addict," by A. R. Bainborough, et
al. CANADIAN MEDICAL ASSOCIATION JOURNAL. 103:
1297-1298, December 5, 1970.

"Corneal complications of topical anesthetic abuse,"
by W. E. Willis, et al. CANADIAN JOURNAL OF OPH-
THALMOLOGY. 5:239-243, July, 1970.

"Effect of intra-arterial injections of barbiturates,"
by D. Albo, Jr., et al. AMERICAN JOURNAL OF SUR-
GERY. 120:676-678, November, 1970.

COMPLICATIONS (cont'd.)
"Endocarditis in the drug addic," by R. G. Ramsey, et al. AMERICAN JOURNAL OF CARIDOLOGY. 25:608-618, May, 1970.

"Endocarditis in the drug user," by V. T. Andriole. CONNECTICUT MEDICINE. 34:327-330, May, 1970.

"Epidemiology of tetanus in narcotic addicts," by C. E. Cherubin. NEW YORK STATE JOURNAL OF MEDICINE. 70:267-271, January 15, 1970.

"Glue sniffing causes heart block in mice," by G. J. Taylor and H. W. Harris. SCIENCE. 170:866-888, November 20, 1970.

"Hepatitis and drug abuse," by I. Mark. UGESKRIFT FOR LAEGER. 132:1109-1116, June 4, 1970.

"Hepatitis associated antigen in young drug abusers with hepatitis in Vestre Hospital," by T. Jersild, et al. NORDISK MEDICIN. 84:1537-1538, November 26, 1970.

"Hepatitis-associated antigen in young narcotic addicts with hepatitis. Qualitative and quantitative determinations," by T. Jersild, et al. UGESKRIFT FOR LAEGER. 132:873-874, May 7, 1970.

"Hepatitis associated with illicit use of intravenous methamphetamine," by L. E. Davis, et al. PUBLIC HEALTH REPORTS. 85:809-813, September, 1970.

"Hepatitis complicated by cirrhosis as a sequel of occasional drug abuse," by H. A. Jensen. UNGESKRIFT FOR LAEGER. 132:880-881, May 7, 1970.

"Hepatitis in young drug abusers--liver pathology and Prince antigen," by T. Jersild, et al. NORDISK MEDICIN. 84:1538, November 26, 1970.

"Hepatitis in young drug users," by T. Jersild, et al. SCANDINAVIAN JOURNAL OF GASTROENTEROLOGY SUPPLEMENT. 7:79-83, 1970.

"Hepatorenal toxicity from sniffing spot-remover (trichloroethylene). Report of 2 cases," by H. R. Clearfield. AMERICAN JOURNAL OF DIGESTIVE DISEASES. 15:851-856, September, 1970.

"Heroin overdose complicated by intravenous injection of milk," by E. J. Drenick, et al. JOUR-

36

COMPLICATIONS (cont'd.)
NAL OF THE AMERICAN MEDICAL ASSOCIATION. 213:
1687, September 7, 1970.

"Intracranial hemorrhage associated with amphetamine
abuse," by S. J. Goodman, et al. JOURNAL OF THE
AMERICAN MEDICAL ASSOCIATION. 212:480, April 20,
1970.

"Intravenous administration of marijuana," by N. E.
Gary, et al. JOURNAL OF THE AMERICAN MEDICAL AS-
SOCIATION. 211:501, January 19, 1970.

"Intravenous drug abuse. Pulmonary, cardiac, and
vascular complications," by R. B. Jaffe, et al.
AMERICAN JOURNAL OF ROENTGENOLOGY, RADIUM THER-
APY AND NUCLEAR MEDICINE. 109:107-120, May, 1970.

"LSD and chromosome damage," by J. Hoey. JOURNAL OF
THE AMERICAN MEDICAL ASSOCIATION. 212:1707, June
8, 1970.

"Leg ulcers and drug abuse," by E. J. Valtonen. LAN-
CET. 2:1192-1193, December 5, 1970.

"Marijuana persistence in the body." SCIENCE NEWS.
98:476, December 26, 1970.

"Mental disorders caused by phenmetrazine abuse,"
by B. Klosinska, et al. PSYCHIATRIA POLSKA. 4:
45-47, January-February, 1970.

"Necrotizing anglitis associated with drug abuse,"
by B. P. Citron, et al. NEW ENGLAND JOURNAL OF
MEDICINE. 283:1003-1011, November 5, 1970.

"Obscure hemolytic anemia due to analgesic abuse.
Does enterogenous cyanosis exist?" by E. A.
Azen, et al. AMERICAN JOURNAL OF MEDICINE. 48:
724-727, June, 1970.

"Periodontal disease in narcotic addicts," by S.
Shapiro, et al. JOURNAL OF DENTAL RESEARCH. 49:
Suppl.:1556, November-December, 1970.

"Pharmacological problems of drug dependence," by
Z. Votava. ACTIVITAS NERVOSA SUPERIOR (Praha).
12:136, 1970.

"Price of a trip? Possibility of chromosome damage
to germ cells by LSD." TIME. 95:43, February
23, 1970.

COMPLICATIONS (cont'd.)
"Propylhexedrine (Benzedrex) psychosis," by E. D.
Anderson. NEW ZEALAND MEDICAL JOURNAL. 71:302,
May, 1970.

"Psychodysleptic drugs. Psychological, physiological
and social complications," by J. P. Chiasson. BUL-
LETIN DES INFIRMIERES CATHOLIQUES DU CANADA. 37:
226-236, September-December, 1970.

"Psychoses due to cannabis abuse," by G. d'Elia, et
al. LAKARTIDNINGEN. 67:3526-3529, August 5, 1970.

"Psychotic symptoms due to cannbis abuse; a survey
of newly admitted mental patients," by W. Keup.
DISEASES OF THE NERVOUS SYSTEM. 31:119-126, February, 1970.

"Pulmonary angiothrombosis caused by 'blue velvet'
addiction," by J. J. Szwed. ANNALS OF INTERNAL
MEDICINE. 73:771-774, November, 1970.

"Pulmonary talc granulomatosis. A complication of
drug abuse," by G. B. Hopkins, et al. AMERICAN
REVIEW OF RESPIRATORY DISEASE. 101:101-104, January, 1970.

"The serum hepatitis related antigen (SH) in illicit
drug users," by C. E. Cherubin, et al. AMERICAN
JOURNAL OF EPIDEMIOLOGY. 91:510-517, May, 1970.

"Skin lesions in drug addicts," by D. I. Vollum.
BRITISH MEDICAL JOURNAL. 2:647-650, June 13, 1970.

"Staphylococcal bacteremia in heroin addicts," by H.
O. Farhoudi, et al. MEDICAL ANNALS OF THE DISTRICT
OF COLUMBIA. 39:187-194, April, 1970.

"Surgical management of infections and other complications resulting from drug abuse," by D. D. Clark.
ARCHIVES OF SURGERY. 101:619-623, November, 1970.

"Visual disturbances experienced by hallucinogenic
drug abusers while driving," by G. E. Woody. AMER-
ICAN JOURNAL OF PSYCHIATRY. 127:683-686, November, 1970.

"Complications caused by anonymous preclinical medication," by A. Voelkel. ARZEIMITTEL-FORSCHUNG. 20:
873-875, July, 1970.

"Complications of narcotic addiction," by R. S. Kurtzman. RADIOLOGY. 96:23-30, July, 1970.

"Compound analgetics with morphine content," by P. Flatberg. TIDSSKRIFT FOR DEN NORSKE LAEGEFORENING. 90:1562, August 15, 1970.

"Comprehensive action model to combat drug abuse in high school," by R. F. Petrillo. JOURNAL OF SCHOOL PSYCHOLOGY. 8,3:226-230, 1970.

"Comprehensive drug abuse prevention and control act of 1970: the President's remarks at the signing ceremony at the Bureau of Narcotics and Dangerous Drugs, October 27, 1970," by R. Nixon. COMPILATION OF PRESIDENTIAL DOCUMENTS. 6:1463, November 2, 1970.

"Conditioned nalorphine-induced abstinence changes: persistence in post morphine-dependent monkeys," by S. R. Goldberg, et al. JOURNAL OF THE EXPERIMENTAL ANALYSIS OF BEHAVIOR. 14:33-46, July, 1970.

"Confronting the drug peril." CHRISTIANITY TODAY. 14: 24-25, April 24, 1970.

"Consumption of psychoactive drugs and illegal drugs by the Zurich university students," by K. Battig. SCHWEIZERISCHE MEDIZINISCHE WOCHENSCHRIFT. 100: 1887-1893, October 31, 1970.

"Continuing studies in the diagnosis and pathology of death from intravenous narcotism," by H. Siegel, et al. JOURNAL OF FORENSIC SCIENCES. 15:179-184, April, 1970.

"Control and distribution of narcotics in the hospital," by L. Banner, et al. HOSPITAL MANAGEMENT. 110:68+, October, 1970.

"Control of amphetamines and L.S.D." LANCET. 1:708, April 4, 1970.

"Control of central stimulants: the Swedish tactics gave the result," by S. Martens. LAKARTIDNINGEN. 67:2269-2272, May 13, 1970.

"Control of drug abuse[from a statement before the United States Senate subcommittee to investigate juvenile delinquency, September 17, 1969]," by Sidney Cohen. FEDERAL PROBATION. 34:32-37, March 7, 1970.

"Control of drugs," by M. M. Glatt. LANCET. 1:889-890,

April 25, 1970.

"Control and psychotropic substances," by W. W. Wigle. CANADIAN MEDICAL ASSOCIATION JOURNAL. 102:873+, April 25, 1970.

"Control of stupefacient drugs," by B. Rolland. ARCHIVES BELGES DE MEDECINE SOCIALE, HYGIENE, MEDECINE DU TRAVAIL ET MEDECINE LEGALE. 28:249-256, April, 1970.

"Control organizations for the restriction of narcotic and drug abuse," by F. Jorgensen. UGESKRIFT FOR LAEGER. 132:2191-2194, November 12, 1970.

"The Controlled Dangerous Substances Act of 1969," by M. R. Sonnenreich. BULLETIN OF THE PARENTERAL DRUG ASSOCIATION. 24:14-22, January-February, 1970.

"Cooperation in drug provision." TIDSKRIFT FOR SVERIGES SJUKSKOTERSKOR. 37:76-77, January, 1970.

"Coping with drug abuse," by S. Lecker and W. Pigott. CANADA'S MENTAL HEALTH. 18:1+ (Suppl. 64), March-April, 1970.

"Coping with drug abuse. I. A community social action approach," by Lecker, et al. CANADIAN JOURNAL OF PSYCHIATRIC NURSING. 11:5-9, July, 1970.

"Coping with drug abuse. II. An indigenous multidisciplinary clinic for youths," by Lecker. CANADIAN JOURNAL OF PSYCHIATRIC NURSING. 11:4-9, August, 1970.

"Cor pulmonale secondary to talc granulomata in the lungs of a drug addict," by A. R. Bainborough, et al. CANADIAN MEDICAL ASSOCIATION JOURNAL. 103:1297-1298, December 5, 1970.

"Corneal complications of topical anesthetic abuse," by W. E. Willis, et al. CANADIAN JOURNAL OF OPHTHALMOLOGY. 5:239-243, July, 1970.

"The costs of Dangerous Drugs legislation in England and Wales," by A. J. Culyer, et al. MEDICAL CARE. 8:501-509, November-December, 1970.

"Counseling the college student drug user," by J. L. Kuehn. BULLETIN OF THE MENNINGER CLINIC. 34:205-214, July, 1970.

"Counselors in the Adolescent Drug Scene." CANADIAN

COUNSELOR. 4,2:131-133, April, 1970.

"Counter-measures against narcotic addiction," by H. Kravitz. IMAGE (New York). 138:55, July, 1970.

"Cracks in the panacea." SCIENCE NEWS. 97:366-367, April 11, 1970.

"The craze for chemical comfort," by K. Keating. AORN JOURNAL. 11:35+, April, 1970.

"A critical review of some psychoanalytic literature on drug addiction," by C. Yorke. BRITISH JOURNAL OF PSYCHIATRY. 43:141-159, June, 1970.

"Criticism on the Department of Welfare. Lack of initiative in incidents of Minamata disease and control of drugs," by M. Hirasawa. JAPANESE JOURNAL OF NURSING. 34:41-45, November, 1970.

"Crossing the marijuana dmz." IMPRINT. 17:3-4, January, 1970.

"Crossvalidation of the Hill-Monroe acceptability for psychotherapy scale for addict males," by J. I. Berzins, et al. JOURNAL OF CLINICAL PSYCHOLOGY. 26: 199-201, April, 1970.

"Curing drug addiction with former addicts help," by V. Brittain. NEW YORK TIMES. p. 9, May 2, 1970.

"A curious situation." SUPERVISOR NURSE. 1:7, November, 1970.

"Current aspects of products causing dependence," by P. J. de Schepper. ARCHIVES BELGES DE MEDECINE SOCIALE, HYGIENE, MEDECINE DU TRAVAIL ET MEDECINE LEGALE. 28: 257-266, April, 1970.

"Current drug addiction: clinical effects of agents in use and common semiologic aspects," by P. Deniker, et al. ANNALES MEDICO-PSYCHOLOGIQUES (Paris). 2: 70-78, June, 1970.

"Current narcotics abuse from the viewpoint of criminalistic practice," by G. Bauer. MUENCHENER MEDIZINISCHE WOCHENSCHRIFT. 112:1562-1569, August 28, 1970.

"Current trends in the treatment of drug dependence and drug abuse," by Nathan B. Eddy. BULLETIN ON NARCOTICS. 22:1-9, January-March, 1970. Prepared at the request of the United States Bureau of Narcotics and Dangerous Drugs.

CYCLAMATES
"Cyclamates, tobacco, and us." NEW YORK JOURNAL OF MEDICINE. 70:757-758, March 15, 1970.

"Why cyclamates were banned." LANCET. 1:1091-1092, May 23, 1970.

"Cyclamates, tobacco, and us." NEW YORK JOURNAL OF MEDICINE. 70:757-758, March 15, 1970.

CYCLAZOCINE
"A cyclazocine typology in opiate dependence," by R. B. Resnick, et al. AMERICAN JOURNAL OF PSYCHIATRY. 126:1256-1260, March, 1970.

"Subjective effects of narcotic antagonists cyclazocine and nalorphine on the Addiction Research Center Inventory (ARCI)," by C. A. Haertzen. PSYCHOPHARMACOLOGIA. 18:366-377, 1970.

"The use of cyclazocine in the treatment of heroin addicts," by E. S. Petursson, et al. DISEASES OF THE NERVOUS SYSTEM. 31:549-551, August, 1970.

"A cyclazocine typology in opiate dependence," by R. B. Resnick, et al. AMERICAN JOURNAL OF PSYCHIATRY. 126:1256-1260, March, 1970.

DAGGA
"Dagga and driving," by T. James. SOUTH AFRICAN MEDICAL JOURNAL. 44:580-581, May 16, 1970.

"Dagga: a review of fact and fancy," by T. James. SOUTH AFRICAN MEDICAL JOURNAL. 44:575-580, May 16, 1970.

"Dagga and driving," by T. James. SOUTH AFRICAN MEDICAL JOURNAL. 44:580-581, May 16, 1970.

"Dagga: a review of fact and fancy," by T. James. SOUTH AFRICAN MEDICAL JOURNAL. 44:575-580, May 16, 1970.

"Damage caused by drugs. I," by M. Messini. CLINICA TERAPEUTICA. 53:197-225, May 15, 1970.

"Dangerous abuses of amphetamines." CANADIAN JOURNAL OF PSYCHIATRIC NURSING. 11:12, March, 1970.

"Dangerous doctors." BRITISH MEDICAL JOURNAL. 1:705-706, March 21, 1970.

"Dangerous drugs at large. II.," by A. Cohen. NURSING MIRROR AND MIDWIVES JOURNAL. 131:22, October 30, 1970.

"Dangers of barbiturates," by E. Tylden, et al. BRITISH MEDICAL JOURNAL. 2:49, April 4, 1970.

"DARE-a thinking, hoping, seeing, feeling, breathing, speaking happening." AORN JOURNAL. 12:52-53, September, 1970.

"Darkening drug mood." TIME. 96:60, August 10, 1970.

"Death from heroin," by P. H. Abelson. SCIENCE. 168: 1289, June 12, 1970.

"Death of a young athlete: possible role of doping. Apropos of 2 cases," by M. Yacoub, et al. MEDECINE LEGALE ET DOMMAGE CORPOREL (Paris). 3:275-277, July-September, 1970.

"Deaths in drug addicts." CANADIAN MEDICAL ASSOCIATION JOURNAL. 103:1309-1310, December 5, 1970.

"Deaths in drug addicts. Cases of death not caused by sickness among abusers of euphorigenic substances, investigated within Copenhagen University's Forensic Medical Institute's field of activity from 1 January 1968 to 1 May 1970," by J. Voight. UGESKRIFT FOR LAEGER. 132:1989-1999, October 15, 1970.

"Deaths in drug addicts. Forensic chemical studies and toxicological considerations," by K. Worm, et al. UGESKRIFT FOR LAEGER. 132:1955-1960, October 15, 1970.

"Deaths in United Kingdom opioid users 1965-69," by R. Gardner. LANCET. 2:650-653, September 26, 1970.

"Deceptions in the illicit drug market," by F. E. Cheek, et al. SCIENCE. 167:1276, February 27, 1970.

"Declaration by the Attorneys General on the narcotics traffic; United States-Mexico joint cooperation." DEPARTMENT OF STATE BULLETIN. 63:300, September 14, 1970.

"Demographic factors in opiate addiction among Mexican-Americans," by C. D. Chambers, et al. PUBLIC HEALTH REPORTS. 85:523-531, June, 1970.

DENTISTRY AND DRUGS
"The oral health of narcotic addicts," by S. Shapiro, et al. JOURNAL OF PUBLIC HEALTH DENTISTRY. 30: 244-249, Fall, 1970.

"Periodontal disease in narcotic addicts," by S. Shapiro, et al. JOURNAL OF DENTAL RESEARCH. 49, Suppl.:1556, November-December, 1970.

"Survey of drug usage in dental practice, 1969. II. Narcotics registry; course taken relating to drug therapy; professional society meetings attended. Bureau of Economic Research and Statistics." JOURNAL OF THE AMERICAN DENTAL ASSOCIATION. 81:1402-1404, December, 1970.

"Department warns of penalties for drug violations abroad; announcement. March 31, 1970." DEPARTMENT OF STATE BULLETIN. 62:549-551, April 27, 1970.

"Dependency habits in delinquent adolescents," by C. I. Backhouse, et al. BRITISH JOURNAL OF ADDICTION. 64: 417-418, January, 1970.

DETECTION
"Amphetamine abuse amongst psychiatric in-patients. The use of gas chromatography," by A. E. Robinson, et al. BRITISH JOURNAL OF PSYCHIATRY. 116: 643-644, June, 1970.

"Amphetamines in human urine: rapid estimation by gas-liquid chromatography," by J. W. Schweitzer, et al. CLINICAL CHEMISTRY. 16:786-788, September, 1970.

"Current drug addiction: clinical effects of agents in use and common semiologic aspects," by P. Deniker, et al. ANNALES MEDICO-PSYCHOLOGIQUES (Paris). 2:70-78, June, 1970.

"Determination and identification of sympathomimetic amines in blood samples from drivers by a combination of gas chromatography and mass spectrometry," by R. Bonnichsen, et al. ZEITSCHRIFT FUER RECHTSMEDIZIN. 67:1926, 1970.

"Determination of drugs in biologic specimens," by

44

DETECTION (cont'd.)
J. E. Wallace, et al. ILLINOIS MEDICAL JOURNAL.
39:512-519, October 9, 1970.

"Diagnosis and treatment of the passively addicted
newborn," by D. Ingall and M. Zukerstatter. HOS-
PITAL PRACTICE. 5:101+, August, 1970.

"Drug detection in urines of commercial blood bank
doners," by R. J. Coumbis, et al. JOURNAL OF
THE AMERICAN MEDICAL ASSOCIATION. 214:596, October 19. 1970.

"Evaluation and treatment of the suspected drug
user in the emergency room," by G. G. Dimijian,
et al. ARCHIVES OF INTERNAL MEDICINE (Chicago).
125:162-170, January, 1970.

"Gas chromatographic determination of amphetamine
in blood, tissue, and urine," by E. Anggard, et
al. SCANDINAVIAN JOURNAL OF CLINICAL AND LABOR-
ATORY INVESTIGATION. 26: 137-143, September, 1970.

"Identification of various amphetamines and amphetamine-like substances in urine using thin-layer
chromatography," by J. P. deMan. PHARMAZEUTISCHE
WEEKBLAD VOOR NEDERLAND. 105:1218-1228, October
16, 1970.

"Monitoring of adverse reactions to drugs in the
United Kingdom," by W. H. Inman. PROCEEDINGS
OF THE AMERICAN PSYCHOPATHOLOGICAL ASSOCIATION.
63:1302-1304, December, 1970.

"Narcotic control and the Nalline test; the addict's
perspective," by S. E. Grupp. JOURNAL OF FORENSIC
SCIENCES. 15:34-50, January, 1970.

"Narcotics detection and industry," by D. Sohn, et al.
JOURNAL OF OCCUPATIONAL MEDICINE. 12:6-9, January,
1970.

"Preliminary report on the detection and quantitation
of opiates and certain other drugs of abuse as
trimethysilyl derivatives by gas-liquid chromatography," by K. D. Parker, et al. JOURNAL OF
THE FORENSIC SCIENCE SOCIETY. 10:17-22, January,
1970.

"Principles of diagnosis and treatment of addictive
drugs overdose," by J. F. Burdon. JOURNAL OF THE
ROYAL COLLEGE OF GENERAL PRACTITIONERS. 20:171-

DETECTION (cont'd.)
174, September, 1970.

"Salicylism revisited. Unusual problems in diagnosis and management," by L. O. Surapathana, et al. CLINICAL PEDIATRICS. 9:658-661, November, 1970.

"Simultaneous measurement technics: urinary CO2 (C14-02) elimination and motor acitivity in mice during metabolic experimentation with amphetamines," by A. Benakis. EXPERIENTIA. 26:1163-1164, October 15, 1970.

"A spectrophotofluorometric method for the determination of amphetamine," by C. R. Nix, et al. JOURNAL OF FORENSIC SCIENCES. 15:595-600, October, 1970.

"Spurious heart disease," by C. B. Upshaw, Jr. MEDICAL TRIAL TECHNIQUE QUARTERLY. 16:27-33, June, 1970.

"Urine testing schedules in methadone maintenance treatment of heroin addiction," by A. Goldstein, et al. JOURNAL OF THE AMERICAN MEDICAL ASSOCIATION. 214:311-315, October 12, 1970.

"Value of serum and urine barbiturate tests in monitoring barbiturate withdrawal," by M. S. Kleckner, et al. JOURNAL OF THE AMERICAN MEDICAL ASSOCIATION. 213:1909, September 14, 1970.

"The youngest addict...and ways to recognize him." EMERGENCY MEDICINE. 2:28+, September, 1970.

"Determination and identification of sympathomimetic amines in blood samples from drivers by a combination of gas chromatography and mass spectrometry," by R. Bonnichsen, et al. ZEITSCHRIFT FUER RECHTS-MEDIZIN. 67:19-26, 1970.

"Determination of drugs in biologic specimens," by J. E. Wallace, et al. INDUSTRIAL MEDICINE AND SURGERY. 39:412-419, October, 1970.

"Developing a new policy on campus drugs," by C. Stauth. COLLEGE MANAGEMENT. 5:15-16, November, 1970.

"The development of international control of drugs," by M. M. Glatt. WHO CHRONICLE. 24:189-197, May, 1970.

"Development of tolerance to and physical dependence on barbiturates in rhesus monkeys," by T. Yanagita, et al. JOURNAL OF PHARMACOLOGY AND EXPERIMENTAL THERAPEUTICS. 172:163-169, March, 1970.

DEXTROMORPHAN
"Toxicomanogenic properties of derivatives of dextromorphan," by J. LaBarre. THERAPIE. 25:565-578, May-June, 1970.

"Diagnosis and treatment of the passively addicted newborn," by D. Ingall and M. Zuckerstatter. HOSPITAL PRACTICE. 5:101+, August, 1970.

DIAZEPAM ABUSE
"Drug abuse and addiction to diazepam," by U. H. Peters, et al. ARZNEIMITTEL-FORSCHUNG. 20: 876-877, July, 1970.

DIET AND DRUGS
"Frozen, preportioned foods meet special needs of narcotics addicts." MODERN HOSPITAL. 114:114-115, June, 1970.

DIET-PILL ABUSE
"How I broke the dangerous diet-pill habit." GOOD HOUSEKEEPING. 176:12+, March, 1970.

"Dimensions of Marijuana Usage in a Land Grant University," by L. B. DeFleur and G. R. Garrett. JOURNAL OF COUNSELING PSYCHOLOGY. 17,5:468-475, September, 1970.

DIMYRIL ABUSE
"Dimyril abuse in the East Midlands," by M. P. Gogan, et al. BRITISH JOURNAL OF ADDICTION. 65:63-66, May, 1970.

"Dimyril abuse in the East Midlands," by M. P. Gogan, et al. BRITISH JOURNAL OF ADDICTION. 65:63-66, May, 1970.

DIPHENOXYLATE
"An oral method of the withdrawal treatment of heroin dependence: a five years' study of a combination of diphenoxylate (Lomotil) and chlormethiazole (Heminevrin)," by M. M. Glatt, et al. BRITISH JOURNAL OF ADDICTION. 65:237-243, November, 1970.

DIPHENYLHDANTOIN
"Comparative effects of amphetamine, scopolamine,

chlordiazepoxide, and diphenylhydantoin on operant
and extinction behavior with brain stimulation and
food reward," by M. E. Olds. NEUROPHARMACOLOGY.
9:519-532, November, 1970.

"Disease course observation in patients with kidney
diseases following abuse of analgesics," by T.
Nitzsche, et al. DEUTSCHE MEDIZINISCHE WOCHEN-
SCHRIFT. 95:927-934, April 24, 1970.

"Disseminated magnesium and aluminum silicate associated
with paregoric addiction," by W. C. Butz. JOURNAL
OF FORENSIC SCIENCES. 15:581-587, October, 1970.

"Distribution and metabolism of neuroleptic drugs. I.
Pharmacokinetics of haloperidol," by P. J. Lewi, et
al. ARZNEIMITTEL-FORSCHUNG. 20:943-948, July, 1970.

"Do drugs lead to violence?" by D. M. Rorvik. LOOK.
34:58+, April 7, 1970.

"Doctor Baird of East Harlem; conductor of group therapy
sessions for narcotic addicts," by W. F. Buckley,Jr.
NATIONAL REVIEW. 22:100, January 27, 1970.

"Doctors at risk." MEDICAL JOURNAL OF AUSTRALIA. 1:
743-744, April 11, 1970.

"Does our Army fight on drugs?" by J. H. Kaplan. LOOK.
34:72+, June 16, 1970.

"Doing it in the road: folkways vs. mores," by E. Schoenfeld. MENTAL HYGIENE. 54:450-452, July, 1970.

"Doing something about amphetamines," by B. Yellen. NEW
ENGLAND JOURNAL OF MEDICINE. 283:1349-1350, December
10, 1970.

DOPAMINE AND DRUGS
"The role of brain dopamine in behavioral regulation
and the actions of psychotropic drugs," by S. H.
Snyder, et al. AMERICAN JOURNAL OF PSYCHIATRY.
127:199-207, August, 1970.

"Dope about dope; publications of the Student association for the study of hallucinogens." SATURDAY
REVIEW OF LITERATURE. 53:80, September 19, 1970.

"Dope Stop--Teen Involvement," by G. E. Conroy. AR-
IZONA MEDICINE. 27:16-17, October, 1970.

"Dope(s)," by G. Lees. HI FI. 20:134, October, 1970.

"A dose of Spanish fly," by A. J. Presto,3rd, et al. JOURNAL OF THE AMERICAN MEDICAL ASSOCIATION. 214: 591-592, October 19, 1970.

DRINAMYL ABUSE
"Successful treatment of 'drinamyl' addicts and associated personality changes," by T. Kraft. CANADIAN PSYCHIATRIC ASSOCIATION JOURNAL. 15:223-227, April, 1970.

"Treatment of drinamyl addiction: two case studies," by T. Kraft. JOURNAL OF NERVOUS AND MENTAL DISEASE. 150:138-145, February, 1970.

"Drug abuse." NOVA SCOTIA MEDICAL BULLETIN. 49:102-103, June, 1970.

"Drug abuse," by J. E. Miale. AORN JOURNAL. 11:7, April, 1970.

"Drug abuse," by W. Wiechowski. WIADOMOSCI LEKARSKIE. 23:2239-2242, December 15, 1970.

"Drug abuse among union members," by L. Perlis. INDUSTRIAL MEDICINE AND SURGERY. 39:54-56, September, 1970.

"Drug abuse and addiction to diazepam," by U. H. Peters, et al. ARZNEIMITTEL-FORSCHUNG. 20:876-877, July, 1970.

"Drug abuse and learning effects," by J. Jacobson. EDUCATIONAL HORIZONS. 48:97-104, Summer, 1970.

"Drug abuse and the school scene; symposium." SCIENCE TEACHER. 37:45-50, September, 1970.

"Drug Abuse and Social Alienation." TODAY'S EDUCATION. 59,6:29-31, September, 1970.

"Drug Abuse and What To Do About It: An Assessment." COMPACT. 4,3:4-11, June, 1970.

"Drug abuse; Comprehensive drug abuse prevention and control act of 1970." NEW REPUBLIC. 163:9, October 10, 1970.

"Drug abuse: a current assessment," by D. B. Louria. AMERICAN FAMILY PHYSICIAN/GP. 1:74-80, June, 1970.

"Drug abuse: The doctor's role," by E. A. Wolfson. JOURNAL OF THE MEDICAL SOCIETY OF NEW JERSEY. 67: 465-471, August, 1970.

"Drug Abuse Education--The Picture in New York City," by I. Tobin. SCIENCE TEACHER. 37,6:47-49, September, 1970.

"Drug abuse: implications for education," by E. B. Luongo. NEW YORK STATE EUCATION. 58:32-33, November, 1970.

"Drug Abuse: Implications for Instruction," by R. K. Means. JOURNAL OF HEALTH, PHYSICAL EDUCATION AND RECREATION. 41,5:23-24+, May, 1970.

"Drug abuse in business." NATURE (London). 227:331-332, July 25, 1970.

"Drug abuse in the Navy," by J. A. Pursch. UNITED STATES NAVAL INSTITUTE PROCEEDINGS. 96:52-56, July, 1970.

"Drug abuse in physicians." JOURNAL OF THE TENNESSEE MEDICAL ASSOCIATION. 63:327-328, April, 1970.

"Drug abuse in the schools; teacher opinion poll. National education association. Research division." TODAY'S EDUCATION. 59:7, December, 1970.

"Drug abuse in the Western world," by G. D. Lundberg. JOURNAL OF THE AMERICAN MEDICAL ASSOCIATION. 213: 2082, September 21, 1970.

"Drug abuse in a young psychiatric population," by M. Cohen and D. F. Klein. AMERICAN JOURNAL OF ORTHO-PSYCHIATRY. 40:448-455, April, 1970.

"Drug abuse is your headache, too; excerpts from Drug abuse as a business problem," by C. Kurtis. NATION'S BUSINESS. 58:38+, November, 1970.

"Drug abuse: Moral considerations," by J. J. Lynch. HOSPITAL PROGRESS. 51:34+, March, 1970.

"Drug abuse: myths and facts about marijuana," by L. Wurmser. ALUMNAE MAGAZINE (Baltimore). 69:3-5, March, 1970.

"Drug abuse: the newest and most dangerous challenge to school boards," by P. C. Barrins. AMERICAN SCHOOL BOARD JOURNAL. 157:15-18, October, 1969; Same cond.

EDUCATION DIGEST. 35:24-26, January, 1970.

"Drug abuse--1970," by J. D. Sapira, et al. DM;
DISEASE-A-MONTH. 1-47, November, 1970.

"Drug abuse--a nursing responsibility?" by L. Blake.
ALASKA NURSE. 24:18-19, December, 1970.

"Drug abuse: pandemic." JOURNAL OF THE AMERICAN MED-
ICAL ASSOCIATION. 214:2327, December 28, 1970.

"Drug abuse prevention," by J. D. Swisher and R. E.
Horman. JOURNAL OF COLLEGE STUDENT PERSONNEL. 11:
337-341, September, 1970.

"The Drug Abuse Program at Milwaukee County Institutions.
A six-month report," by R. L. Wiesen, et al. WISCON-
CIN MEDICAL JOURNAL. 69:141-144, May, 1970.

"Drug abuse programs--timely efforts." JOURNAL OF THE
AMERICAN PHARMACEUTICAL ASSOCIATION. 10:299, June,
1970.

"Drug abuse rehabilitation program for youth," by C. J.
Katz, et al. ROCKY MOUNTAIN MEDICAL JOURNAL. 67:
57-60, July, 1970.

"Drug Abuse. Schools Find Some Answers." SHOOL MAN-
AGEMENT. 14,4:22-28, April, 1970.

"Drug abuse, self abuse and the abuse of authority,"
by K. S. Adam, et al. CANADIAN PSYCHIATRIC ASSO-
CIATION JOURNAL. 15:79-81, February, 1970.

"Drug abuse topic at state meeting." BULLETIN; TEXAS
NURSES ASSOCIATION. 43:2-3, May, 1970.

"Drug Abuses." ECONOMIST. 234:40, January 17, 1970.

"Drug addiction." DENTAL DIGEST. 76:236, May, 1970.

"Drug addiction," by H. Grant-Whyte. SOUTH AFRICAN
MEDICAL JOURNAL. 44:520, April 25, 1970.

"Drug addiction among juveniles with special consider-
ation of hashish smoking," by P. Kielholz, et al.
DEUTSCHE MEDIZINISCHE WOCHENSCHRIFT. 95:101-105,
January 16, 1970.

"Drug addiction and abuse." THE JOURNAL OF PRACTICAL
NURSING. 20:22+, January, 1970.

"Drug addiction and drug misuse," by R. H. Hemphill. SOUTH AFRICAN MEDICAL JOURNAL. 44:307-317, March 14, 1970.

"Drug addiction and the law," by D. A. Cahal. JOURNAL OF THE ROYAL COLLEGE OF GENERAL PRACTITIONERS. 20: 32-38, July, 1970.

"Drug addiction and personality disorder," by T. Kraft. BRITISH JOURNAL OF ADDICTION. 64:403-408, January, 1970.

"Drug addiction. A crime or a disease?" MEDICAL ANNALS OF THE DISTRICT OF COLUMBIA. 39:113-114+, February, 1970.

"Drug addiction: An effective therapeutic approach," by R. C. Wolfe, et al. MEDICAL TIMES. 98:185-193, September, 1970.

"Drug addiction--a menace to youth in Great Britain. A pilot epidemiological study," by D. C. Watt, et al. ACTIVITAS NERVOSA SUPERIOR (Praha). 12:284-287, 1970.

"Drug addiction of adolescents in Sweden," by B. Jansson. NORDISK PSYKIATRISK TIDSSKRIFT. 24:44-56, 1970.

"Drug addiction prevention program," by A. J. Friedhoff. JOURNAL OF THE AMERICAN MEDICAL ASSOCIATION. 214: 1564, November 23, 1970.

"Drug addiction--treatment or punishment?" by N. Retterstol. TIDSSKRIFT FOR DEN NORSKE LAEGEFORENING. 90: 2095, November 15, 1970.

"Drug addiction treatment with maintenance doses of methdone," by M. Nimb. NORDISK MEDICIN. 83:1412, October 29, 1970.

"Drug addicts getting younger; with study-discussion program, by E. Harris and D. Harris," by C. Winick. PTA MAGAZINE. 65:6-8+, September, 1970.

"The "drug" and drug addiction in Americans before the conquest," by C. Coury. PRESSE MEDICALE. 78:979-981, April 25, 1970.

"Drug controlled addiction," by A. Bauer. ARZNEIMITTEL-FORSCHUNG. 20:875-876, July, 1970.

"Drug crutches," by V. A. Donner. NEW ENGLAND MEDICAL JOURNAL. 282:876, April 9, 1970.

"Drug culture: use of stimulants, sedatives and tranquilizers by office workers." BUSINESS WEEK. p. 83-84, August 15, 1970.

"Drug deceptions," by S. Krippner. SCIENCE. 168:654, May 8, 1970.

"Drug dependence among patients attending a Department of Venereology," by L. I. Ponting, et al. BRITISH JOURNAL OF VENEREAL DISEASES. 46:111-113, April, 1970.

"Drug dependence among physicians," by D. L. Farnsworth. NEW ENGLAND JOURNAL OF MEDICINE. 282:392-393, February 12, 1970.

"Drug dependence and addiction among patients of the Vienna Psychiatric-Neurological University Hospital with special reference to psychotropic drugs," by G. Hofman, et al. ARZNEIMITTEL-FORSCHUNG. 20: 871-873, July, 1970.

"Drug dependence and its treatment. I.," by D. X. Freedman. POSTGRADUATE MEDICINE. 47:110-114, January, 1970.

"Drug dependence and its treatment. II.," by D. X. Freedman. POSTGRADUATE MEDICINE. 47:150-154, February, 1970.

"Drug dependence and pregnancy: a review of the problems and their management," by R. Neuberg. JOURNAL OF OBSTETRICS AND GYNAECOLOGY OF THE BRITISH COMMONWEALTH. 77:1117-1122, December, 1970.

"Drug dependence in Brisbane," by M. J. Abrahams, et al. MEDICAL JOURNAL OF AUSTRALIA. 2:397-404, August 29, 1970.

"Drug dependence in isophrenaline inhalation. Argument against a concentrated preparation," by K. Naess. TIDSSKRIFT FOR DEN NORSKE LAEGEFORENING. 90:505-506, March 1, 1970.

"Drug dependence in Italy: some statistical, clinical, and social observations," by A. Madeddu and G. Malagoli. BULLETIN ON NARCOTICS. 22:1-11, October-December, 1970.

"Drug dependence in the United States of America," by
I. A. Lowe. JOURNAL OF THE ROYAL COLLEGE OF GENERAL
PRACTITIONERS. 19:16-21, January, 1970.

"Drug dependence: a problem for society," by J. M. Benforado. WISCONSIN MEDICAL JOURNAL. 69:145-147,
May, 1970.

"Drug dependence: some research issues," by D. C. Cameron. BULLETIN OF THE WORLD HEALTH ORGANIZATION.
43:589-598, 1970.

"Drug detection in urines of commercial blook bank
donors," by R. J. Coumbis, et al. JOURNAL OF THE
AMERICAN MEDICAL ASSOCIATION. 214:596, October
19, 1970.

"Drug education and our children." BEDSIDE NURSE.
3:13, May, 1970.

"Drug education and training: statement by the President [March 11, 1970] announcing an expanded federal
program." COMPILATION OF PRESIDENTIAL DOCUMENTS.
6:351-353, March 16, 1970.

"Drug education begins before kindergarten: the Glen
Cove, New York pilot program," by R. M. Daniels.
JOURNAL OF SCHOOL HEALTH. 40:242-248, May, 1970.

"Drug Education: A Challenge for the 70's." EDUCATION-
AL PRODUCT REPORT. 3,7:2-3, April, 1970.

"Drug Education Does't Work Unless Kids Care," by W.
Rasberry. COMPACT. 4,3:36, June, 1970.

"Drug education in the primary grades," by R. Daniels.
JOURNAL OF THE NEW YORK STATE SCHOOL NURSE-TEACHER
ASSOCIATION. 1:37-38, June, 1970.

"Drug education in schools, by whose values?" by M.
E. Doster. DELTA KAPPA GAMMA BULLETIN. 36:47-49,
Summer, 1970.

"Drug education in the schools; panel discussion."
COMPACT. 4:41-44, October, 1970.

"Drug education in the states," Special Suppl.: COMPACT.
4,6:21-28, December, 1970.

"Drug education: take out the glamor!" by R. Carpenter.
INSTRUCTOR. 80:130-133, August, 1970.

"Drug epidemic: what's a teacher to do?" by C. H. Harrison. SCHOLASTIC TEACHER SECONDARY TEACHER SUPPLEMENT. 4-6+, May 4, 1970.

"Drug Explosion." ECONOMIST. 235-252+, April 4, 1970.

"Drug glossary." SATURDAY REVIEW OF LITERATURE. 53: 21, November 14, 1970.

"Drug glossary." SOCIAL EDUCATION. 34:892-894, December, 1970.

"Drug habit. Multiplication of preventive measures," by C. Vaille. PRESSE MEDICALE. 78:755-757, March 28, 1970.

"Drug-induced changes of urinary catecholamines in the rat: role of the adrenal medulla," by P. Del Basso, et al. EUROPEAN JOURNAL OF PHARMACOLOGY. 13:83-89, 1970.

"Drug menace: how serious? dangers in dope: teen-age addicts: interview with John E. Ingersoll, director, Federal Bureau of Narcotics." U.S. NEWS AND WORLD REPORT. 68:38-42, May 25, 1970.

"Drug-metabolizing capacity and drug dependence," by I. H. Stevenson, et al. CLINICAL SCIENCE. 39:11, September, 1970.

"Drug misuse in teenagers," by D. Lloyd. APPLIED THERAPEUTICS. 12:19-25, March, 1970.

"Drug Offenses and the University." UNIVERSITIES QUARTERLY. 24,3:243-257, Summer, 1970.

"Drug peril hits home in U.S." IRISH NURSING NEWS. p. 12-14, March-April, 1970.

"Drug prevention clubs in France," by J. Ellul. INTERPLAY. 3:39-41, August, 1970.

"The drug problem and industry," by F. M. Garfield. INDUSTIRAL MEDICINE AND SURGERY. 39:366-368, August, 1970.

"The drug problem as it stands in Hong Kong," by T. G. Garner. BRITISH JOURNAL OF ADDICTION. 65:45-50, May, 1970.

"Drug problem; treating preaddictive adolescents," by

P. Caroff, et al. SOCIAL CASEWORK. 51:527-532, November, 1970. Reply: D. Hallowitz and G. N. Cohen. 52:46-47, January, 1971.

"Drug Problems and the High School Principal." NATIONAL ASSOCIATION OF SECONDARY SCHOOL PRINCIPALS BULLETIN. 54,346:52-59, May, 1970.

"Drug pushers in the United Kingdom," by D. MacSweeney, et al. NATURE (London). 228:422-424, October 31, 1970.

"Drug registration in the county of Jamtland: Clinical experiences of the preliminary study in 1968," by I. Bergstrom, et al. LAKARTIDNINGEN. 67:Suppl. III: 91+, October 12, 1970.

"Drug scene." by S. M. Spencer and R. Severo. READER'S DIGEST. 96:67-75, January, 1970.

"The Drug Scene." SCHOOL PROGRESS. 39,5:46-47, May, 1970.

"The drug scene," by S. F. Yolles. NURSING OUTLOOK. 18:24-26, July, 1970.

"Drug scene: high schools are higher now." NEWSWEEK. 75:66-67, February 16, 1970.

"Drug scene in East Egg," by E. Diamond. NEW YORK TIMES MAGAZINE. pp. 28-29+, May 17, 1970. Discussion, 56-57, June 28, 1970.

"Drug screening in industrial nursing," by D. Sohn, et al. OCCUPATIONAL HEALTH NURSING. 18:7-10, August, 1970.

"The drug syndrome in the affluent society," by J. Finlator. JOURNAL OF FORENSIC SCIENCES. 13:293-301, July, 1968.

"Drug-taking in delinquent boys," by P. J. Noble. BRITISH MEDICAL JOURNAL. 1:102-105, January 10, 1970.

"Drug therapy. II. Treatment of drug misuse," by J. S. Holcenberg, et al. NORTHWEST MEDICINE. 69:31-33, January, 1970.

"Drug therapy today. Use and abuse of the amphetamines," by M. J. Rodman. RN. 33:55+, August, 1970.

"Drug threat in business." NATION. 211:484, November 16, 1970.

"A drug to lick a drug," by F. Warshofsky. FAMILY HEALTH. 2:22+, May, 1970.

"Drug traffic in the middle east; a lesson for the west?" by R. Alan. NEW LEADER. 53:16-19, September 7, 1970.

"Drug treatment and prevention; Hope house, inc, Albany, N.Y.," by H. Hubbard. NATIONAL ASSOCIATION OF SECONDARY SCHOOL PRINCIPALS BULLETIN. 54:95-105, November, 1970.

"Drug use-abuse: quo vadimus," by W. R. Lipscomb. NEBRASKA STATE MEDICAL JOURNAL. 55:671-675, November, 1970.

"Drug use among the young: As teenagers see it," by E. Herzog, et al. CHILDREN. 17:207+, November-December, 1970.

"Drug use and health," by J. T. Ungerleider. AORN JOURNAL. 12:111-112, September, 1970.

"Drug use by university freshmen," by K. R. Mitchell, et al. JOURNAL OF COLLEGE STUDENT PERSONNEL. 11:332-336, September, 1970.

"Drug use on a university campus," by B. C. Smith. JOURNAL OF THE AMERICAN COLLEGE HEALTH ASSOCIATION. 18:360-364, June, 1970.

"The drug-using adolescent as a pediatric patient," by I. F. Litt, et al. JOURNAL OF PEDIATRICS. 77:195-202, August, 1970.

"Drugs," by D. P. Mogal, et al. INDEPENTENT SCHOOL BULLETIN. 29:7-13, May, 1970.

"Drugs--addicts. Helping the nurse to understand the needs expressed by the addicted person," by C. Kelly. PENNSYLVANIA NURSE. 25:4-6+, October, 1970.

"Drugs, adolescents and society," by O. Jeanneret. ZEITSCHRIFT FUR KRANKENPFLEGE. 63:9-13, January, 1970.

"Drugs and the college student," by C. Knipmeyer. NEBRASKA NURSE. 3:8-9, July, 1970.

"Drugs and death in the run-down world of rock music; J. Hendrix and J. Joplin," by A. Goldman. LIFE. 69:32-33, October 16, 1970.

"Drugs and the educational antidote." NATION'S SCHOOLS. 85:49-52+, April, 1970.

"Drugs and the law," by D. M. Dozer. FREEMAN. 20:131-135, March, 1970.

"Drugs and modern drug addiction," by P. Deniker. ANNALES MEDICO-PSYCHOLOGIQUES (Paris). 2:68-70, June, 1970.

"Drugs and our children: a White House report; questions and answers." LADIES HOME JOURNAL. 87:112-113+, May, 1970.

"Drugs and reality in captive society. Some observations on chemical adaptation," by G. D. Scott. CANADIAN PSYCHIATRIC ASSOCIATION JOURNAL. 15:215-222, April, 1970.

"Drugs and the Schools: Two Case Studies." EDUCATIONAL PRODUCT REPORT. 3,7:4-15, April, 1970.

"Drugs and the Small College," by C. S. Olton. NATIONAL ASSOCIATION OF STUDENT PERSONNEL ADMINISTRATORS BULLETIN. 8,2:83-89, October, 1970.

"Drugs and Youth," by D. P. Mogol. INDEPENDENT SCHOOL BULLETIN. 29,4:7-9, May, 1970.

"Drugs are not the problem," by V. A. Dohner. COMPACT. 4:20-24, June, 1970; Same cond. EDUCATION DIGEST. 36:25-28, November, 1970.

"Drugs are your problem," by D. C. King. AMERICA. 122:497-498, May 9, 1970.

"Drugs Bill; Piecing it all together." ECONOMIST. 234:23-24, March 14, 1970.

"Drugs, a contagious disease," by R. Page. DAILY TELEGRAPH. p. 8, December 23, 1970.

"Drugs: development and use." LANCET. 2:972, November 7, 1970.

" 'Drugs'--do they produce open or closed minds?" by D. L. Farnsworth. Part I. MEDICAL INSIGHT. 2:34+,

July, 1970. Part 2. MEDICAL INSIGHT. 2:22+, August, 1970.

"Drugs, drug dependence and traffic safety. Psycho-physical capacity under the influence of drugs and their effect on traffic," by B. Dokert. PHARMA-ZEUTISCHE PRAXIS; BEILAGE ZUR DIE PHARMAZIE. 1: 1-6, 1970.

"Drugs, drunken driving, the delivery of medical care, the high cost of hospitalization," by S. D. Simon. RHODE ISLAND MEDICAL JOURNAL. 53:276-281+, May, 1970.

"Drugs for Escape or Religious Experience," by T. Reinhardt. RELIGIOUS EDUCATION. 65:176-183, March, 1970.

"Drugs: hard and soft distinguished." NATURE (London). 225:1089, March 21, 1970.

"Drugs in decline?" CHRISTIANITY TODAY. 15:54, November 6, 1970.

"Drugs in modern society," by C. R. Henwood. NEW ZEALAND NURSING JOURNAL. 63:9+, April, 1970.

"Drugs in suburbia." WALL STREET JOURNAL. 176:1+, November 12, 1970; 1+, November 18, 1970.

"Drugs: the landscape of grass and snow," by H. S. Resnik. SATURDAY REVIEW OF LITERATURE. 53:23-25+, August 15, 1970.

"Drugs: Letter to Parents," by H. S. Frost. INDEPENDENT SCHOOL BULLETIN. 29,4:12-13, May, 1970.

"Drugs: Letter to a Trustee," by E. S. Van Gorder. INDEPENDENT SHCOOL BULLETIN. 29,4:10-11, May, 1970.

"Drugs on the college campus," by H. B. Bruyn. JOURNAL OF SCHOOL HEALTH. 40:91-98, February, 1970.

"Drugs raise a specter." BUSINESS WEEK. 80-82, May 9, 1970.

"Drugs--the role of the teacher and youth leader," by D. A. Lane. COMMUNITY HEALTH (Bristol). 1:327-329, May-June, 1970.

"Drugs, sports and doping," by K. S. Clarke. JOURNAL OF THE MAINE MEDICAL ASSOCIATION. 61:55-58, March, 1970.

"Drugs: stopping the supply is not enough," by G. Birdwood. DAILY TELEGRAPH. p. 12, April 4, 1970.

"Drugs, talk makes sixth formers queasy," by T. Devlin.
TIMES (London) EDUCATIONAL SUPPLEMENT. 2854:11,
January 30, 1970.

"Drugs/teens=alcohol/parents," by T. Lawrence and J.
Velleman. SCIENCE DIGEST. 68:46-48+, October, 1970.

"Drugs: Ten years to doomsday?" by H. Sutton. SATURDAY
REVIEW OF LITERATURE. 53:18+, November 14, 1970.

"Drugs: the tools of medical progress," by S. Boe. JOUR-
NAL OF SCHOOL HEALTH. 40:65-70, February, 1970.

"Drugs used against addiction," by M. J. Rodman. RN.
33:71-80, October, 1970.

"Drugs: we are just plain ignorant," by J. R. Moskin.
LOOK. 34:108+, October 6, 1970.

"Drugs; what can the schools do about the problem?" by
L. D. Hamilton. EDUCATION CANADA. 10,4:30-36,
December, 1970.

"Drunkenness, drugs and manslaughter," by G. F. Orchard.
CRIMINAL LAW REVIEW. 211-218, April, 1970.

"EEG arousal reactions to amphetamine and 2,5-dimethoxy-
4-methylamphetamine in reserpine-pretreated rabbits,"
by M. Fujimori, et al. BIOLOGICAL PSYCHIATRY. 2:
241-250, July, 1970.

"Each other's victim's; excerpts," by M. Travers. MC-
CALLS. 97:70-71+, June, 1970.

"Early steps toward preventing drug abuse; with study-
discussion program, by E. Harris and D. Harris," by
R. E. Gould. PTA MAGAZINE. 64:6-9+, March, 1970.

"Ecological variations in heroin abuse," by L. J. Redlinger and J. B. Michel. SOCIOLOGICAL QUARTERLY.
11:219-229, Spring, 1970.

"Editorial: drug addiction, anesthetists and injections."
ANAESTHESIA. 25:163-164, April, 1970.

"Editorially speaking: youth and drug abuse," by R. Cumming. MUSIC JOURNAL. 28:4, March, 1970.

EDUCATION
"Adolescents and adults: the prism of drugs," by W. J. Cook. ILLINOIS EDUCATION. 58:293-296, March, 1970.

"Checkpoints for fighting the drug menace in camp; education program at Camp Narrin, Michigan," by S. C. Huck and P. A. Denomme. CAMPING MAGAZINE. 42:19+, September, 1970.

"Classroom drug scene; training sessions for educators," by M. V. Gelinas. AMERICAN EDUCATION. 6: 3-5, November, 1970.

"Counseling the college student drug user," by J. L. Kuehn. BULLETIN OF THE MENNINGER CLINIC. 34: 205-214, July, 1970.

"Counselors in the adolescent drug scene," by W. Penner. CANADIAN COUNSELOR. 4,2:131-133, April, 1970.

"Drug abuse and learning effects," by J. Jacobson. EDUCATIONAL HORIZONS. 48:97-104, Summer, 1970.

"Drug abuse education--the picture in New York City," by I. Tobin. SCIENCE TEACHER. 37,6:47-49, September, 1970.

"Drug abuse: implications for education," by E. B. Luongo. NEW YORK STATE EDUCATION. 58:32-33, November, 1970.

"Drug abuse: implications for instruction," by R. K. Means. JOURNAL OF HEALTH, PHYSICAL EDUCATION AND RECREATION. 41,5:23-24+, May, 1970.

"Drug abuse programs--timely efforts." JOURNAL OF THE AMERICAN PHARMACEUTICAL ASSOCIATION. 10:299, June, 1970.

"Drug education and our children (editorial)." BEDSIDE NURSE. 3:13, May, 1970.

"Drug education and training; statement by the President (March 11, 1970) announcing an expanded Federal program." COMPILATION OF PRESIDENTIAL DOCUMENTS. 6:351-353, March 16, 1970.

EDUCATION (cont'd.)

"Drug education begins before kindergarten; the Glen Cove, New York pilot program," by R. M. Daniels. JOURNAL OF SCHOOL HEALTH. 40:242-248, May, 1970.

"Drug education; a challenge for the 70's," by D. C. Lewis. EDUCATIONAL PRODUCT REPORT. 3,7:2-3, April, 1970.

"Drug education doesn't work unless kids care," by W. Rasberry. COMPACT. 4,3:36+, June, 1970.

"Drug education in the primary grades," by R. Daniels. JOURNAL OF THE NEW YORK STATE SCHOOL NURSE-TEACHER ASSOCIATION. 1:37-38, June, 1970.

"Drug education in schools; by whose values?" by M. E. Doster. DELTA KAPPA GAMMA BULLETIN. 36: 47-49, Summer, 1970.

"Drug education in the schools; panel discussion." COMPACT. 4:41-44, October, 1970.

"Drug education in the States." COMPACT. Special Supplement. 4,6:21-28, December, 1970.

"Drug education; take out the glamor," by R. Carpenter. INSTRUCTOR. 80:130-133, August, 1970.

"Drug epidemic; what's a teacher to do?" by C. H. Harrison. SCHOLASTIC TEACHER SECONDARY TEACHER SUPPLEMENT. 4-6+, May 4, 1970.

"Drugs and the educational antidote." NATION'S SCHOOLS. 85:49-52+, April, 1970.

"Drugs--the role of the teacher and youth leader," by D. A. Lane. COMMUNITY HEALTH (Bristol). 1: 327-329, May-June, 1970.

"Drugs: what can the schools do about the problem?" by L. D. Hamilton. EDUCATION CANADA. 10,4:30-36, December, 1970.

"Early steps toward preventing drug abuse: with study-discussion program, by E. Harris and D. Harris," by R. E. Gould. PTA MAGAZINE. 64:6-9+, March, 1970.

"Education programs in the State Legislature," by R. M. Webster. COMPACT. 4,3:40+, June, 1970.

EDUCATION (cont'd.)

"Educational philosophy for drug abuse programs,"
by R. L. Prettyman. SCIENCE TEACHER. 37:45-47,
September, 1970.

"An educational program on drug usage," by R. E.
Benion, et al. JOURNAL OF THE AMERICAN COLLEGE
HEALTH ASSOCIATION. 18:270-273, April, 1970.

"The great drug education hoax," by S. Halleck. PRO-
GRESSIVE. 34:30-33, July, 1970.

"Guilty, who?" by L. L. Taylor. JOURNAL OF SCHOOL
HEALTH. 40:74-75, February, 1970.

"High school drug education, an iterim measure,"
by M. A. LaCombe, et al. JOURNAL OF THE AMERICAN
MEDICAL ASSOCIATION. 214:1327-1328, November 16,
1970.

"Inservice education for teachers," by C. P. Tate.
SCIENCE TEACHER. 37:49-50, September, 1970.

"Is knowledge of most worth in drug abuse education?"
JOURNAL OF SCHOOL HEALTH. 40:453, October, 1970.

"Lack of drug education." CANADIAN JOURNAL OF PSY-
CHIATRIC NURSING. 11:12-13, April-May, 1970.

"Narcotics; a crucial area of secondary school responsibility; fully credited courses needed," by
R. Elliott. EDUCATION DIGEST. 36:44-47, September, 1970.

"Narcotics; a new area of secondary school responsi-
bility," by R. Elliott. NORTH CENTRAL ASSOCIATION
QUARTERLY. 44:325-334, Spring, 1970; also in
EDUCATION DIGEST. 36:44-47, September, 1970.

"New skills for teachers," by J. Spillane. COMPACT.
4,3:26-27, June, 1970.

"On teaching about drugs; guide to books and audio-
visual aids," by S. J. Feinglass. MEDIA AND
MEDHODS. 7:36-39+, September, 1970.

"The pharmacist and drug abuse education." JOURNAL
OF THE AMERICAN PHARMACEUTICAL ASSOCIATION. 10:
678-679, December, 1970.

"Planning and implementation of an effective drug
abuse education program," by C. A. Rodowskas, Jr.,

EDUCATION (cont'd.)
>>et al. JOURNAL OF THE AMERICAN PHARMACEUTICAL ASSOCIATION. 10:563-565+, October, 1970.

"A positive approach to drug education." JOURNAL OF SCHOOL HEALTH. 40,8:450-452, October, 1970.

"Presenting the facts. Drug abuse education." JOURNAL OF THE AMERICAN PHARMACEUTICAL ASSOCIATION. 10:628, November, 1970.

"Private enterprise and dope; creative learning group, distributor of scientific educational materials on drug damage," by W. F. Buckley, Jr. NATIONAL REVIEW. 22:964, September 8, 1970.

"The role of a school of pharmacy. Drug abuse education programming for a rural state--one approach," by P. Zanowiak. JOURNAL OF THE AMERICAN PHARMACEUTICAL ASSOCIATION. 10:566-568+, October, 1970.

"Should the drug education bandwagon be rerouted?" by C. H. Harrison. SCHOLASTIC TEACHER JR/SR HIGH. 18-19+, October 5, 1970.

"Special supplement: drug education in the states." COMPACT. 4:21-28, December, 1970.

"Strengthening drug education." SCHOOL AND SOCIETY. 98:400, November, 1970.

"Teacher evaluation of the school drug education program," by D. Pargman. SCHOOL HEALTH REVIEW. 1:14, April, 1970.

"The therapeutic community and the school," by B. Sugarman. INTERCHANGE. 1,2:77-96, 1970.

"Training teachers to deal with drugs." SCHOOL JOURNAL. 118:258-261+, May, 1970.

"Unselling drugs; antidrug education and advertising," by D. Sanford. NEW REPUBLIC. 162:15-16, February 28, 1970.

"Education Programs in the State Legislature," by R. M. Webster. COMPACT. 4,3:40, June, 1970.

"Educational philosophy for drug abuse programs," by R. L. Prettyman. SCIENCE TEACHER. 37:45-47, September, 1970.

"An educational program on drug usage," by R. E. Benion, et al. JOURNAL OF THE AMERICAN COLLEGE HEALTH ASSOCIATION. 18:270-273, April, 1970.

"Effect of intra-arterial injections of barbiturates," by D. Albo, Jr., et al. AMERICAN JOURNAL OF SURGERY. 120:676-678, November, 1970.

"The effect of nialamide, pargyline and tranylcypromine on the removal of amphetamine by the perfused liver," by F. R. Trinker, et al. JOURNAL OF PHARMACY AND PHARMACOLOGY. 22:496-499, July, 1970.

"Effect of psychoton and dexfenmetrazin on maximum physical performance," by K. Barták, et al. PHYSIOLOGIA BOHEMOSLOVACA. 19:117-121, 1970.

"The effect of various neurohumoral modulators on the activity of morphine and the narcotic antagonists in the tail-flick and phenylquinone tests," by W. L. Dewey, et al. JOURNAL OF PHARMACOLOGY AND EXPERIMENTAL THERAPEUTICS. 175:435-442, November, 1970.

"Effect of withdrawal of corticotrophin in patients on long-term treatment for multiple sclerosis," by J. H. Millar, et al. LANCET. 1:700-701, April 4, 1970.

"An effective therapeutic method for the LSD user," by C. Torda. PERCEPTUAL AND MOTOR SKILLS. 30:79-88, February, 1970.

"The effects of altered brain norepinephrine levels on continuous avoidance responding and the action of amphetamines," by F. P. Miller, et al. NEUROPHARMACOLOGY. 9:511-517, November, 1970.

"Effects of amphetamine upon relearning pattern and black-white discriminations following neocortical lesions in rats," by K. R. Jonason, et al. JOURNAL OF COMPARATIVE AND PHYSIOLOGICAL PSYCHOLOGY. 73:47-55, October, 1970.

"Effects of cocaine and amphetamine on the metabolism of tryptophan and 5-hydroxytryptamine in mouse brain in vivo," by J. Schubert, et al. JOURNAL OF PHARMACY AND PHARMACOLOGY. 22:860-862, November, 1970.

"Effects of diphenylhydantoin (Dilantin) withdrawal on non-epileptics: preliminary report," by J. A. Rosenblum, et al. CURRENT THERAPEUTIC RESEARCH. 12:31-33,

January, 1970.

"Effects of lithium pretreatment on amphetamine and DMI tetrabenazine produced psychomotor behavior," by P. S. D'Encarnacao, et al. DISEASES OF THE NERVOUS SYSTEM. 31:494-496, July, 1970.

"Effects of short and long-term administration of pentazocine in man," by D. R. Jasinski, et al. CLINICAL PHARMACOLOGY AND THERAPEUTICS. 11:385-403, May-June, 1970.

"Effects of systemically administered drugs on intraocular pressure in rabbits," by P. Burberi, et al. ARZNEIMITTEL-FORSCHUNG. 20:1143-1147, August, 1970.

"Eighteen narcotic-addiction buildings in eighteen months; Arthur Kill Rehabilitation Center, Staten Island." AMERICAN CITY. 85:152+, June, 1970.

"Electroencephalographic study of morphine tolerance and withdrawal phenomena in rats," by F. Lipparini, et al. THERAPIE. 25:929-937, September-October, 1970.

"Emergency care of acute drug intoxication," by E. A. Wolfson. JOURNAL OF THE MEDICAL SOCIETY OF NEW JERSEY. 67:820, December, 1970.

"Emergency treatment of drug abuse," by J. DeGross. RESIDENT AND STAFF PHYSICIAN. 16:43+, February, 1970.

ENDOCARDITIS
"Endocarditis in the drug addict," by R. G. Ramsey, et al. AMERICAN JOURNAL OF CARDIOLOGY. 25:608-618, May, 1970.

"Endocarditis in the drug user," by V. T. Andriole. CONNECTICUT MEDICINE. 34:327-330, May, 1970.

"Endocarditis in the drug addict," by R. G. Ramsey, et al. AMERICAN JOURNAL OF CARDIOLOGY. 25:608-618, May, 1970.

"Endocarditis in the drug user," by V. T. Andriole. CONNECTICUT MEDICINE. 34:327-330, May, 1970.

EPIDEMIOLOGY
"Drug abuse: pandemic." JOURNAL OF THE AMERICAN MEDICAL ASSOCIATION. 214:2327, December 28, 1970.

EPIDEMIOLOGY (Cont'd.)
"Drug addiction--a menace to youth in Great Britain,
a pilot epidemiological study," by D. C. Watt, et
al. ACTIVITAS NERVOSA SUPERIOR (Praha). 12:284-
287, 1970.

"The epidemiology of cannabism in France ," by B.
Defer, et al. ANNALES MEDICO-PSYCHOLOGIQUES
(Paris). 2:113-120, June, 1970.

"The epidemiology of drug dependence in the UK," by
D. V. Hawks. BULLETIN ON NARCOTICS. 22:15-24,
July-September, 1970.

"The epidemiology of drug overdosage," by L. K.
Morgan. MEDICAL JOURNAL OF AUSTRALIA. 2:338,
August 15. 1970.

"The epidemiology of drug overdosage," by F. A. Whitlock. MEDICAL JOURNAL OF AUSTRALIA. 1:1195-
1199, June, 1970.

"Epidemiology of tetanus in narcotic addicts," by
C. E. Cherubin. NEW YORK STATE JOURNAL OF MED-
ICINE. 70:267-271, January 15, 1970.

"A pandemic disease surrounds us," by V. Spencer.
HOSPITAL MANAGEMENT. 110:20+, October, 1970.

"The epidemiology of cannabism in France," by B. Defer,
et al. ANNALES MEDICO-PSYCHOLOGIQUES (Paris). 2:
113-120, June, 1970.

"The epidemiology of drug dependence in the UK," by D.
V. Hawks. BULLETIN ON NARCOTICS. 22:15-24, July-
September, 1970.

"The epidemiology of drug overdosage," by L. K. Morgan.
MEDICAL JOURNAL OF AUSTRALIA. 2:338, August 15, 1970.

"The epidemiology of drug overdosage," by F. A. Whitlock. MEDICAL JOURNAL OF AUSTRALIA. 1:1195-1199,
June 13, 1970.

"Epidemiology of tetanus in narcotic addicts," by C.
E. Cherubin. NEW YORK STATE JOURNAL OF MEDICINE.
70:267-271, January 15, 1970.

ETHANOL ABUSE
"Morphine and ethanol physical dependence; a critique
of a hypothesis," by M. H. Seevers, et al. SCIENCE.
170:1113-1115, December 4, 1970.

ETIOLOGY
"Etiology of drug addiction of adolescents," by E.
Varilo. NORDISK PSYKIATRISK TIDSSKRIFT. 24:56-
71, 1970.

"Let the physician beware," by M. S. Rapp. CANADIAN
MEDICAL ASSOCIATION JOURNAL. 102:1188+, May 30,
1970.

"The pharmacological basis of drug dependence," by
H. F. Marlow. SOUTH AFRICAN MEDICAL JOURNAL. 44:
610-615, May 23, 1970.

"Pharmacological problems of drug dependence," by Z.
Votava. ACTIVITAS NERVOSA SUPERIOR (Praha). 12:
136, 1970.

"The problem of drugs. Motives, prevention, and
measures to be taken," by H. Baruk. ANNALES MED-
ICO-PSYCHOLOGIQUES (Paris). 2:136-139, June,
1970.

"Social and psychological correlates of drug abuse.
A comparison of addict and non-addict populations
from the perspective of self-theory," by H. B.
Kaplan, et al. SOCIAL SCIENCE AND MEDICINE. 4:
203-225, August, 1970.

"The syndrome of barbiturate dependence," by F. A.
Whitlock. MEDICAL JOURNAL OF AUSTRALIA. 2:391-
396, August 29, 1970.

"Etiology of drug addiction of adolescents," by E.
Varilo. NORDISK PSYKIATRISK TIDSSKRIFT. 24:56-
71, 1970.

"Euphomania in New York City," by J. Simonsen. UGE-
SKRIFT FOR LAEGER. 132:1642-1646, August 27, 1970.

"European mental hygienists and drug abuse," by R.
Sarro, et al. NERVENARZT. 41:364, July, 1970.

"Evaluation and treatment of the suspected drug user in
the emergency room," by G. G. Dimijian, et al.
ARCHIVES OF INTERNAL MEDICINE (Chicago). 125:162-
170, January, 1970.

"Evolution of a day program," by C. J. Dromberg and J.
B. Proctor. AMERICAN JOURNAL OF NURSING. 70:2575+,
December, 1970.

"Experience with young narcomaniacs in a provincial
hospital," by N. Pape. NORDISK MEDICIN. 83:1413,
October 29, 1970.

"An experimental clinic for narcotic abusers--the nurse
as a research coordinator," by F. Kerman. ALUMNAE
MAGAZINE (Baltimore). 69:5-7, March, 1970.

"The experimental use of psychedelic (LSD) psychotherapy," by W. N. Pahnke, et al. JOURNAL OF THE
AMERICAN MEDICAL ASSOCIATION. 212:1856-1863, June
15, 1970.

"Extramural psychiatric work among narcomaniacs," by
M. Schioler. NORDISK MEDICIN. 83:1413, October 29,
1970.

"Fact is: we like to be drugged," by J. C. Oates.
McCALLS. 97:69, June, 1970.

"Facts and hypothesis on the use and current abuses of
modifying substances of the state of consciousness,"
by P. A. Bensoussan. ANNALES MEDICO-PSYCHOLOGIQUES
(Paris). 2:101-106, June, 1970.

"Factors influencing drug abuse in young people," by
D. I. Carson, et al. TEXAS MEDICINE. 66:50-57,
January, 1970.

"Family and differential involvement with marijuana;
a study of suburban teenagers," by N. Tec. JOURNAL
OF MARRIAGE AND THE FAMILY. 32:656-664, November,
1970.

"Father tells how drugs invaded his family; anonymous
report." LIFE. 68:50-52+, March 20, 1970; Same abr.
with title "Story of my son's heroin addiction."
READER'S DIGEST. 97:64-69, July, 1970.

"Fathers and sons." NEWSWEEK. 75:24+, February 9,
1970.

"Federal Bureau of Narcotics lists 15 don'ts as physician safeguards." JOURNAL OF THE INDIANA STATE
MEDICAL ASSOCIATION. 63:140, February, 1970.

"The Federal Drug Abuse Program." PUBLIC HEALTH RE-

PORTS. 85:565-568, July, 1970.

FEDERAL DRUG PROGRAMS
"The federal drug abuse program." PUBLIC HEALTH
REPORTS. 85:565-568, July, 1970.

"National drug abuse prevention program." COMPACT.
4,3:25+, June, 1970.

"National policy on drug abuse," by M. C. Gabel.
PEDIATRICS. 45:152, January, 1970.

"Federal Narcotics and Dangerous Drug Laws." COMPACT.
4,3:44, June, 1970.

"Federal plan for narcotics and dangerous drugs," by
F. M. Garfield. BULLETIN OF THE PARENTERAL DRUG
ASSOCIATION. 24:11-13, January-February, 1970.

FENFLURAMINE
"Unusual effect of fenfluramine," by D. V. Hawks.
BRITISH MEDICAL JOURNAL. 1:238, January 24,
1970.

FILMS
"16mm films on drug, alcohol and tobacco abuse."
Product information supplement no. 6. EDUCA-
TIONAL PRODUCT REPORT. 3,7:1-36, April, 1970.

"Ten drug abuse films; what students and professionals think of them." EDUCATIONAL PRODUCT
REPORT. 3,7:16-27, April, 1970.

"Video recordings," by S. H. Griffiths. NURSING
TIMES. 66:1208+, September 17, 1970.

"Frequency--specific relation between hippocampal theta
rhythm, behavior, and amobarbital action," by J.
A. Gray and G. G. Ball. SCIENCE. 168:1246-1248,
June, 1970.

"Fresh disclosures on drugs and GI's; Senate investigation into marijuana smoking." U.S. NEWS AND
WORLD REPORT. 68:32-33, April 6, 1970.

"Frisking for drugs," by C. H. Rolph. NEW STATESMAN.
79:688, May 15, 1970.

"From soft to hard drugs," by M. M. Glatt. BRITISH
MEDICAL JOURNAL. 1:756, March 21, 1970.

70

"Frozen, preportioned foods meet special needs of narcotics addicts." MODERN HOSPITAL. 114:114-115, June, 1970.

"Furor over drugs; physicians vs. the Attorney General." NEWSWEEK. 75:65+, March 30, 1970.

"Gas chromatographic determination of amphetamine in blood, tissue, and urine," by E. Anggard, et al. SCANDINAVIAN JOURNAL OF CLINICAL AND LABORATORY INVESTIGATION. 26:137-143, September, 1970.

"General observations on drug habituation," by R. E. Reinert. BULLETIN OF THE MENNINGER CLINIC. 34: 195-204, July, 1970.

"Getting the adolescent to worry about drug abuse... and his parents not to," by V. R. Allen. CONSULTANT. 10:5+, March-April, 1970.

"Getting heroin into U.S.: how the smugglers operate; excerpts from What everyone needs to know about drugs." U.S. NEWS AND WORLD REPORT. 69:41-44, December 7, 1970.

"Global headache; use of drugs spreads abroad spurring drive for international curbs," by G. Melloan. WALL STREET JOURNAL. 175:1+, March 25, 1970.

GLOSSARIES
   "Drug glossary." SATURDAY REVIEW OF LITERATURE. 53:21, November 14, 1970.

   "Drug glossary." SOCIAL EDUCATION. 34:892-894, December 4, 1970.

   "Lexicon for today--2nd edition." NEW ENGLAND JOURNAL OF MEDICINE. 282:756, March 26, 1970.

GLUE SNIFFING
   "Glue sniffing cuases heart block in mice," by G. J. Taylor and W. S. Harris. SCIENCE. 170:866-868, November 20, 1970.

"Glue sniffing cuases heart block in mice," by G. J. Taylor and W. S. Harris. SCIENCE. 170:866-868, November 20, 1970.

GLUTETHIMIDE ABUSE
"A case of glutethimide and meprobamate dependence with delirium as a drug withdrawal symptom," by J. Svestka, et al. ACTIVITAS NERVOSA SUPERIOR (Praha). 12:70-71, January 12, 1970.

"Goodbye junkies. A general practitioner takes leave of his addicts," by A. J. Hawes. LANCET. 2:258-260, August 1, 1970.

"Governor's Panel Explores Drug Abuse in Utah," by C. L. Rampton. COMPACT. 4,3:15, June, 1970.

"A graduate student looks at the drug problem," by R. R. Shibuya. JOURNAL OF SCHOOL HEALTH. 40:435-437, October, 1970.

"Grams and damns," by H. Beckelhymer. CHRISTIAN CENTURY. 87:267-268, March 4, 1970.

"Grass & the brass," by D. Sanford. NEW REPUBLIC. 162:11-12, April 25, 1970.

"The great drug education hoax," by S. Halleck. PROGRESSIVE. 34:30-33, July, 1970.

"The great medico-social problems of neuropsychiatry: drugs," by L. Businco. POLICLINICO (Prat). 77:950-954, July 20, 1970.

"Greener grass, grimmer jails: the scene abroad." NEWSWEEK. 75:51+, June 15, 1970.

"Group therapy and group work with addicted females," by R. von Battegay, et al. BRITISH JOURNAL OF ADDICTION. 65:89-98, August, 1970.

"Growing menace of pep pills," by B. Surface. SEVENTEEN. 29:146-147+, May, 1970.

"Guide to drug abuse." CANADIAN JOURNAL OF PSYCHIATRIC NURSING. 11:9-13, September, 1970.

"Guidelines for Program Development," by D. B. Louria. COMPACT. 4,3:13-14, June, 1970.

"Guidelines for using methadone in the outpatient treatment of narcotic addicts," by C. B. Scrignar, et al. JOURNAL OF THE LOUISIANA MEDICAL SOCIATY. 122:167-172, June, 1970.

"Guilty! Who?" by L. L. Taylor. JOURNAL OF SCHOOL
HEALTH. 40:74-75, February, 1970.

"Hallucinogenic drug reactions," by L. P. Solursh.
MEDICAL TRIAL TECHNIQUE QUARTERLY. 16:23-28, March,
1970.

"Hallucinogenic drugs: an unconstitutional delegation
of authority," by W. J. Curran. AMERICAN JOURNAL OF
PUBLIC HEALTH AND THE NATION'S HEALTH. 60:1314-
1315, July, 1970.

HALLUCINOGENS
"Abuse of halluncinogenic drugs: some observations
of a college psychiatrist," by P. K. Munter.
INTERNATIONAL PSYCHIATRY CLINICS. 7:153-168,
1970.

"The abuse of psychodelics: a social and medical
problem," by S. Nowak, et al. POLSKI TYGODNIK
LEKARSKI. 25:698-701, May 11, 1970.

"Hallucinogenic drug reactions," by L. P. Solursh.
MEDICAL TRIAL TECHNIQUE QUARTERLY. 16:23-28,
March, 1970.

"Hallucinogenic drugs; an unconstitutional delegation of authority," by W. J. Curran. AMERICAN
JOURNAL OF PUBLIC HEALTH AND THE NATION'S HEALTH.
60:1314-1315, July, 1970.

"Hallucinogens," by R. M. Mowbray. MEDICAL JOURNAL
OF AUSTRALIA. 1:1215-1218, June 13, 1970.

"Hallucinogens," by R. M. Mowbray. MEDICAL JOURNAL
OF AUSTRALIA. 1:1215-1218, June 13, 1970.

"Harlem group performs drug drama; King Heroin," by
G. Lichenstein. TIMES (London) EDUCATIONAL SUPPLE-
MENT. 2859:9, March 6, 1970.

HASHISH
"Drug addiction among juveniles with special con-
sideration of hashish smoking," by P. Kielholz,
et al. DEUTSCHE MEDIZINISCHE WOCHENSCHRIFT. 95:
101-105, January 16, 1970.

HASHISH (cont'd.)
"How dangerous is hashish?" by H. Sattes. SCHWESTERN
REVUE. 8:15-16, October, 1970.

"Toxicological research on hashish. Apropos of
some recent observations collected in the North,"
by T. Van Ky, et al. MEDECINE LEGALE ET DOMMAGE
CORPOREL (Paris). 3:245-250, July-September, 1970.

"Hassle over narcotics control." SCIENCE NEWS. 97:339,
April 4, 1970.

"Hazards implicit in prescribing psychoactive drugs,"
by H. L. Lennard, et al. SCIENCE. 169:438-441,
July 31, 1970.

"Health aspects of drug addiction," by F. J. Yuste
Grijalba. REVISTA DE SANIDAD E HIGIENE PUBLICA. 44:
611-624, June, 1970.

"A health fair," by M. Hurster, et al. JOURNAL OF
SCHOOL HEALTH. 40,10:539-541, December, 1970.

"Help from methadone." NEWSWEEK. 75:52, June 8, 1970.

"A halping hand to victims of drugs," by N. Blais.
INFIRMIERE CANADIENNE. 12:22-24, October, 1970.

HEMINEVRIN
"An oral method of the withdrawal treatment of
heroin dependence: a five years' study of a combination of diphenoxylate (Lomotil) and chlormethiazole (Heminevrin)," by M. M. Glatt, et al.
BRITISH JOURNAL OF ADDICTION. 65:237-243, November, 1970.

HEPATITIS AND DRUGS
"Hepatitis and drug abuse," by I. Mark. UGESKRIFT
FOR LAEGER. 132:1109-1116, June 4, 1970.

"Hepatitis associated antigen in young drug abusers.
With hepatitis in Vestre hospital," by T. Jersild,
et al. NORDISK MEDICIN. 84:1537-1538, November
26, 1970.

"Hepatitis-associated antigen in young narcotic
addicts with hepatitis. Qualitative and quantitative determinations," by T. Jersild, et al.
UGESKRIFT FOR LAEGER. 132:873-874, May 7, 1970.

"Hepatitis associated with illicit use of intra-

74

HEPATITIS AND DRUGS (cont'd.)
venous methamphetamine," by L. E. Davis, et al.
PUBLIC HEALTH REPORTS. 85:809-813, September,
1970.

"Hepatitis complicated by cirrhosis as a sequel of
occasional drug abuse," by H. A. Jensen. UGE-
SKRIFT FOR LAEGER. 132:880-881, May 7, 1970.

"Hepatitis in young drug users," by T. Jersild, et
al. SCANDINAVIAN JOURNAL OF GASTROENTEROLOGY
SUPPLEMENT. 7:79-83, 1970.

"Hepatitis and drug abuse," by I. Mark. UGESKRIFT
FOR LAEGER. 132:1109-1116, June 4, 1970.

"Hepatitis associated antigen in young drug abusers
with hepatitis in Vestre hospital," by T. Jersild,
et al. NORDISK MEDICIN. 84:1537-1538, November 26,
1970.

"Hepatitis-associated antigen in young narcotic addicts
with hepatitis. Qualitative and quantitative determinations," by T. Jersild, et al. UGESKRIFT FOR
LAEGER. 132:873-874, May 7, 1970.

"Hepatitis associated with illicit use of intravenous
methamphetamine," by L. E. Davis, et al. PUBLIC
HEALTH REPORTS. 85:809-813, September, 1970.

"Hepatitis complicated by cirrhosis as a sequel of
occasional drug abuse," by H. A. Jensen. UGESKRIFT
FOR LAEGER. 132:880-881, May 7, 1970.

"Hepatitis in young drug users," by T. Jersild, et al.
SCANDINAVIAN JOURNAL OF GASTROENTEROLOGY SUPPLEMENT.
7:79-83, 1970.

"Hepatitis in young drug abusers--liver pathology and
Prince antigen," by T. Jersild, et al. NORDISK
MEDICIN. 84:1538, November 26, 1970.

"Hepatorenal toxicity from sniffing spot-remover (trichloroethylene). Report of 2 cases," by H. R. Clearfield. AMERICAN JOURNAL OF DIGESTIVE DISEASES. 15:
851-856, September, 1970.

HEROIN
"The acute pulmonary edema of heroin intoxication,"
by W. J. Morrison, et al. RADIOLOGY. 97:347-351,
November, 1970.

HEROIN (cont'd.)

"Alarm grows in U. S. as youth moves on to heroin,"
by F. Hechinger. TIMES (London) EDUCATIONAL
SUPPLEMENT. 2859:9, March 6, 1970.

"$C_{21}H_{23}NO_3$: a primer for parents and children," by
L. Edson. NEW YORK TIMES MAGAZINE. pp. 92-93+,
May 24, 1970.

"Conditioned nalorphine-induced abstinence changes:
persistence in post morphine-dependent monkeys,"
by S. R. Goldberg, et al. JOURNAL OF THE EXPERI-
MENTAL ANALYSIS OF BEHAVIOR. 14:33-46, July, 1970.

"Death from heroin," by P. H. Abelson. SCIENCE. 168:
1289, June 12, 1970.

"Ecological variations in heroin abuse," by L. J. Redlinger and J. B. Michel. SOCIOLOGICAL QUARTERLY.
11:219-229, Spring, 1970.

"Father tells how drugs invaded his family; anonymous
report." LIFE. 68:50-52+, March 20, 1970; also
in READERS DIGEST. 97:64-69, July, 1970.

"Getting heroin into U.S.; how the smugglers operate;
excerpts from What everyone needs to know about
drugs." U.S. NEWS AND WORLD REPORT. 69:41-44,
December 7, 1970.

"Heroin addiction," by R. L. Worsnop. EDITORIAL
RESEARCH REPORTS. 385-402, May 27, 1970.

"Heroin addiction; a comparison of two inpatient
treatment methods," by M. L. LaRouche, et al.
MICHIGAN MEDICINE. 69:751-754, September, 1970.

"Heroin addiction: the epidemic of the 70's," by
J. W. Speiman. ARCHIVES OF ENVIRONMENTAL HEALTH.
21:589-590, November, 1970.

"Heroin addiction in adolescents," by P. Boyd. JOUR-
NAL OF PSYCHOSOMATIC RESEARCH. 14:295-301, September, 1970.

"Heroin and crime in the streets." AMERICA. 122:
34, January 17, 1970.

"Heroin dependence and delinquency in women--a study
of heroin addicts in Holloway prison," by P. T.
d'Orban. BRITISH JOURNAL OF ADDICTION. 65:67-
78, May, 1970.

HEROIN (cont'd.)
"Heroin in the schools." CHRISTIANITY TODAY. 14:
32, March 13, 1970.

"Heroin overdose complicated by intravenous injection
of milk," by E. J. Drenick, et al. JOURNAL OF THE
AMERICAN MEDICAL ASSOCIATION. 213:1687, September 7, 1970.

"Heroin withdrawal syndrome," by C. Zelson, et al.
JOURNAL OF PEDIATRICS. 76:483-484, March, 1970.

"Horrors of heroin; Hunts Point scene," by R. Severo.
READERS DIGEST. 96:72-75, January, 1970.

"Kids and heroin; the adolescent epidemic." TIME.
95:16-20+, March 16, 1970; also in READERS DIGEST.
96:88-92, June, 1970.

"Life on two grams a day; heroin in the high
schools." LIFE. 68:24-32, February 20, 1970.

"Main line to an early grave," by D. Gray. GUARD-
IAN. p. 10, March 18, 1970.

"Methadone and heroin addiction; rehabilitation
without a cure," by J. Walsh. SCIENCE. 168:
684-686, May 8, 1970.

"Methadone maintenance in heroin addiction," by
B. A. Pearson. AMERICAN JOURNAL OF NURSING.
70:2571+, December, 1970.

"Methadone maintenance treatment is successful for
heroin addicts," by R. E. Trussell and H. Gollance. HOSPITAL MANAGEMENT. 110:56+, October,
1970.

"Methadone management of heroin addiction." BUL-
LETIN OF THE NEW YORK ACADEMY OF MEDICINE. 46:
391-395, June, 1970.

"Miliary tuberculosis, tuberculosis of ribs and
heroin addiction," by J. Merry, et al. BRITISH
JOURNAL OF PSYCHIATRY. 116:645-646, June, 1970.

"New heroin substitute." SCIENCE DIGEST. 67:56,
June, 1970.

"An oral method of the withdrawal treatment of
heroin dependence; a five years' study of a
combination of diphenoxylate (Lomotil) and

77

HEROIN (cont'd.)
chlormethiazole (Heminevrin)," by M. M. Glatt,
et al. BRITISH JOURNAL OF ADDICTION. 65:237-243,
November, 1970.

"The political economy of junk," by S. Yurick.
MONTHLY REVIEW. 22:22-31+, December, 1970.

"Programme on heroin." NATURE (London). 227:773-
774, August 22, 1970.

"Reaction-times of methadone treated ex-heroin addicts," by N. B. Gordon. PSYCHOPHARMACOLOGIA
(Berlin). 16:337-344, 1970.

"The road to H: the same old opium of the masses,"
by D. Rosenblatt. INTERPLAY. 3:42-45, August,
1970.

"The role of occupational therapy in heroin detoxification," by F. W. Slobetz. AMERICAN JOURNAL
OF OCCUPATIONAL THERAPY. 24:340-342, July-August,
1970.

"Sedative abuse by heroin addicts," by M. Mitcheson,
et al. LANCET. 1:606-607, March 21, 1970.

"Sexual aspects of heroin addiction," by J. L. Mathis.
MEDICAL ASPECTS OF HUMAN SEXUALITY. 4,9:98-109,
September, 1970.

"Staphylococcal bacteremia in heroin addicts," by
H. O. Farhoudi, et al. MEDICAL ANNALS OF THE
DISTRICT OF COLUMBIA. 39:187-194, April, 1970.

"A survey of a representative sample of addicts prescribed heroin at London clinics," by G. V. Stimson and A. C. Ogborne. BULLETIN ON NARCOTICS.
22:12-13, October-December, 1970.

"Teenage heroin epidemic that has alarmed US," by
V. Brittain. TIMES (London). p. 11, March 13,
1970.

"Teenagers take over a slum, to quit heroin," by V.
Waite. DAILY TELEGRAPH. p. 17, April 10, 1970.

"Treating heroin addiction at Simmons House," by G.
M. Greaves and K. Ryz. NURSING TIMES. 66:49+,
January 8, 1970.

"Treatment of heroin dependence with opiate antag-

onists," by M. Fink, et al. CURRENT PSYCHIATRIC
THERAPIES. 10:161-170, 1970.

"Urine testing schedules in methadone maintenance
treatment of heroin addiction," by A. Goldstein,
et al. JOURNAL OF THE AMERICAN MEDICAL ASSOCI-
ATION. 214:311-315, October 12, 1970.

"The use of cyclazocine in the treatment of heroin
addicts," by E. S. Petursson, et al. DISEASES
OF THE NERVOUS SYSTEM. 31:549-551, August, 1970.

"Using methadone to treat the heroin addict," by H.
R. Williams. CANADA'S MENTAL HEALTH. 18:4+,
March-April, 1970.

"What the English are doing about heroin," by M.
Simons. LOOK. 34:47+, April 7, 1970.

"Heroin addiction," by R. L. Worsnop. EDITORIAL RE-
SEARCH REPORTS. pp. 385-402, May 27, 1970.

"Heroin addiction. A comparison of two inpatient
treatment methods," by M. L. LaRouche, et al. MICH-
IGAN MEDICINE. 69:751-754, September, 1970.

"Heroin addiction: the epidemic of the 70's," by J.
W. Speiman. ARCHIVES OF ENVIRONMENTAL HEALTH. 21:
589-590, November, 1970.

"Heroin addiction in adolescents," by P. Boyd. JOUR-
NAL OF PSYCHOSOMATIC RESEARCH. 14:295-301, September, 1970.

"Heroin and crime in the streets." AMERICA. 122:34,
January 17, 1970.

"Heroin dependence and delinquency in women--a study
of heroin addicts in Holloway prison," by P. T. d'
Orbán. BRITISH JOURNAL OF ADDICTION. 65:67-78,
May, 1970.

"Heroin in the schools." CHRISTIANITY TODAY. 14:32,
March 13, 1970.

"Heroin overdose complicated by intravenous injection
of milk," by E. J. Drenick, et al. JOURNAL OF THE
AMERICAN MEDICAL ASSOCIATION. 213:1687, September
7, 1970.

"Heroin withdrawal syndrome," by C. Zelson, et al.

JOURNAL OF PEDIATRICS. 76:483-484, March, 1970.

"The Hidden Addiction," by A. D. Moffett and C. D. Chambers. SOCIAL WORK. 15,3:54-59, July, 1970.

"High school drug education, an interim measure," by M. A. LaCombe, et al. JOURNAL OF THE AMERICAN MEDICAL ASSOCIATION. 214:1327-1328, November 16, 1970.

"A High School Principal Looks at Drug Abuse," by R. W. Joly. COMPACT. 4,3:37-39, June, 1970.

"High school sports flunk the saliva test," by T. Irwin. TODAY'S HEALTH. 48:44-46+, October, 1970.

HILL-MONROE ACCEPTABILITY SCALE
"Crossvalidation of the Hill-Monroe acceptability for psychotherapy scale for addict males," by J. I. Berzins, et al. JOURNAL OF CLINICAL PSYCHOLOGY. 26:199-201, April, 1970.

"Hippy communities may cure drug addicts." TIMES (London) EDUCATIONAL SUPPLEMENT. 2886:14, September 11, 1970.

HISTORY
"The 'drug' and drug addiction in Americans before the conquest," by C. Coury. PRESSE MEDICALE. 78: 979-981, April 25, 1970.

"Horrors of heroin: Hunts Point scene," by R. Severo. READER'S DIGEST. 96:72-75, January, 1970.

HOSPITALS AND DRUG ABUSE
"How Scarborough General handles drug abuse victims," by D. Charter. CANADIAN HOSPITAL. 47:42+, September, 1970.

"Narcotics control in the hospital," by K. deVahl. LAKARTIDNINGEN. 67:3622-3624, August 12, 1970.

"Prescribing and handling drugs in hospital," by B. J. Lewis. NURSING MIRROR AND MIDWIVES JOURNAL. 131:24-27, October 16, 1970.

"A study of patients with a record of drug dependence or drug abuse admitted to a private psychiatric hospital, 1882-1969," by R. W. Medlicott, et al. NEW ZEALAND MEDICAL JOURNAL. 72:92-95, August, 1970.

"Hospitals in the Canadian drug scene," by L. P. Solursh.
CANADIAN HOSPITAL. 47:56-59, August, 1970.

"Hospitals responsible for alcohol and drug addicts,"
by W. Rooen. CANADIAN HOSPITAL. 47:5+, February,
1970.

"Hotline for troubled teen-agers: Los Angeles," by J.
N. Bell. READER'S DIGEST. 97:41-46, November, 1970.

"How addicts are treated." TIME. 95:20, March 16,
1970.

"How the American marijuana market works," by E. Goode.
NEW SOCIETY. 992-994, June 11, 1970.

"How can you tell if your child is taking drugs?" by
I. Mothner. LOOK. 34:42+, April 7, 1970.

"How dangerous is hashish?" by H. Sattes. SCHWESTERN
REVIEW. 8:15-16, October, 1970.

"How I broke the dangerous diet-pill habit." GOOD
HOUSEKEEPING. 170:12+, March, 1970.

"How I faced my son's drug arrest," by G. Astor. LOOK.
34:87-88+, December 15, 1970.

"How long Congress how long? features of the Controlled
dangerous substance bill: address, June 19, 1970," by
J. N. Mitchell. VITAL SPEECHES. 36:610-612, August
1, 1970.

"How many new employees are drug abusers?" by G. P.
Bisgeier. INDUSTRIAL MEDICINE AND SURGERY. 39:369-
370, August, 1970.

"How many of your personnel are captives of drugs?" by
E. Lewis. HOSPITAL MANAGEMENT. 110:30+, October,
1970.

"How Missouri high school principals deal with student
use of tobacco, alcohol, narcotics, drugs," by R.
M. Taylor and J. Rackers. SCHOOL AND COMMUNITY. 56:
7+, March, 1970.

"How nice drugs killed my sister," by M. Davidson.
GOOD HOUSEKEEPING. 171:96-97+, September, 1970.

"How Scarborough General handles drug abuse victims,"
by D. Charter. CANADIAN HOSPITAL. 47:42+, September, 1970.

"How the Schools Can Prevent Drug Abuse," by D. C. Lewis. NATIONAL ASSOCIATION OF SECONDARY SCHOOL PRINCIPALS BULLETIN. 54,346:43-51, May, 1970.

"How to face up to drug abuse in your schools and your community," by P. C. Barrins. AMERICAN SCHOOL BOARD JOURNAL. 158:17-20+, August, 1970.

"How to talk with your teen-ager about drugs; excerpt from What you can do about drugs and your child," by H. W. Land. READER'S DIGEST. 97:69-72, August, 1970.

"How to thwart the law on Rx drugs: Asthmador." CONSUMER REPORTS. 35:192-193, April, 1970.

"Hudegarden and its underground clinic," by O. Henriksen. UGESKRIFT FOR LAEGER. 132:2190-2192, November 12, 1970.

"Hygeia or hysteria." NEW ENGLAND JOURNAL OF MEDICINE. 282:926-927, April 16, 1970.

"Hyperkineticism in children." ILLINOIS MEDICAL JOURNAL. 138:618, December, 1970.

"Hypnosis and the adolescent drug abuser," by F. Baumann. AMERICAN JOURNAL OF CLINICAL HYPNOSIS. 13:17-21, July, 1970.

HYPNOSIS AND DRUGS
"Hypnosis and the adolescent drug abuser," by F. Baumann. AMERICAN JOURNAL OF CLINICAL HYPNOSIS. 13:17-21, July, 1970.

"Hypnosis in living systems theory: a living systems autopsy in a polysurgical, polymedical, polypsychiatric patient addicted to talwin," by F. T. Kolouch. AMERICAN JOURNAL OF CLINICAL HYPNOSIS. 13:22-34, July, 1970.

"Hypnosis in living systems theory: a living systems autopsy in a polysurgical, polymedical, polypsychiatric patient addicted to talwin," by F. T. Kolouch. AMERICAN JOURNAL OF CLINICAL HYPNOSIS. 13:22-34, July, 1970.

"Hypothalamic-pituitary-adrenal axis in methadone-treated heroin addicts," by P. Cushman, Jr., et al. JOURNAL OF CLINICAL ENDOCRINOLOGY AND METABOLISM.

30:24-29, January, 1970.

"I am a junkie. Is that what you are?" by J. Steele.
GUARDIAN. p. 10, October 5, 1970.

"I can take it or leave it." PTA MAGAZINE. 64:5-7,
May, 1970.

"I took a trip," by J. T. Ungerleider. AORN JOURNAL.
12:41-50, September, 1970.

"Identification of various amphetamines and amphetamine-like substances in urine using thin-layer chromatography," by J. R. deMan. PHARMAZEUTISCHE WEEKBLAD
VOOR NEDERLAND. 105:1218-1228, October 16, 1970.

"If pot were legal." TIME. 96:41, July 20, 1970.

"Illicit drug use and addiction in the United States,"
by L. G. Richards, et al. PUBLIC HEALTH REPORTS.
85:1035-1041, December, 1970.

"Illicit LSD Users: Their Personality Characteristics
and Psychopathology," by R. G. Smart and D. Jones.
ABNORMAL PSYCHOLOGY. 75,3:286-292, June, 1970.

"In prison," by I. P. James, et al. LANCET. 1:37,
January 3, 1970.

"The incidence of drug use among Halifax adolescents,"
by P. C. Whitehead. BRITISH JOURNAL OF ADDICTION.
65:159-165, August, 1970.

INDUSTRY AND DRUGS
    "The drug problem and industry," by F. M. Garfield.
    INDUSTRIAL MEDICINE AND SURGERY. 39:366-368,
    August, 1970.

    "Drug screening in industrial nursing," by D. Sohn,
    et al. OCCUPATIONAL HEALTH NURSING. 18:7-10,
    August, 1970.

    "Narcotics detection and industry," by D. Sohn, et
    al. JOURNAL OF OCCUPATIONAL MEDICINE. 12:6-9,
    January, 1970.

    "A program for control of drug abuse in industry,"

83

by C. H. Hine and J. A. Wright. OCCUPATIONAL
HEALTH NURSING. 18:17+, April, 1970.

INFANTS AND DRUGS
"Diagnosis and treatment of the passively addicted
newborn," by D. Ingall and M. Zukerstatter. HOS-
PITAL PRACTICE. 5:101+, August, 1970.

"Inhibition by p-chloroamphetamine of the conversion
of 5-hydroxytryptamine to 5-hydroxyindoleacetic acid
in rat brain," by R. W. Fuller, et al. JOURNAL OF
PHARMACY AND PHARMACOLOGY. 22:634-635, August, 1970.

"The inhibitory effect of amphetamine on exploration
in mice," by J. G. Bainbridge. PSYCHOPHARMACOLOGIA.
18:314-319, 1970.

"Inservice education for teachers," by C. P. Tate.
SCIENCE TEACHER. 37:49-50, September, 1970.

"Instead of police raids," by K. Kettner. SCHWESTERN
REVIEW. 8:13-14, June, 1970.

"Interagency council on drug abuse," by E. R. Bloomquist.
CALIFORNIA MEDICINE. 112:71-72, April, 1970.

"International agreement on narcotic control as a legal
basis for the prevention of narcotic addiction,"
by M. B. Khodakov. FARMATSEVTYCHNYI ZHURNAL (Kiev).
25:69-74, 1970.

"International control of central stimulants: five drugs
are considered as dangerous as opium. Every state
can privately sharpen the control." LAKARTIDNINGEN.
67:2267-2268, May 13, 1970.

"International narcotics control," by I. G. Waddell.
AMERICAN JOURNAL OF INTERNATIONAL LAW. 64:310-323,
April, 1970.

"An international problem: Department of State joins
fight against drug smuggling," by E. L. Richardson.
DEPARTMENT OF STATE NEWS LETTER. pp. 18-21, April, 1970

"Interns and narcotic drugs," by D. E. Miller. AMERICAN
JOURNAL OF HOSPITAL PHARMACY. 27:799, October, 1970.

"Intoxicants and their action. Causes and effects of
drug abuse." AGNES KARLL-SCHWESTER. 24:314-317,
August, 1970.

84

"Intra-arterial administration of oral pentazocine,"
by A. M. Harrison, et al. JOURNAL OF THE AMERICAN
MEDICAL ASSOCIATION. 214:914, November 2, 1970.

"Intra-arterial injection of propoxphene into brachial
artery," by H. S. Pearlman, et al. JOURNAL OF THE
AMERICAN MEDICAL ASSOCIATION. 214:2055-2057, December 14, 1970.

"Intracranial hemorrhage associated with amphetamine
abuse," by S. J. Goodman, et al. JOURNAL OF THE
AMERICAN MEDICAL ASSOCIATION. 212:480+, April 20,
1970.

"Intravenous administration of marijuana," by N. E.
Gary, et al. JOURNAL OF THE AMERICAN MEDICAL ASSO-
CIATION. 211:501, January 19, 1970.

"Intravenous amphetamine poisoning. Report of three
cases," by R. H. Cravey, et al. JOURNAL OF FORENSIC
SCIENCES. 10:109-112, April, 1970.

"Intravenous drug abuse. Pulmonary, cardiac, and
vascular complications," by R. B. Jaffe, et al.
AMERICAN JOURNAL OF ROENTGENOLOGY, RADIUM THERAPY
AND NUCLEAR MEDICINE. 109:107-120, May, 1970.

"Investigation into the possible influence of chlorinated amphetamine derivatives on 5-hydroxytryptamine
synthesis in man," by H. M. van Praag, et al. PSY-
CHOPHARMACOLOGIA. 18:412-420, 1970.

"Investigations on the origin and development of drug
dependence," by R. Battegay. SOUTH AFRICAN MEDICAL
JOURNAL. 44:289-293, March 7, 1970.

IPECAC
"Ipecac may not halt drug abuse," by J. M. Gowdy.
NEW ENGLAND JOURNAL OF MEDICINE. 283:936, October
22, 1970.

"Ipecac may not halt drug abuse," by J. M. Gowdy. NEW
ENGLAND JOURNAL OF MEDICINE. 283:936, October 22,
1970.

"Is knowledge of most worth in drug abuse education?"
JOURNAL OF SCHOOL HEALTH. 40:453, October, 1970.

ISOPRENALINE ABUSE
"Drug dependence in isoprenaline inhalation. Argument against a concentrated preparation," by K.

Naess. TIDSSKRIFT FOR DEN NORSKE LAEGEFORENING.
90:505-506, March 1, 1970.

JEWS AND DRUGS
"Alcoholism and drug dependence amongst Jews," by
M. M. Glatt. BRITISH JOURNAL OF ADDICTION. 64:
297-304, January, 1970.

"John Dewey is Alive and Well in New England," by R. H.
and S. T. deLone. SATURDAY REVIEW OF LITERATURE.
53,47:69-71+, November 21, 1970.

JOHNS HOPKINS HOSPITAL DRUG ABUSE CENTER
"The program of the Johns Hopkins Hospital drug
abuse center," by L. Wurmser. ALUMNAE MAGAZINE
(Baltimore). 69:10-12, March, 1970.

JOURNALISM AND DRUGS
"Tripping on the drug scene; some coverage of narcotics problems has been admirable, but moralizing, misinformation, and sensationalizing predominate; why not an embargo on non-news?" by
M. K. Sanders. COLUMBIA JOURNALISM REVIEW. 9:
35-42, Fall, 1970.

"Junior junkie." TIME. 95:36, February 16, 1970.

"Junkie doctors," by J. R. Wilson. SPECTATOR. p. 359,
October 30, 1970.

"Junkie personality," by A. J. Snider. SCIENCE DIGEST.
68:62, December, 1970.

"Kicks, drugs, and politics," by N. Adler. PSYCHOANA-
LYTIC REVIEW. 57:432-441, 1970.

"Kids and heroin: the adolescent epidemic." TIME .
95:16-20+, March 16, 1970; Same abr. READER'S DI-
GEST. 96:88-92, June, 1970.

"The Kilburn Square drug abuse centre," by B. M. Garvey.
BRITISH JOURNAL OF ADDICTION. 64:383-394, January,
1970.

"Knowledge and experience of young people regarding drug abuse," by J. D. Wright. PROCEEDINGS OF THE ROYAL SOCIETY OF MEDICINE. 63:725-729, July, 1970.

LSD

"Acid by accident; case of mass hallucinogenic poisoning." TIME. 95:8, April 20, 1970.

"Acid report on acid." NATURE (London). 226:4-5, April 4, 1970.

"Behavioural effects of some derivative of amphetamines and LSD and their significance," by J. R. Smythies, et al. NATURE (London). 226:644-645, May 16, 1970.

"Body image and defensiveness in an LSD-taking subculture," by J. R. Hartung, et al. JOURNAL OF PROJECTIVE TECHNIQUES AND PERSONALITY ASSESSMENT. 34:316-323, August, 1970.

"Caring for the 'bad trip,' a review of current status of LSD," by C. M. Martin. HAWAII MEDICAL JOURNAL. 29:555-560, September-October, 1970.

"Chromosomal aberrations induced by barley by LSD," by M. P. Singh, et al. SCIENCE. 169:491-492, July 31, 1970.

"Chromosome abnormality in offspring of LSD user. D trisomy with D-D translocation," by L. Y. Hsu, et al. JOURNAL OF THE AMERICAN MEDICAL ASSOCIATION. 1:987-990, February 9, 1970.

"A clinical examination of chronic LSD use in the community," by S. P. Barron, et al. COMPREHENSIVE PSYCHIATRY. 11:69-79, January, 1970.

"Control of amphetamines and LSD." LANCET. 1:708, April 4, 1970.

"An effective therapeutic method for the LSD user," by C. Torda. PERCEPTUAL AND MOTOR SKILLS. 30: 79-88, February, 1970.

"The experimental use of psychedelic (LSD) psychotherapy," by W. N. Pahnke, et al. JOURNAL OF THE

LSD (cont'd.)
AMERICAN MEDICAL ASSOCIATION. 212:1856-1863, June 15, 1970.

"Illicit LSD users; their personality character-
istics and psychopathology," by R. G. Smart and
D. Jones. ABNORMAL PSYCHOLOGY. 75,3:286-292,
June, 1970.

"LSD and chromosome damage," by J. Hoey. JOURNAL
OF THE AMERICAN MEDICAL ASSOCIATION. 212:1707,
June 8, 1970.

"LSD exposure in utero," by R. J. Warren, et al.
PEDIATRICS. 45:466-469, March, 1970.

"LSD: no teratogenic actions in rats, mice, or
hamsters," by C. Roux, et al. SCIENCE. 169:
588-589, August 7, 1970; Reply: R. Auerbach.
SCIENCE. 170:558, October 30, 1970.

"New warning on LSD: defective children." NEWS-
WEEK. 75:98, May 18, 1970.

"Observations on an effective method to shorten
the psychotherapy of LSD-users," by C. Torda.
AMERICAN JOURNAL OF PSYCHOTHERAPY. 24:499-508,
July, 1970.

"Price of a trip? Possibility of chromosome damage
to germ cells by LSD." TIME. 95:43, February
23, 1970.

"Princess Leda's castle in the air," by T. Burke.
ESQUIRE. 73:104-111+, March, 1970.

"A spoonful of sugar," by C. M. Wallace. NURSING
MIRROR. 130:32, May 8, 1970.

"The termination of an LSD freakout through the
use of relaxation," by R. M. Suinn and J. Brittain. JOURNAL OF CLINICAL PSYCHOLOGY. 27,1:
127-128, January, 1970.

"Wave of LSD-taking hitting Britain," by E. Clark.
OBSERVER. p. 1+, December 20, 1970.

"LSD and chromosome damage," by J. Hoey. JOURNAL OF
THE AMERICAN MEDICAL ASSOCIATION. 212:1707, June
8, 1970.

"LSD exposure in utero," by R. J. Warren, et al.

PEDIATRICS. 45:466-469, March, 1970.

"LSD: no teratogenic actions in rats, mice, or hamsters," by C. Roux, et al. SCIENCE. 169:588-589, August 7, 1970; Reply: R. Auerbach. SCIENCE. 170:558, October 30, 1970.

"Lack of drug education." CANADIAN JOURNAL OF PSY-CHIATRIC NURSING. 11:12-13, April-May, 1970.

"The Laguna Beach experiments as a community approach to family counselling for drug abuse problems in youth," by L. A. Gottschalk, et al. COMPREHENSIVE PSYCHIATRY. 11:226-234, May, 1970.

"Late brain recovery processes after drug overdose," by I. Haider, et al. BRITISH MEDICAL JOURNAL. 1: 318-322, May 9, 1970; also in ELECTROENCEPHALOGRAPHY AND CLINICAL NEUROPHYSIOLOGY. 29:326, September, 1970.

"The Law and Drugs in the Schools," by J. D. McKevitt. COMPACT. 4,3:45-46, June, 1970.

"Law and maryjane," by M. B. Hering. AMERICAN LIBRARIES. 1:896-899, October, 1970.

LAW ENFORCEMENT
  "The addict: criminal or cripple? hard drug dilemma," by G. Samuels. NEW LEADER. 53:10-12, March 15, 1970.

  "The addict today--1970," by K. P. O'Brien and R. C. Sullivan. POLICE. 14:35-41, May-June, 1970.

  "Current narcotics abuse from the viewpoint of criminalistic practice," by G. Bauer. MUENCHENER MEDIZINISCHE WOCHENSCHRIFT. 112:1562-1569, August 28, 1970.

  "Drug addiction and the law," by D. A. Cahal. JOUR-NAL OF THE ROYAL COLLEGE OF GENERAL PRACTITIONERS. 20:32-38, July, 1970.

  "Law'n order in Dallas; case of four black students from the University of California." NATION. 211:582, December 7, 1970.

  "Of plumbing and privacy; no-knock drug raids." EBONY. 25:154-155, April, 1970.

"Town deals sternly with its own; six young drug offenders sent to prison in Rupert, Idaho," by L. Wainwright. LIFE. 69:10-12+, November 6, 1970.

"U.S. Journal: Houston: thirty year sentence to L. O. Johnson for giving away one marijuana cigarette," by C. Trillin. NEW YORKER. 46:164+, December 12, 1970.

"Vacationing in jail." SENIOR SCHOLASTIC. 96: 19, May 18, 1970.

"When a holiday ends in a prison sentence," by H. Sieve. DAILY TELEGRAPH. p. 16+, October 9, 1970.

"Law'n order in Dallas; case of four black students from the University of California." NATION. 211: 582, December 7, 1970.

LAWS AND LEGISLATION
"Addiction, medicine and the law." SCIENTIFIC AMERICAN. 223:50, July, 1970.

"Bust insurance; organization free weed, dedicated to the legalization of marijuana." TIME. 96: 15, July 20, 1970.

"Comprehensive drug abuse prevention and control act of 1970: the President's remarks at the signing ceremony at the Bureau of Narcotics and Dangerous Drugs, October 27, 1970," by R. Nixon. COMPILATION OF PRESIDENTIAL DOCUMENTS. 6:1463, November 2, 1970.

"The controlled dangerous substances Act of 1969," by M. R. Sonnenreich. BULLETIN OF THE PARENTERAL DRUG ASSOCIATION. 24:14-22, January-February, 1970.

"The costs of dangerous drugs legislation in England and Wales," by A. J. Culyer, et al. MEDICAL CARE. 8:501-509, November-December, 1970.

"Declaration by the Attorneys General on the narcotics traffic; United States-Mexico joint cooperation." DEPARTMENT OF STATE BULLETIN. 63: 300, September 14, 1970.

"Department warns of penalties for drug violations

LAWS AND LEGISLATION (cont'd.)
   abroad: announcement, March 31, 1970." DEPART-
   MENT OF STATE BULLETIN. 62:549-551, April 27,
   1970.

"Drug abuse; comprehensive drug abuse prevention
   and control act of 1970." NEW REPUBLIC. 163:
   9, October 10, 1970.

"Drug addiction and the law," by D. A. Cahal. JOUR-
   NAL OF THE ROYAL COLLEGE OF GENERAL PRACTITIONERS.
   20:32-38, July, 1970.

"Drug offenses and the university." UNIVERSITIES
   QUARTERLY. 24,3:243-257, Summer, 1970.

"Drugs and the law," by D. M. Dozer. FREEMAN. 20:
   131-135, March, 1970.

"Drugs bill; piecing it all together." ECONOMIST.
   234:23-24, March 14, 1970.

"Education programs in the State Legislature," by
   R. M. Webster. COMPACT. 4,3:40+, June, 1970.

"Federal narcotic and dangerous drug laws." COMPACT.
   4,3:44+, June, 1970.

"Furor over drugs; physicians vs. the Attorney General." NEWSWEEK. 75:65+, March 20, 1970.

"Governor's panel explores drug abuse in Utah,"
   by C. L. Rampton. CAMPACT. 4,3:15+, June, 1970.

"Hassle over narcotics control." SCIENCE NEWS. 97:
   339, April 4, 1970.

"How long congress how long? features of the controlled dangerous substance bill: address, June 19,
   1970," by J. N. Mitchell. VITAL SPEECHES. 36:
   610-612, August 1, 1970.

"How to thwart the law on Rx drugs; Asthmador."
   CONSUMER REPORTS. 35:192-193, April, 1970.

"If pot were legal." TIME. 96:41, July 29, 1970.

"International agreement on narcotic control as a
   legal basis for the prevention of narcotic addiction," by M. B. Khodakov. FARMATSEVTYCHNYI
   ZHURNAL (Kiev). 25:69-74, 1970.

LAWS AND LEGISLATION (cont'd.)
"International control of central stimulants: five
drugs are considered as dangerous as opium. Every
state can privately sharpen the control." LAKAR-
TIDNINGEN. 67:2267-2268, May 13, 1970.

"International narcotics control," by I. G. Waddell.
AMERICAN JOURNAL OF INTERNATIONAL LAW. 64:310-
323, April, 1970.

"The law and drugs in the schools," by J. D. McKevitt.
COMPACT. 4,3:45-46, June, 1970.

"Law and maryjane," by M. B. Hering. AMERICAN LI-
BRARIES. 1:896-899, October, 1970.

"Legal prescription of narcotics," by J. J. Bellizzi.
NEW YORK STATE JOURNAL OF MEDICINE. 70:1677-1680,
June 15, 1970.

"Legalize marijuana?" MEDICAL JOURNAL OF AUSTRALIA.
1:1237-1238, June 20, 1970.

"Legalized flight from reality?" by F. H. van Os.
PHARMAZEUTISCHE WEEKBLAD VOOR NEDERLAND. 105:
1054-1058, September 11, 1970.

"Legislative proposals on drug abuse," by W. G. Mil-
liken. COMPACT. 4,3:18-19, June, 1970.

"Marijuana," by D. K. Cash, et al. MEDICO-LEGAL
BULLETIN. 212:1-7, December, 1970.

"Marijuana: is it time for a change in our laws?
with views of J. Mitchell." NEWSWEEK. 76:20-
22+, September 7, 1970; also in READER'S DIGEST.
97:88-92, December, 1970.

"Methadone; the law and the clinics," by R. O'Mara.
NATION. 211:242-244, September 21, 1970.

"Model narcotic drug legislation (prepared by criminal law education and research center study
group, New York University)." CRIMINOLOGY. 8:
156-172, August, 1970.

"Moving forward; drug abuse bill." U.S. NEWS AND
WORLD REPORT. 68:4, February 9, 1970.

"The narcotic addict rehabilitation act; a change
in the federal response to the treatment of narcotic addiction," by C. B. Scrignar, et al.

LAWS AND LEGISLATION (cont'd.)
SOUTHERN MEDICAL JOURNAL. 63:109-112, January, 1970.

"New look; the Dodd drug bill." NEWSWEEK. 75:24, February 9, 1970.

"New medico-legal aspects of toxicomania," by A. Franchini. MINERVA MEDICA. 61:4331-4338, October 3, 1970.

"New York's statutory scheme for the rehabilitation of narcotics addicts through civil commitment," by M. M. D'Auria. NEW YORK STATE BAR JOURNAL. 42:436-443, August, 1970.

"Nixon approves drug guidelines, gives role to narcotics bureau," by D. Bonafede. NATIONAL JOURNAL. 2:1532-1534, July 18, 1970.

"No knock?" by W. F. Buckley, Jr. NATIONAL REVIEW. 23:220, February 24, 1970.

"No knock drug bill." TIME. 95:11-12, February 9, 1970.

"Of plumbing and privacy; no-knock drug raids." EBONY. 25:154-155, April 5, 1970.

"Pot and the law; the legalization of marijuana on a provisional basis." CHRISTIAN CENTURY. 87: 1275, October 28, 1970; Discussion: 87:1461, December 2, 1970.

"Pot hard drugs, and the law," by G. Samuels. NEW YORK TIMES MAGAZINE. p. 4+, February 15, 1970.

"Pot in prison," by W. F. Buckley, Jr. NATIONAL REVIEW. 22:221, February 24, 1970.

"Relationship between criminal law and health protection, tasks of public health organs and institutions," by H. G. Keune. PHARMAZEUTISCHE PRAXIS; BEILAGE ZUR DIE PHARMAZIE. 5:97-101, 1970.

"Some ambiguities for research in Senate's drug bill," by J. Walsh. SCIENCE. 167:849, February 6, 1970.

"Some legal and ethical aspects of addiction," by D. F. Robb. JOURNAL OF THE ROYAL COLLEGE OF

LAWS AND LEGISLATION (cont'd.)
GENERAL PRACTITIONERS. 20:98-99, August, 1970.

"State action against drug abuse." COMPACT. 4,3:
28-33, June, 1970.

"State-initiated community programs," by H. Levander. COMPACT. 4,3:49+, June, 1970.

"The state versus the addict: uncivil commitment,"
by J. C. Kramer. BOSTON UNIVERSITY LAW REVIEW.
40:1-22, Winter, 1970.

"Statement on the Federal Drug Abuse and Drug Dependence, Prevention, Treatment and Rehabilitation
Act of 1970 (S. 3562) by The New York Academy of
Medicine." BULLETIN OF THE NEW YORK ACADEMY OF
MEDICINE. 46:642, August, 1970.

"Strengthened programs of international cooperation
for halting the illicit supply of drugs; address,
April 2, 1970, by E. L. Richardson. DEPARTMENT
OF STATE BULLETIN. 62:544-549, April 27, 1970.

"Tough bill plus research: comprehensive drug abuse
and control act of 1970." SCIENCE NEWS. 98:332-
333, October 24, 1970.

"Traveling Americans warned against drug abuse."
DEPARTMENT OF STATE NEWS LETTER. pp. 21-22,
April, 1970.

"What legal status for marijuana?" by J. Kaplan.
CURRENT. 123:44-47, November, 1970.

"Leadership by Local School Boards," by D. H. Kurtzman.
COMPACT. 4,3:34-35, June, 1970.

"Leaving the drug world behind; results from the Awareness house project," by R. Moskowitz. AMERICAN
EDUCATION. 6:3-6, January, 1970; Same. EDUCATION
DIGEST. 35:5-7, May, 1970.

"Leg ulcers and drug abuse," by E. J. Valtonen. LANCET.
2:1192-1193, December 5, 1970.

"Legal prescription of narcotics," by J. J. Bellizzi.
NEW YORK STATE JOURNAL OF MEDICINE. 70:1677-1680,
June 15, 1970.

"Legalize marijuana?" MEDICAL JOURNAL AUSTRALIA. 1:
1237-1238, June 20, 1970.

"Legalized flight from reality?" by F. H. van Os.
PHARMAZEUTISCHE WEEKBLAD VOOR NEDERLAND. 105:1054-
1058, September 11, 1970.

"Legislative Proposals on Drug Abuse," by W. G. Mil-
liken. COMPACT. 4,3:18-19, June, 1970.

"Let the physician beware," by M. S. Rapp. CANADIAN
MEDICAL ASSOCIATION JOURNAL. 102:1188+, May 30,
1970.

"Lethal amphetamine intoxication. A report of three
cases," by S. Orrenius, et al. ZEITSCHRIFT FUER
RECHTSMEDIZIN. 67:184-189, 1970.

"Lexicon for today--2nd edition." NEW ENGLAND JOURNAL
OF MEDICINE. 282:756, March 26, 1970.

LEXINGTON HOSPITAL
    "Readmission rates at Lexington Hospital for 43,215
    narcotic drug addicts," by J. C. Ball, et al.
    PUBLIC HEALTH REPORTS. 85:610+, July, 1970.

"Life on two grams a day; heroin in the high schools."
LIFE. 68:24-32, February 20, 1970.

"Lifeboat: Phoenix house survival therapy." MOTOR
BOATING. 126:42-43, December, 1970.

LIVER DISEASES AND DRUGS
    "Australia-SH-antigen and diseases of the liver.
    Preliminary investigations of Danish drug ad-
    dicts and patients with chronic liver diseases,"
    by V. Reinicke, et al. SCANDINAVIAN JOURNAL OF
    GASTROENTEROLOGY SUPPLEMENT. 7:85-88, 1970.

LOMOTIL
    "An oral method of the withdrawal treatment of
    heroin dependence; a five years' study of a com-
    bination of diphenoxylate (Lomotil) and chlor-
    methiazole (Heminerin)," by M. M. Glatt, et al.
    BRITISH JOURNAL OF ADDICTION. 65:237-243, No-
    vember, 1970.

"The long-term outcome for adolescent drug users: a
follow-up study of 76 users and 146 nonusers," by
L. N. Robins, et al. PROCEEDINGS OF THE AMERICAN
PSYCHOPATHOLOGICAL ASSOCIATION. 59:159-180, 1970.

"Love, delights and drugs. Some considerations on the
body, the erotical relations and nirvanic ascesis

95

under toxicomaniac influence," by P. Bailly-Salin, et al. ANNALES MEDICO-PSYCHOLOGIQUES (Paris). 2: 120-126, June, 1970.

"Magic garden." TIME. 96:14, July 27, 1970.

"Main line to an early grave," by D. Gray. GUARDIAN (U.S.). p. 10, March 18, 1970.

"Maintaining the methadone patient," by Sister R. Mc Dermott. NURSING OUTLOOK. 18:22+, December, 1970.

"Man Alive is alive, and well," by G. B. Whitman. ALUM-NAE MAGAZINE (Baltimore). 69:8-9, March, 1970.

"Man and his drugs," by P. Christie. CANADIAN PSY-CHIATRIC ASSOCIATION JOURNAL. 15:1-2, February, 1970.

"Management of 'bad trips' in an evolving drug scene," by R. L. Taylor, et al. JOURNAL OF THE AMERICAN MEDICAL ASSOCIATION. 213:422-425, July 20, 1970.

"Management of the narcotic-addicted surgical patient: concepts of medical and surgical care," by T. E. Splaver, et al. JOURNAL OF ORAL SURGERY. 28:346-352, May, 1970.

MARIJUANA
"Alcohol or marijuana: a follow up survey at Ithaca College." JOURNAL OF THE AMERICAN COLLEGE HEALTH ASSOCIATION. 18,5:366-367, June, 1970.

"America should not 'go to pot'," by T. F. Coon. POLICE. 14:65-68, March-April, 1970.

"Appraising marijuana; the new American pastime," by J. Keats. HOLIDAY. pp. 47:52-53+, April, 1970.

"At least a million people smoke pot." OBSERVER. 1-2, March 15, 1970.

"Bust insurance; organization Free weed, dedicated to the legalization of marijuana." TIME. 96: 15, July 20, 1970.

"Chemical basis of hashish activity," by R. Mechoulam, et al. SCIENCE. 169:611-612, August 7, 1970.

96

MARIJUANA (cont'd.)

"College student attitudes toward marijuana," by
M. F. Amo and J. R. Bittner. COLLEGE STUDENT
SURVEY. 4,2:52-54, February, 1970.

"Crossing the marijuana dmz." IMPRINT. 17:3-4,
January, 1970.

"Dimensions of marijuana usage in a land grant university," by L. B. DeFleur and G. R. Garrett.
JOURNAL OF COUNSELING PSYCHOLOGY. 17,5:468-
475, September, 1970.

"Drug abuse: myths and facts about marijuana," by
L. Wurmser. ALUMNAE MAGAZINE (Baltimore). 69:
3-5, March, 1970.

"Family and differential involvement with marijuana;
a study of suburban teenagers," by N. Tec. JOUR-
NAL OF MARRIAGE AND THE FAMILY. 32:656-664, November, 1970.

"Fresh disclosures on drugs and GIs; Senate investigation into marijuana smoking." U.S. NEWS AND
WORLD REPORT. 68:32-33, April 6, 1970.

"How the American marijuana market works," by E.
Goode. NEW SOCIETY. pp. 992-994, June 11, 1970.

"Intravenous administration of marijuana," by N. E.
Gary, et al. JOURNAL OF THE AMERICAN MEDICAL
ASSOCIATION. 211:501, January 19, 1970.

"Law and maryjane," by M. B. Hering. AMERICAN LI-
BRARIES. 1:896-899, October, 1970.

"Legalize marijuana." MEDICAL JOURNAL OF AUSTRALIA.
1:1237-1238, June 20, 1970.

"Marijuana," by D. K. Cash, et al. MEDICO-LEGAL BUL-
LETIN. 212:1-7, December, 1970.

"Marijuana; L. Grinspoon; reply with rejoinder,"
by D. W. Goodwin. SCIENTIFIC AMERICAN. 222:6-7,
February, 1970.

"Marijuana, by J. Kaplan. Review," by L. DuBois.
NATIONAL REVIEW. 22:955-956, September 8, 1970.

"Marijuana," by D. Perna. JOURNAL OF THE AMERICAN
MEDICAL ASSOCIATION. 214:760, October 26, 1970.

MARIJUANA (cont'd.)

"Marijuana and behavior; the unfilled gaps," by L.
Massett. SCIENCE NEWS. 97:156-158, February 7,
1970.

"Marijuana and the pediatrician; an attitude survey,"
by A. L. Abrams, et al. PEDIATRICS. 46:462-464,
September, 1970.

"Marijuana and temporal disintegration," by F. T.
Melges, et al. SCIENCE. 168:1118-1120, May
29, 1970.

"Marijuana and the use of other drugs," by W. Mc
Glothlin, et al. NATURE (London). 228:1227-1229,
December 19, 1970.

"Marijuana chemistry," by R. Mechoulam. SCIENCE.
168:1159-1166, June 5, 1970.

"Marijuana clouds the generation gap," by S. Blum.
NEW YORK TIMES MAGAZINE. pp. 28-29+, August 23,
1970; Discussion: p. 16+, September 6, 1970.

"The marijuana habit," by J. Scher. JOURNAL OF THE
AMERICAN MEDICAL ASSOCIATION. 214:1120, November
9, 1970.

"Marijuana; how dangerous is it?" by S. M. Spencer.
READER'S DIGEST. 96:67-71, January, 1970.

"Marijuana in junior high school," by G. W. Wohlberg.
NEW ENGLAND JOURNAL OF MEDICINE. 283:318-319,
August 6, 1970.

"Marijuana-induced social high," by J. E. Hildebrand.
JOURNAL OF THE AMERICAN MEDICAL ASSOCIATION. 214:
1565, November 23, 1970.

"Marijuana; is it time for a change in our laws?
with views of J. Mitchell." NEWSWEEK. 76:20-22+,
September 7, 1970; also in READER'S DIGEST. 97:
88-92, December, 1970.

"Marijuana; it's big business now; House select committee on crime report." U.S. NEWS AND WORLD RE-
PORT. 68:103, April 20, 1970.

"Marijuana; Mary Jane faces the identity crisis
or three blind men study the elephant," by H. B.
Bruyn. JOURNAL OF THE AMERICAN COLLEGE HEALTH
ASSOCIATION. 18:323-324, June, 1970.

MARIJUANA (cont'd.)
"Marijuana--not to be compared with alochol," by
E. L. Dembicki. JOURNAL OF PSYCHIATRIC NURSING.
8:35, November-December, 1970.

"Marijuana; the other enemy in Vietnam." U.S. NEWS
AND WORLD REPORT. 68:68-69, January 26, 1970.

"Marijuana persistence in the body." SCIENCE NEWS.
98:476, December 26, 1970.

"The marijuana problem," by N. Q. Brill, et al. AN-
NALS OF INTERNAL MEDICINE. 73:449-465, September,
1970.

"Marijuana; should it be controlled?" by S. Heinemann. SOUTHWESTERN MEDICINE. 51:267-268, December, 1970.

"Marijuana use among adults," by W. H. McGlothlin,
et al. PSYCHIATRY. 33:433-443, November, 1970.

"Marijuana users' views of marijuana use," by R.
Brotman, et al. PROCEEDINGS OF THE AMERICAN
PSYCHOPATHOLOGICAL ASSOCIATION. 59:258-274,
1970.

"Marijuana. The watched pot," by P. K. Kaufman.
NEW YORK STATE JOURNAL OF MEDICINE. 70:1793-
1799, July 1, 1970.

"No marijuana for adolescents," by K. Angel. NEW
YORK TIMES MAGAZINE. p. 9+, January 25, 1970.

"One father's war on marijuana," by W. F. Buckley,
Jr. NATIONAL REVIEW. 22:1072, October 6, 1970.

"The pediatrician and the marijuana question," by C.
H. Gleason. PEDIATRICS. 45:1037, June, 1970.

"The pediatrician and the marijuana question," by
V. A. Dohner, et al. PEDIATRICS. 45:1039-1040,
June, 1970.

"The pediatrician and the marijuana question," by
Johnson, et al. PEDIATRICS. 45:1037-1038, June,
1970.

"Personality correlates of undergraduate marijuana
use," by R. Hogan, et al. JOURNAL OF CONSULTING
AND CLINICAL PSYCHOLOGY. 35:58-63, August, 1970.

MARIJUANA (cont'd.)

"The physician, marijuana and reason," by A. S. Norris. JOURNAL OF THE IOWA MEDICAL SOCIETY. 60:623-630, September, 1970.

"Pot and the law: the legalization of marijuana on a provisional basis." CHRISTIAN CENTURY. 87: 1275, October 28, 1970; Discussion: 87:1461, December 2, 1970.

"Pot boils over," by F. Poland. SCIENCE NEWS. 97: 620, June 27, 1970.

"Pot bust." NEWSWEEK. 75:92+, May 11, 1970.

"Pot facing stringent scientific examination," by B. J. Culliton. SCIENCE NEWS. 97:102-105, January 24, 1970.

"Pot, hard drugs and the law," by G. Samuels. NEW YORK TIMES MAGAZINE. p. 4+, February 15, 1970.

"Pot, pills and people; Camp JCA, California," by M. Schlesinger. CAMPING MAGAZINE. 42:10-11+, March, 1970.

"Pot samplers may be dabbling with psychosis." TODAY'S HEALTH. 48:71, August, 1970.

"Pot-smoking young executives," by S. Margetts. DUNS. 95:42-43, February, 1970.

"Pot to prison," by W. F. Buckley, Jr. NATIONAL REVIEW. 22:221, February 24, 1970.

"Prohibition of marijuana," by J. Kaplan. NEW REPUBLIC. 163:11-12, November 21, 1970.

"Psychiatrist and his daughter talk frankly about marijuana; interview, edited by A. Bramson," by M. and S. F. Yolles. SEVENTEEN. 29:134-135+, October, 1970.

"Psychoses due to cannabis abuse," by G. d'Elia, et al. LAKARTIDNINGEN. 67:3526-3529, August 5, 1970.

"Psychotic symptoms due to cannabis abuse; a survey of newly admitted mental patients," by W. Keup. DISEASES OF THE NERVOUS SYSTEM. 31:119-126, February, 1970.

MARIJUANA (cont'd.)
"Putting pot in its place," by G. Tindall. GUARDIAN
(U.S.). p. 9, January 14, 1970.

"A scale to measure attitude toward smoking marijuana," by R. J. Vincent. JOURNAL OF SCHOOL
HEALTH. 40:454-456, October, 1970.

"Sparks fly over pot." NATION'S BUSINESS. 58:24,
March, 1970.

"Talk about pot," by C. Adam. NEW STATESMAN. 80:
674, November 20, 1970.

"To parents; plain talk on marijuana." BUSINESS
WEEK. p. 127, March 21, 1970.

"Turning off the Tijuana grass; operation intercept,"
by C. Kentfield. ESQUIRE. 73:8+, May, 1970.

"U.S. Journal; Houston: thirty year sentence to L.
O. Johnson for giving away one marijuana ciga-
rette," by C. Trillin. NEW YORKER. 46:164+,
December 12, 1970.

"Users and nonusers of marijuana; some attitudinal
and behavioral correlates," by F. W. King. JOUR-
NAL OF THE AMERICAN COLLEGE HEALTH ASSOCIATION.
18:213-217, February, 1970.

"What legal status for marijuana?" by J. Kaplan.
CURRENT. 123:44-47, November, 1970.

"What? Pot? Not Laredo." FORBES. 106:48, November
1, 1970.

"What we have forgotten about pot, a pharmacologist's
history: cannabis sativa," by S. H. Snyder. NEW
YORK TIMES MAGAZINE. pp. 26-27+, December 13, 1970.

"What's it like to smoke marijuana?" SCIENCE DIGEST.
68:18-19, October, 1970.

"Marijuana," by D. K. Cash, et al. MEDICO-LEGAL BULLE-
TIN. 212:1-7, December, 1970.

"Marijuana, L. Grinspoon; reply with rejoinder," by D.
W. Goodwin. SCIENTIFIC AMERICAN. 222:6-7, Fall,
1970.

"Marijuana, by J. Kaplan. Review," by L. DuBois.
NATIONAL REVIEW. 22:955-956, September 8, 1970.

"Marijuana," by D. Perna. JOURNAL OF THE AMERICAN MEDICAL ASSOCIATION. 214:760, October 26, 1970.

"Marijuana and behavior; the unfilled gaps," by L. Massett. SCIENCE NEWS. 97:156-158, February 7, 1970.

"Marijuana and the pediatrician: an attitude survey," by A. L. Abrams, et al. PEDIATRICS. 46:462-464, September, 1970.

"Marijuana and temporal disintegation," by F. T. Melges, et al. SCIENCE. 168:1118-1120, May 29, 1970.

"Marijuana and the use of other drugs," by W. McGlothlin, et al. NATURE (London). 228:1227-1229, December 19, 1970.

"Marijuana chemistry," by R. Mechoulam. SCIENCE. 168: 1159-1166, June 5, 1970.

"Marijuana clouds the generation gap," by S. Blum. NEW YORK TIMES MAGAZINE. pp. 28-29+, August 23, 1970; Discussion. p. 4+, September 6, 1970; p. 16+, September 20, 1970.

"The marijuana habit," by J. Scher. JOURNAL OF THE AMERICAN MEDICAL ASSOCIATION. 214:1120, November 9, 1970.

"Marijuana: how dangerous is it?" by S. M. Spencer. READER'S DIGEST. 96:67-71, January, 1970.

"Marijuana in junior high school," by G. W. Wohlberg. NEW ENGLAND JOURNAL OF MEDICINE. 283:318-319, August 6, 1970.

"Marijuana-induced 'social high'," by J. E. Hildebrand. JOURNAL OF THE AMERICAN MEDICAL ASSOCIATION. 214: 1565, November 23, 1970.

"Marijuana: is it time for a change in our laws? with views of J. Mitchell." NEWSWEEK. 76:20-22+, September 7, 1970; Same abr. with title, "What to do about marijuana?" READER'S DIGEST. 97:88-92, December, 1970.

"Marijuana: it's big business now; House select committee on crime report." U.S. NEWS AND WORLD REPORT. 68:103, April 20, 1970.

"Marijuana: Mary Jane faces the identity crisis or three blind men study the elephant," by H. B. Bruyn.

JOURNAL OF THE AMERICAN COLLEGE HEALTH ASSOCIATION. 18:323-324, June, 1970.

"Marijuana--not to be compared with alcohol," by E. L. Dembicki. JOURNAL OF PSYCHIATRIC NURSING. 8:35, November-December, 1970.

"Marijuana: the other enemy in Vietnam." U.S. NEWS AND WORLD REPORT. 68:68-69, January 26, 1970.

"Marijuana persistence in the body." SCIENCE NEWS. 98: 476, December 26, 1970.

"The marijuana problem," by N. Q. Brill, et al. ANNALES OF INTERNAL MEDICINE. 73:449-465, September, 1970.

"Marijuana: should it be controlled?" by S. Heinemann. SOUTHWESTERN MEDICINE. 51:267-268, December, 1970.

"Marijuana use among adults," by W. H. McGlothlin, et al. PSYCHIATRY. 33:433-443, November, 1970.

"Marijuana users' views of marijuana use," by R. Brotman and F. Suffet. PROCEEDINGS OF THE AMERICAN PSYCHOPATHOLOGICAL ASSOCIATION. 59:258-274, 1970.

"Marijuana. The watched pot," by P. K. Kaufman. NEW YORK STATE JOURNAL OF MEDICINE. 70:1793-1799, July 1, 1970.

"Medical Society on care of drug addicts: forms of care for those not yet ready to ask for care." LAKAR-TIDNINGEN. 67:2872-2876, June 17, 1970.

"Medicine in modern society. Some remarks on consumption, distribution and manufacture," by F. Jorgensen. UGESKRIFT FOR LAEGER. 132:2150-2151, November 5, 1970.

"Medico-psychological contribution to the comprehension of young drug addicts," by A. Gorceix, et al. ANNALS MEDICO-PSYCHOLOGIQUES (Paris). 2:126-132, June, 1970.

"Medi-Rock: a bridge between two cultures," by K. H. Dansky. ALUMNAE MAGAZINE (Baltimore). 69:65+, September, 1970.

"Menace and the malady." NATION. 211:228-229, September 21, 1970.

"Mental disorders caused by phenmetrazine abuse," by B. Klosinska, et al. PSYCHIATRIA POLSKA. 4:45-47, January-February, 1970.

MEPHENTERMINE ABUSE
"Mephentermine psychosis; misuse of the Wyamine inhaler," by B. M. Angrist, et al. AMERICAN JOURNAL OF PSYCHIATRY. 126:1315-1317, March, 1970.

"Mephentermine psychosis; misuse of the Wyamine inhaler," by B. M. Angrist, et al. AMERICAN JOURNAL OF PSYCHIATRY. 126:1315-1317, March, 1970.

MEPROBAMATE ABUSE
"A case of glutethimide and meprobamate dependence with delirium as a drug withdrawal sympton," by J. Svestka, et al. ACTIVITAS NERVOSA SUPERIOR (Praha). 12:70-71, January 12, 1970.

METHADONE
"Antagonist of the behavioral effects of morphine and methadone by narcotic antagonists in the pigeon," by D. E. McMillan, et al. JOURNAL OF PHARMACOLOGY AND EXPERIMENTAL THERAPEUTICS. 175:443-458, November, 1970.

"Cracks in the panacea." SCIENCE NEWS. 97:366-367, April 11, 1970.

"Drug addiction treatment with maintenance doses of methadone," by M. Nimb. NORDISK MEDICIN. 83:1412, October 29, 1970.

"Guidelines for using methadone in the outpatient treatment of narcotic addicts," by C. B. Scrignar, et al. JOURNAL OF THE LOUISIANA MEDICAL SOCIETY. 122:167-172, June, 1970.

"Help from methadone." NEWSWEEK. 75:52, June 8, 1970.

"Hypothalamic-pituitary-adrenal axis in methadone-treated heroin addicts," by P. Cushman, Jr., et al. JOURNAL OF CLINICAL ENDOCRINOLOGY AND METABOLISM. 30:24-29, January, 1970.

"Maintaining the methadone patient," by R. McDermott, Sr. NURSING OUTLOOK. 18:22+, December, 1970.

"Man alive is alive and well," by G. B. Whitman.

METHADONE (cont'd.)
ALUMNAE MAGAZINE (Baltimore). 69:8-9, March, 1970.

"Methadone," by J. Bishop. CANADIAN MEDICAL ASSOCIA-
TION JOURNAL. 104:164, January 23, 1971.

"Methadone and heroin addiction; rehabilitation without a cure," by J. Walsh. SCIENCE. 168:684-686,
May 8, 1970.

"Methadone and the private practitioner," by H. W.
Freymuth. JOURNAL OF THE MEDICAL SOCIETY OF NEW
JERSEY. 67:128-130, March, 1970.

"Methadone; a drug to lick a drug?" by F. Warshofsky.
READER'S DIGEST. 96:88-92, May, 1970.

"Methadone for the pentazocine-dependent patient,"
by N. N. Raskin. NEW ENGLAND JOURNAL OF MEDICINE.
283:1349, December 10, 1970.

"Methadone; the law and the clinics," by R. O'Mara.
NATION. 211:242-244, September 21, 1970.

"Methadone maintenance for opiate dependence," by
J. C. Kramer. CALIFORNIA MEDICINE. 113:6-11,
December, 1970.

"Methadone maintenance in heroin addiction," by B.
A. Pearson. AMERICAN JOURNAL OF NURSING. 70:
2571+, December, 1970.

"Methadone maintenance treatment is successful for
heroin addicts," by R. E. Trussell and H. Gollance. HOSPITAL MANAGEMENT. 110:56+, October,
1970.

"Methadone maintenance treatment program," by P. R.
Torrens. HOSPITALS. 44:76+, December 1, 1970.

"Methadone management of heroin addiction." BUL-
LETIN OF THE NEW YORK ACADEMY OF MEDICINE. 46:
391-395, June, 1970.

"Methadone misuse and death by overdosage," by R.
Gardner. BRITISH JOURNAL OF ADDICTION. 65:113-
118, August, 1970.

"Methadone treatment of opiate addicts in Sweden,"
by J. H. Erikson. LAKARTIDNINGEN. 67:849-852,

METHADONE (cont'd.)
February 18, 1970.

"On treating drug addiction with methadone." CURRENT.
120:35-38, August, 1970.

"Reaction-times of methadone treated ex-heroin addicts," by N. B. Gordon. PSYCHOPHARMACOLOGIA
(Berlin). 16:337-344, 1970.

"Urine testing schedules in methadone maintenance
treatment of heroin addiction," by A. Goldstein,
et al. JOURNAL OF THE AMERICAN MEDICAL ASSOCIA-
TION. 214:311-315, October 12, 1970.

"Using methadone to treat the heroin addicted," by
H. R. Williams. CANADA'S MENTAL HEALTH. 18:4+,
March-April, 1970.

"What price methadone addiction?" by R. F. Alsop.
NEW ENGLAND JOURNAL OF MEDICINE. 282:756, March
26, 1970.

"Methadone," by J. Bishop. CANADIAN MEDICAL ASSOCIA-
TION JOURNAL. 104:164, January 23, 1971.

"Methadone and heroin addiction: rehabilitation without a cure," by J. Walsh. SCIENCE. 168:684-686,
May 8, 1970.

"Methadone and the private practitioner," by H. W. Freymuth. JOURNAL OF THE MEDICAL SOCIETY OF NEW JERSEY.
67:128-130, March, 1970.

"Methadone: a drug to lick a drug?" by F. Warshofsky.
READER'S DIGEST. 96:88-92, May, 1970.

"Methadone for the pentazocine-dependent patient," by
N. N. Raskin. NEW ENGLAND JOURNAL OF MEDICINE. 283:
1349, December 10, 1970.

"Methadone: the law and the clinics," by R. O'Mara.
NATION. 211:242-244, September 21, 1970.

"Methadone maintenance for opiate dependence," by J.
C. Kramer. CALIFORNIA MEDICINE. 113:6-11, December, 1970.

"Methadone maintenance in heroin addiction," by B. A.
Pearson. AMERICAN JOURNAL OF NURSING. 70:2571+,

December, 1970.

"Methadone maintenance treatment is successful for heroin addicts," by R. E. Trussell and H. Gollance. HOSPITAL MANAGEMENT. 110:56+, October, 1970.

"Methadone maintenance treatment program," by P. R. Torrens. HOSPITALS. 44:76+, December 1, 1970.

"Methadone management of heroin addiction." BULLETIN OF THE NEW YORK ACADEMY OF MEDICINE. 46:391-395, June, 1970.

"Methadone misuse and death by overdosage," by R. Gardner. BRITISH JOURNAL OF ADDICTION. 65:113-118, August, 1970.

"Methadone treatment of opiate addicts in Sweden," by J. H. Erikson. LAKARTIDNINGEN. 67:849-852, February 18, 1970.

METHADRINE
"Speed kills: the adolescent methedrine addict," by R. R. Rodewald. PERSPECTIVES IN PSYCHIATRIC CARE. 8:160-167, July-August, 1970.

"A method for the prevention of drug abuse," by L. Párkányi. ORVOSI HETILAP. 111:1855, August 2, 1970.

"The metro drug scene," by G. MacKinnon. TORONTO BOARD OF TRADE JOURNAL. 60:2-5, October, 1970.

MEXICAN-AMERICANS AND DRUGS
"Demographic factors in opiate addiction among Mexican-Americans," by C. D. Chambers, et al. PUBLIC HEALTH REPORTS. 85:523-531, June, 1970.

"Miliary tuberculosis, tuberculosis of ribs and heroin addiction," by J. Merry, et al. BRITISH JOURNAL OF PSYCHIATRY. 116:645-646, June, 1970.

"The misuse of drugs." NEW ZEALAND MEDICAL JOURNAL. 71:163, March, 1970.

"Model narcotic drug legislation (prepared by Criminal law education and research center study group, New York University)." CRIMINOLOGY. 8:156-172, August, 1970.

"Moderation in drug use at Michigan; survey of University of Michigan students." SCHOOL AND SOCIETY. 98: 134-135, March, 1970.

"Modern pharmacy practice: new treatment for addicts, new control problem for pharmacist," by G. C. Bowles, Jr. MODERN HOSPITAL. 114:126, April, 1970.

"Modest proposal; responsibility of record industry," by G. Lees. HI FI. 20:sec I,116, June, 1970.

"Monitoring of adverse reactions to drugs in the United Kingdom," by W. H. Inman. PROCEEDINGS OF THE ROYAL SOCIETY OF MEDICINE. 63:1302-1304, December, 1970.

"Mood-altering substances: a behavior inventory," by M. B. Pollock. JOURNAL OF EDUCATIONAL MEASUREMENT. 7: 211-212, Fall, 1970.

"Mood, Behavior, and Drugs, AAAS Symposium, 27-28 December 1970, Chicago," by C. D. Leake. SCIENCE. 170, 3957:559-560, October, 1970.

MORPHINE
"Antagonism of the behavioral effects of morphine and methadone by narcotic antagonists in the pigeon," by D. E. McMillan, et al. JOURNAL OF PHARMACOLOGY AND EXPERIMENTAL THERAPEUTICS. 175:443-458, November, 1970.

"Compound analgetics with morphine content," by P. Flatberg. TIDSSKRIFT FOR DEN NORSKE LAEGE-FORENING. 90:1562, August 15, 1970.

"Electroencephalographic study of morphine tolerance and withdrawal phenomenon in rats," by F. Lipparini, et al. THERAPIE. 25:929-937, September-October, 1970.

"Morphine and ethanol physical dependence; a critique of a hypothesis," by M. H. Seevers, et al. SCIENCE. 170:1113-1115, December 4, 1970.

"Morphine dependent rats as a model for evaluating potential addiction liability of analgesic compounds," by O. J. Lorenzetti, et al. ARCHIVES INTERNATIONALES DE PHARMACODYNAMIE ET DE THERAPIE. 183:391-402, February, 1970.

"Persistence of 'relapse-tendencies' of rats pre-

MORPHINE (cont'd.)
viously made physically dependent on morphine,"
by A. Wikler, et al. PSYCHOPHARMACOLOGIA. 16:
375-384, 1970.

"Physiologic parameters of morphine dependence in
man--tolerance, early abstinence, protracted
abstinence," by W. R. Martin, et al. PSYCHIATRY
DIGEST. 31:37+, July, 1970.

"Unchanged rate of brain serotonin synthesis during
chronic morphine treatment and failure of para-
chlorophenylalanine to attenuate withdrawal syndrome in mice," by I. Marshall, et al. NATURE
(London). 228:1206-1208, December 19, 1970.

"Morphine and ethanol physical dependence: a critique
of a hypothesis," by M. H. Seevers, et al. SCIENCE.
170:1113-1115, December 4, 1970.

"Morphine dependent rats as a model for evaluating
potential addiction liability of analgesic compounds," by O. J. Lorenzetti, et al. ARCHIVES
INTERNATIONALES DE PHARMACODYNAMIE ET DE THERAPIE.
183:391-402, February, 1970.

MORTALITY
"Causes of death among institutionalized narcotic
addicts," by J. D. Sapira, et al. JOURNAL OF
CHRONIC DISEASES. 22:733-742, April, 1970.

"Continuing studies in the diagnosis and pathology
of death from intravenous narcotism," by H. Siegel, et al. JOURNAL OF FORENSIC SCIENCES. 15:
179-184, April, 1970.

"Death from heroin," by P. H. Abelson. SCIENCE.
168:1289, June 12, 1970.

"Death of a young athlete: possible role of doping
apropos of 2 cases," by M. Yacoub, et al. MEDICO-
LEGAL BULLETIN. 3:275-277, July-September, 1970.

"Deaths in drug addicts." CANADIAN MEDICAL ASSOCIA-
TION JOURNAL. 103:1309-1310, December 5, 1970.

"Deaths in drug addicts. Cases of death not caused
by sickness among abusers of euphorigenic substances, investigated within Copenhagen University's Forensic Medical Institute's field of

MORTALITY (cont'd.)
    activity from 1 January 1968 to 1 May 1970," by
    J. Voigt. UGESKRIFT FOR LAEGER. 132:1989-1999,
    October 15, 1970.

    "Deaths in drug addicts. Forensic chemical studies
    and toxicological considerations," by K. Worm,
    et al. UGESKRIFT FOR LAEGER. 132:1955-1980,
    October 15, 1970.

    "Deaths in United Kingdom opioid users 1965-1969,"
    by R. Gardner. LANCET. 2:650-653, September
    26, 1970.

    "How nice drugs killed my sister," by M. Davidson.
    GOOD HOUSEKEEPING. 171:96-97+, September, 1970.

    "Lethal amphetamine intoxication. A report of
    three cases," by S. Orrenius, et al. ZEITSCHRIFT
    FUER RECHTSMEDIZIN. 67:184-189, 1970.

    "Methadone misuse and death by overdosage," by R.
    Gardner. BRITISH JOURNAL OF ADDICTION. 65:113-
    118, August, 1970.

"Motivation for addiction to amphetamine and reducing
    drugs," by S. Robinson, et al. PSYCHIATRY DIGEST.
    31:26+, July, 1970.

"Moving forward: drug-abuse bill." U.S. NEWS AND
    WORLD REPORT. 68:4, February 9, 1970.

MUSIC AND DRUGS
    "Drugs and death in the run-down world of rock
    music; Hendrix and Joplin," by A. Goldman. LIFE.
    69:32-33, October 16, 1970.

"NIMH tune-in." MEDICAL INSIGHT. 2:109+, September,
    1970.

NALLINE TEST
    "Narcotic control and the Nalline test; the addict's
    perspective," by S. E. Grupp. JOURNAL OF FORENSIC
    SCIENCES. 15:34-50, January, 1970.

NALORPHINE

"Conditioned nalorphine-induced abstinence changes:
persistence in post morphine-dependent monkeys,"
by S. R. Goldberg, et al. JOURNAL OF THE EXPERI-
MENTAL ANALYSIS OF BEHAVIOR. 14:33-46, July, 1970.

"Subjective effects of narcotic antagonists Cycla-
zocine and nalorphine on the Addiction Research
Center Inventory (ARCI)," by C. A. Haertzen.
PSYCHOPHARMACOLOGIA. 18:366-377, 1970.

NARCOMANIA

"Experience with young narcomaniacs in a provincial
hospital," by N. Pape. NORDISK MEDICIN. 83:
1413, October 29, 1970.

"Extramural psychiatric work among narcomaniacs,"
by M. Schioler. NORDISK MEDICIN. 83:1413, October 29, 1970.

"Narcomanism in the youth. Report from the Massa-
chusetts Medical Society," by N. Retterstol.
TIDSSKRIFT FOR DEN NORSKE LAEGEFORENING. 90:
878, May 1, 1970.

"Narcomanism in the youth. Report from the Massa-
chusetts Medical Society," by N. Retterstol. TIDS-
SKRIFT FOR DEN NORSKE LAEGEFORENING. 90:878, May
1, 1970.

"Narcotic abuse by adolescents," by R. Langmann. OEF-
FENTLICHE GESUNDHEITSWESEN. 32:43-46, January, 1970.

"The Narcotic Addict Rehabilitation Act: a change in
the federal response to the treatment of narcotic
addiction," by C. B. Scrignar, et al. SOUTHERN
MEDICAL JOURNAL. 63:109-112, January, 1970.

"Narcotic antagonists in opiate dependence; report
of meeting," by M. Fink. SCIENCE. 169:1005-1006,
September 4, 1970.

"Narcotic control and the Nalline test: the addict's
perspective," by S. E. Grupp. JOURNAL OF FORENSIC
SCIENCE. 15:34-50, January, 1970.

"Narcotic detoxification and rehabilitation service,"
by F. D. Alley and C. Simons. HOSPITAL MANAGEMENT.
110-164+, October, 1970.

"Narcotic problems among youth in Randers. A 10-month study of incidence," by E. Hansen, et al. UGESKRIFT FOR LAEGER. 132:2187-2189, November 12, 1970.

"Narcotics abuse in England," by K. Lie. SYKEPIEIEN. 57:422, June 15, 1970.

"Narcotics and the nurse," by M. M. Hennigh. BULLETIN; TEXAS NURSES ASSOCIATION. 43:5-7, March, 1970.

"Narcotics control in the hospital," by K. de Vahl. LARKARTIDNINGEN. 67:3622-3624, August 12, 1970.

"Narcotics: a crucial area of secondary school responsibility; fully credited courses needed," by R. Elliott. EDUCATION DIGEST. 36:44-47, September, 1970.

"Narcotics: the customs service; address, June 23, 1970," by M. J. Ambrose. VITAL SPEECHES. 36:612-615, August 1, 1970.

"Narcotics detection and industry," by D. Sohn, et al. JOURNAL OF OCCUPATIONAL MEDICINE. 12:6-9, January, 1970.

"Narcotics in prisons," by K. G. Gotestam. LARKARTID-NINGEN. 67:3277-3280, July 15, 1970.

"Narcotics: a new area of secondary school responsibility," by R. Elliott. NORTH CENTRAL ASSOCIATION QUARTERLY. 44:325-334, Spring, 1970; Same cond. EDUCATION DIGEST. 36:44-47, September, 1970.

"National Drug Abuse Prevention Program." COMPACT. 4,3:25, June, 1970.

"National policy on drug abuse," by M. C. Gabel. PEDIATRICS. 45:152, January, 1970.

"Necrotizing angiitis associated with drug abuse," by B.P. Citron, et al. NEW ENGLAND JOURNAL OF MEDICINE. 283:1003-1011, November 5, 1970.

"The need for therapeutic and administrative partnerships," by R. S. Garber. HOSPITAL AND COMMUNITY PSYCHIATRY. 21:349+, November, 1970.

"Needle sharing in the Haight: some social and psychological functions," by J. Howard, et al. JOUR-

NAL OF HEALTH AND SOCIAL BEHAVIOR. 11:220-230,
September, 1970.

"New heroin substitute." SCIENCE DIGEST. 67:56, June,
1970.

"New hope for the hopeless. Drug addiction: its treatment, management and the nurse's role," by J. N.
Chappel. CHART. 67:251-255, October, 1970.

"New look; the Dodd drug bill." NEWSWEEK. 75:24, February 9, 1970.

"New medico-legal aspects of toxicomania," by A. Franchini. MINERVA MEDICA. 61:4331-4338, October 3,
1970.

"A new method for treatment of barbiturate dependence,"
D. E. Smith, et al. JOURNAL OF THE AMERICAN MEDICAL
ASSOCIATION. 213:294-295, July 13, 1970.

"New Skills for Teachers," by J. Spillane. COMPACT.
4,3:26-27, June, 1970.

"New warning on LSD: defective children." NEWSWEEK.
75:98, May 18, 1970.

"New York's statutory scheme for the rehabilitation of
narcotics addicts through civil commitment," by M.
M. D'Auria. NEW YORK STATE BAR JOURNAL. 42:436-
443, August, 1970.

"Newark, narcotics, and the medical school," by E. A.
Wolfson. JOURNAL OF THE MEDICAL SOCIETY OF NEW
JERSEY. 67:207-210, May, 1970.

"Nixon approves drug guidelines, gives role to nar-
cotics bureau," by D. Bonafede. NATIONAL JOURNAL:
INDEXED STUDIES AND SUMMARIES OF FEDERAL GOVERNMENT
ACTIONS. 2:1532-1534, July 18, 1970.

"No knock?" by W. F. Buckley, Jr. NATIONAL REVIEW. 22:
220, February 24, 1970.

"No knock drug bill." TIME. 95:11-12, February 9,
1970.

"No marijuana for adolescents," by K. Angel. NEW
YORK TIMES MAGAZINE. p. 9+, January 25, 1970.

"Nonaddictive psychotropic medication for imprisoned narcotic addicts," by H. S. Feldman, et al. JOURNAL OF THE MEDICAL SOCIETY OF NEW JERSEY. 67:278-283, June, 1970.

"Nonmedical drug use among college student psychiatric patients," by R. G. Hinckley. JOURNAL OF THE AMERICAN COLLEGE HEALTH ASSOCIATION. 18:333-341, June, 1970.

"Non-medical use of drugs," by D. A. Geekie. CANADIAN MEDICAL ASSOCIATION JOURNAL. 102:421-422, February 28, 1970.

"Not my son!" by M. Baldwin. WOMAN'S DAY. 33:20+, June, 1970.

"Note on sex differences in student drug usage," by K. R. Mitchell, et al. PSYCHOLOGICAL REPORTS. 27:116, August, 1970.

"Nurses at risk." NURSING TIMES. 66:737, June 11, 1970.

NURSING AND DRUGS
"Drug abuse--a nursing responsibility?" by L. Blake. ALASKA NURSE. 24:18-19, December, 1970.

"Drug screening in industrial nursing," by D. Sohn, et al. OCCUPATIONAL HEALTH NURSING. 18:7-10, August, 1970.

"Drugs--addicts. Helping the nurse to understand the needs expressed by the addicted person," by C. Kelly. PENNSYLVANIA NURSE. 25:4-6+, October, 1970.

"An experimental clinic for narcotic abusers--the nurse as a research coordinator," by F. Kerman. ALUMNAE MAGAZINE (Baltimore). 69:5-7, March, 1970.

"Narcotics and the nurse," by M. M. Hennigh. BULLETIN; TEXAS NURSES ASSOCIATION. 43:5-7, March, 1970.

"New hope for the hopeless. Drug addiction; its treatment, management and the nurse's role," by J. N. Chappel. CHART. 67:251-255, October, 1970.

"Nurses at risk." NURSING TIMES. 66:737, June 11, 1970.

NURSING AND DRUGS (cont'd.)
"Nursing in a narcotic-detoxification unit," by E.
H. Russaw. AMERICAN JOURNAL OF NURSING. 70:
1720-1723, August, 1970.

"Participation of the nursing service department in
programs related to drug habituation." PRACTICAL
APPROACHES TO NURSING SERVICE ADMINISTRATION. 9:
1+, Fall, 1970.

"The role of the nurse with the drug abuser and addict," by G. Childress. JOURNAL OF PSYCHIATRIC
NURSING. 8:21+, March-April, 1970.

"The school nurse and drug abusers," by K. K. Caskey,
et al. NURSING OUTLOOK. 18:27-30, December, 1970.

"Staff-patient problems in drug dependence treatment
clinics," by T. H. Bewley, et al. JOURNAL OF
PSYCHOSOMATIC RESEARCH. 14:303-306, September,
1970.

"Nursing in a narcotic-detoxification unit," by E. H.
Russaw. AMERICAN JOURNAL OF NURSING. 70:1720-
1723, August, 1970.

NUTRITION AND DRUGS
"Alcoholism, drug addiction, and nutrition," by C.
M. Leevy, et al. MEDICAL CLINICS OF NORTH AMERICA.
54:1567-1575, November, 1970.

"Obscure hemolytic anemia due to analgesic abuse.
Does enterogenous cyanosis exist?" by E. A. Azen,
et al. AMERICAN JOURNAL OF MEDICINE. 48:724-727,
June, 1970.

"Observations about and from narcotic addiction," by
V. Borg. SYKEPLEIEN. 57:581-583, September 1, 1970.

"Observations on the current drug scene," by R. F. Aubrey.
NATIONAL ASSOCIATION OF COLLEGE ADMISSIONS COUNSE-
LORS JOURNAL. 15:24-26, November, 1970.

"Observations on an effective method to shorten the
psychotherapy of LSD-users," by C. Torda. AMERICAN

JOURNAL OF PSYCHOTHERAPY. 24:499-508, July, 1970.

OCCURRENCE

"Adolescent drug abuse in a North London suburb," by A. Anumonye, et al. BRITISH JOURNAL OF AD-DICTION. 65:25-33, May, 1970.

"Alcoholism and drug dependence amongst Jews," by M. M. Glatt. BRITISH JOURNAL OF ADDICTION. 64: 297-304, January, 1970.

"Anonymous versus identifiable questionnaires in drug usage surveys," by F. W. King. AMERICAN PSYCHOLOGIST. 25:982-985, October, 1970.

"Another checkup on drug use by GI's." U.S. NEWS AND WORLD REPORT. 69:33, August 31, 1970.

"At least a million people smoke pot." OBSERVER. pp. 1-2, March 15, 1970.

"Australian patterns of drug abuse." MEDICAL JOUR-NAL OF AUSTRALIA. 2:1105-1106, December 12, 1970.

"Consumption of psychoactive drugs and illegal drugs by the Zurich university students," by K. Battig. SCHWEIZERISCHE MEDIZINISCHE WOCHENSCHRIFT. 100: 1887-1893, October 31, 1970.

"Demographic factors in opiate addiction among Mex-ican-Americans," by C. D. Chambers, et al. PUBLIC HEALTH REPORTS. 85:523-531, June, 1970.

"Dimensions of marijuana usage in a land grant uni-versity," by L. B. DeFleur and G. R. Garrett. JOURNAL OF COUNSELING PSYCHOLOGY. 17,5:468-475, September, 1970.

"Drug abuse among union members," by L. Perlis. INDUSTRIAL MEDICINE AND SURGERY. 39:54-56, Sep-tember, 1970.

"Drug abuse in business." NATURE (London). 227: 331-332, July 25, 1970.

"Drug abuse in the Navy," by J. A. Pursch. UNITED STATES NAVAL INSTITUTE PROCEEDINGS. 96:52-56, July, 1970.

"Drug abuse in physicians." JOURNAL OF THE TENNESSEE

MEDICAL ASSOCIATION. 63:327-328, April, 1970.

"Drug abuse in the schools; teacher opinion poll.
National Education Association. Research Division." TODAY'S EDUCATION. 59:7, December, 1970.

"Drug abuse in the western world," by G. D. Lundberg. JOURNAL OF THE AMERICAN MEDICAL ASSOCIA-
TION. 213:2082, September 21, 1970.

"Drug abuse in a young psychiatric population," by
M. Cohen and D. F. Klein. AMERICAN JOURNAL OF
ORTHOPSYCHIATRY. 40:448-455, April, 1970.

"Drug abuse; pandemic." JOURNAL OF THE AMERICAN
MEDICAL ASSOCIATION. 214:2327, December 28, 1970.

"Drug addiction--a menace to youth in Great Britain,
a pilot epidemiological study," by D. C. Watt,
et al. ACTIVITAS NERVOSA SUPERIOR (Praha). 12:
284-287, 1970.

"Drug addiction of adolescents in Sweden," by B.
Jansson. NORDISK PSYKIATRISK TIDSSKRIFT. 24:
44-56, 1970.

"Drug culture; use of stimulants, sedative, and
tranquilizers by office workers." BUSINESS WEEK.
pp. 83-84, August 15, 1970.

"Drug dependence in Brisbane," by M. J. Abrahams,
et al. MEDICAL JOURNAL OF AUSTRALIA. 2:397-404,
August 29, 1970.

"Drug dependence in Italy: some statistical, clinical,
and social observations," by A. Madeddu and G.
Malagoli. BULLETIN ON NARCOTICS. 22:1-11, October-December, 1970.

"Drug dependence in the United States of America,"
by I. A. Lowe. JOURNAL OF THE ROYAL COLLEGE OF
GENERAL PRACTITIONERS. 19:16-21, January, 1970.

"Drug peril hits home in US." IRISH NURSING NEWS.
12-14, March-April, 1970.

"The drug problem and industry," by F. M. Garfield.
INDUSTRIAL MEDICINE AND SURGERY. 39:366-368,
August, 1970.

OCCURRENCE (cont'd.)

"The drug problem as it stands in Hong Kong," by
T. G. Garner. BRITISH JOURNAL OF ADDICTION.
65:45-50, May, 1970.

"Drug scene in East Egg," by E. Diamond. NEW YORK
TIMES MAGAZINE pp. 28-29+, May 17, 1970; Discussion, pp. 56-57, June 28, 1970.

"Drug threat in business." NATION. 211:484, November 16, 1970.

"Drugs in suburbia." WALL STREET JOURNAL. 176:1+,
November 12, 1970; 1+, November 18, 1970.

"Ecological variations in heroin abuse," by L. J.
Redlinger and J. B. Michel. SOCIOLOGICAL QUARTERLY. 11:219-229, Spring, 1970.

"The epidemiology of cannabism in France," by B.
Defer, et al. ANNALES MEDICO-PSYCHOLOGIQUES
(Paris). 2:113-120, June, 1970.

"The epidemiology of drug dependence in the UK,"
by D. V. Hawks. BULLETIN ON NARCOTICS. 22:15-
24, July-September, 1970.

"The epidemiology of drug overdosage," by L. K.
Morgan. MEDICAL JOURNAL OF AUSTRALIA. 2:338,
August 15, 1970.

"The epidemiology of drug overdosage," by F. A.
Whitlock. MEDICAL JOURNAL OF AUSTRALIA. 1:
1195-1199, June, 1970.

"Euphomania in New York City," by J. Simonsen.
UGESKRIFT FOR LAEGER. 132:1642-1646, August
27, 1970.

"Heroin dependence and delinquency in women--a
study of heroin addicts in Holloway prison," by
P. T. d'Orban. BRITISH JOURNAL OF ADDICTION.
65:67-78, May, 1970.

"How many new employees are drug abusers?" by G.
P. Bisgeier. INDUSTRIAL MEDICINE AND SURGERY.
39:369-370, August, 1970.

"How many of your personnel are captives of drugs?"
by E. Lewis. HOSPITAL MANAGEMENT. pp. 110-130+,

OCCURRENCE (cont'd.)
October, 1970.

"The incidence of drug use among Halifax adolescents," by P. C. Whitehead. BRITISH JOURNAL OF ADDICTION. 65:159-165, August, 1970.

"Marijuana," by D. Perna. JOURNAL OF THE AMERICAN MEDICAL ASSOCIATION. 214:760, October 26, 1970.

"Marijuana use among adults," by W. H. McGlothlin, et al. PSYCHIATRY. 33:433-443, November, 1970.

"Narcotics abuse in England," by K. Lie. SYKEPLEIEN. 57:422, January 15, 1970.

"Note on sex differences in student drug usage," by K. R. Mitchell, et al. PSYCHOLOGICAL REPORTS. 27:116, August, 1970.

"A pandemic disease surrounds us," by V. Spencer. HOSPITAL MANAGEMENT. 110:20+, October, 1970.

"Patterns of drug use among college students; a preliminary report," by G. L. Mizner, et al. AMERICAN JOURNAL OF PSYCHIATRY. 127:15-24, July, 1970.

"Patterns of drug use in a provincial university," by I. Hindmarch. BRITISH JOURNAL OF ADDICTION. 64:395-402, January, 1970.

"Patterns of drug use in school-age children," by H. B. Randall. JOURNAL OF SCHOOL HEALTH. 40:296-301, June, 1970.

"Patterns of drug use; a study of 5,482 subjects," by S. Black, et al. AMERICAN JOURNAL OF PSYCHIATRY. 127:420-423, October, 1970.

"Purposes, patterns, and protection in a campus drug using community," by E. Schaps, et al. JOURNAL OF HEALTH AND SOCIAL BEHAVIOR. 11: 135-145, June, 1970.

"Rarity of drug problems during political protest," by W. T. Carpenter, Jr., et al. JOURNAL OF THE AMERICAN MEDICAL ASSOCIATION. 213:1193, August 17, 1970.

OCCURRENCE (cont'd.)
"Readmission rates at Lexington Hospital for 43,
215 narcotic drug addicts," by J. C. Ball, et al.
PUBLIC HEALTH REPORTS. 85:610+, July, 1970.

"Social and psychological correlates of drug abuse.
A comparison of addict and non-addict populations
from the perspective of self-theory," by H. B.
Kaplan, et al. SOCIAL SCIENCE AND MEDICINE. 4:
203-225, August, 1970.

"The spread of drug addiction in the UK," by P. A.
Chapple. ROYAL SOCIETY OF HEALTH JOURNAL. 90:
196-197+, July-August, 1970.

"The use of catha edulis among Yemenite Jews," by
J. P. Hes. HAREFUAH. 78:283-284, March 15, 1970.

"Wave of LSD-taking hitting Britain," by E. Clark.
OBSERVER. p. 1+, December 20, 1970.

"Of plumbing and privacy; no-knock drug raids." EBONY.
25:154-155, April, 1970.

"On campus: drugs vs. drinking." MADEMOISELLE. 70:230,
March, 1970.

"On the edge of a cliff," by M. C. Ricks. INFIRMIERE
CANADIENNE. 12:24-27, December, 1970.

"On teaching about drugs; guide to books and audio-
visual aids," by S. J. Feinglass. MEDIA AND METHODS.
7:36-39+, September, 1970.

"On treating drug addiction with methadone." CURRENT.
120:35-38, August, 1970.

"One father's war on marijuana," by W. F. Buckley, Jr.
NATIONAL REVIEW. 22:1072, October 6, 1970.

"1 years admission of young drug abusers in the psychiatric clinic of Greater Copenhagen--preliminary
report," by S. Haastrup. NORDISK MEDICIN. 83:1412-
1413, October 29, 1970.

"Open Letter to Policy Makers," by A. Y. Cohen. COMPACT.
4,3:16-17, June, 1970.

"Open season on drug-smugglers; with interview by W.
B. Leithead, ed. by J. Fincher," by R. Chelminski.

LIFE. 68:28-35, June 26, 1970.

OPIATES
"Absence of major medical complications among chronic opiate addicts," by J. C. Ball, et al. BRITISH JOURNAL OF ADDICTION. 65:109-112, August, 1970.

"A cyclazocine typology in opiate dependence," by R. B. Resnick, et al. AMERICAN JOURNAL OF PSYCHIATRY. 126:1256-1260, March, 1970.

"Deaths in United Kingdom opioid users 1965-1969," by R. Gardner. LANCET. 2:650-653, September 26, 1970.

"Demographic factors in opiate addiction among Mexican-Americans," by C. D. Chambers, et al. PUBLIC HEALTH REPORTS. 85:523-531, June, 1970.

"Methadone maintenance for opiate dependence," by J. C. Kramer. CALIFORNIA MEDICINE. 113:6-11, December, 1970.

"Methadone treatment of opiate addicts in Sweden," by J. H. Erikson. LAKARTIDNINGEN. 67:849-852, February 18, 1970.

"Narcotic antagonists in opiate dependence; report of meeting," by M. Fink. SCIENCE. 169:1005-1006, September 4, 1970.

"Pursuit of the poppy." TIME. 96:28+, September 14, 1970.

"Opinion: Phoenix house, a celebration of life," by F. Natale. MADEMOISELLE. 72:46+, December, 1970.

OPIUM
"Ventilatory capacity in a group of opium smokers," by L. H. Koon, et al. SINGAPORE MEDICAL JOURNAL. 11:75-79, June, 1970.

"Opium and the Miao; a study in ecological adjustment," by W. R. Geddes. OCEANIA. 41:1-11, September, 1970.

OPIUM TRADE
"Opium and the Miao; a study in ecological adjustment," by W. R. Geddes. OCEANIA. 41:1-11, September, 1970.

"The oral health of narcotic addicts," by S. Shapiro,
et al. JOURNAL OF PUBLIC HEALTH DENTISTRY. 30:
244-249, Fall, 1970.

"An oral method of the withdrawal treatment of heroin
dependence: a five years' study of a combination of
diphenoxylate (Lomotil) and chlormethiazole (Heminevrin)," by M. M. Glatt, et al. BRITISH JOURNAL OF
ADDICTION. 65:237-243, November, 1970.

"Our drug-oriented society," by A. Van Hoff. NEBRASKA
NURSE. 3:5-6, July, 1970.

"An overdose of sleep." EMERGENCY MEDICINE. 2:78+,
September, 1970.

"Pain medications--for what reason?" by P. Jarvinen,
et al. SAIRAANHOITAJA. 46:383-385, May 10, 1970.

"A pandemic disease surrounds us," by V. Spencer. HOS-
PITAL MANAGEMENT. 110:20+, October, 1970.

"Paraphernalia, inc." TIME. 96:15, July 20, 1970.

PAREGORIC ABUSE
"Disseminated magnesium and aluminum silicate as-
sociated with paregoric addiction," by W. C.
Butz. JOURNAL OF FORENSIC SCIENCES. 15:581-587,
October, 1970.

"Participation of the Nursing Service Department in
programs related to drug habituation." PRACTICAL
APPROACHES TO NURSING SERVICE ADMINISTRATION. 9:
1+, Fall, 1970.

PATHOLOGY
"Continuing studies in the diagnosis and pathology
of death from intravenous narcotism," by H. Siegel,
et al. JOURNAL OF FORENSIC SCIENCES. 15:179-
184, April, 1970.

"Hepatitis in young drug abusers--liver pathology
and Prince antigen," by T. Jersild, et al. NOR-
DISK MEDICIN. 84:1538, November 26, 1970.

"Patient values on an adolescent drug unit," by E. L.

Burke. AMERICAN JOURNAL OF PSYCHOTHERAPY. 24:400-410, July, 1970.

"Patterns of drug use among college students: a preliminary report," by G. L. Mizner, et al. AMERICAN JOURNAL OF PSYCHIATRY. 127:15-24, July, 1970.

"Patterns of drug use in a provincial university," by I. Hindmarch. BRITISH JOURNAL OF ADDICTION. 64:395-402, January, 1970.

"Patterns of drug use in school-age children," by H.B. Randall. JOURNAL OF SCHOOL HEALTH. 40:296-301, June, 1970.

"Patterns of drug use: a study of 5,482 subjects," by S. Black, et al. AMERICAN JOURNAL OF PSYCHIATRY. 127:420-423, October, 1970.

"P-chloroamphetamine: in vivo investigations on the mechanism of action of the selective depletion of cerebral serotonin," by E. Sanders-Bush, et al. JOURNAL OF PHARMACOLOGY AND EXPERIMENTAL THERAPEUTICS. 175:419-426, November, 1970.

"p-Chloroamphetamine. Temporal relationship between psychomotor stimulation and metabolism of brain norepinephrine," by S. J. Strada, et al. BIOCHEMICAL PHARMACOLOGY. 19:2621-2629, September, 1970.

"The pediatrician and the marijuana question," by V. A. Donner, et al. PEDIATRICS. 45:1039-1040, June, 1970.

"The pediatrician and the marijuana question," by C. H. Gleason. PEDIATRICS. 45:1037, June, 1970.

"The pediatrician and the marijuana question," by Johnson, et al. PEDIATRICS. 45:1037-1038, June, 1970.

PENTAZOCINE ABUSE
"Addiction to pentazocine (Fortral)," by J. Geerling. PHARMAZEUTISCHE WEEKBLAD VOOR NEDERLAND. 105:405, March 27, 1970.

"Addiction to pentazocine: report of two cases," by W. F. Weber, et al. JOURNAL OF THE AMERICAN MEDICAL ASSOCIATION. 212:1708, June 8, 1970.

PENTAZOCINE ABUSE (cont'd.)
"Effects of short-and long-term administration of
pentazocine in man," by D. R. Jasinski, et al.
CLINICAL PHARMACOLOGY AND THERAPEUTICS. 11:385-
403, May-June, 1970.

"Intra-arterial administration of oral pentazocine,"
by A. M. Harrison, et al. JOURNAL OF THE AMERI-
CAN MEDICAL ASSOCIATION. 214:914, November 2,
1970.

"Methadone for the pentazocine-dependent patient,"
by N. N. Raskin. NEW ENGLAND JOURNAL OF MEDICINE.
283:1349, December 10, 1970.

"Pentazocine," by R. K. Ferguson. JOURNAL OF THE
IOWA MEDICAL SOCIETY. 60:112-113, February, 1970.

"Pentazocine dependence," by P. Idanpaan-Heikkila.
DUODECIM. 86:1386-1387, 1970; also DUODECIM.
86:519-522, 1970.

"Pentazocine," by R. K. Ferguson. JOURNAL OF THE IOWA
MEDICAL SOCIETY. 60:112-113, February, 1970.

"Pentazocine dependence," by P. Idanpaan-Heikkila.
DUODECIM. 86:1386-1387, 1970; also DUODECIM. 86:
519-522, 1970.

"Pep pills common in secondary schools," by C. Moorehead. TIMES (London) EDUCATIONAL SUPPLEMENT. 2895:
6, November 13, 1970.

"Pep pills for youngsters: treatment of hyperactive
children in Omaha." U.S. NEWS AND WORLD REPORT.
69:49, July 13, 1970.

"Periodontal disease in narcotic addicts," by S. Shapiro,
et al. JOURNAL OF DENTAL RESEARCH. 49:Suppl:1556,
November-December, 1970.

"Persistence of "relapse-tendencies" of rats previously
made physically dependent on morphine," by A. Wikler,
et al. PSYCHOPHARMACOLOGIA. 16:375-384, 1970.

PERSONALITY AND DRUGS
"Atypical reasoning errors in sociopathic, paranoid,
and schizophrenic personality types," by J. Fracchia, et al. JOURNAL OF PSYCHOLOGY. 76:91-95,
September, 1970.

PERSONALITY AND DRUGS (cont'd.)
"Drug addiction and personlaity disorder," by T.
Kraft. BRITISH JOURNAL OF ADDICTION. 64:403-408, January, 1970.

"Illicit LSD users; their personality character-istics and psychopathology," by R. G. Smart and
D. Jones. ABNORMAL PSYCHOLOGY. 75,3:286-292,
June, 1970.

"Personality correlates of undergraduate marijuana
use," by R. Hogan, et al. JOURNAL OF CONSULTING
AND CLINICAL PSYCHOLOGY. 35:58-63, August, 1970.

"Personality factors and barbiturate dependence,"
by A. Anumonye. BRITISH JOURNAL OF ADDICTION.
64:365-370, January, 1970.

"The personality of drug addicts and their treatment,"
by P. Delteil, et al. ANNALES MEDICO-PSYCHOLOGI-QUES (Paris). 2:107-113, June, 1970.

"Successful treatment of 'drinamyl' addicts and asso-ciated personality changes," by T. Kraft. CAN-ADIAN PSYCHIATRIC ASSOCIATION JOURNAL. 15:223-227, April, 1970.

"Personality correlates of undergraduate marijuana use,"
by R. Hogan, et al. JOURNAL OF CONSULTING AND CLIN-ICAL PSYCHOLOGY. 35:58-63, August, 1970.

"Personality factors and barbiturate dependence," by
A. Anumonye. BRITISH JOURNAL OF ADDICTION. 64:
365-370, January, 1970.

"The personality of drug addicts and their treatment,"
by P. Delteil, et al. ANNALES MEDICO-PSYCHOLOGIQUES
(Paris). 2:107-113, June, 1970.

PHARMACEUTICAL INDUSTRY
"Psychotropic drug therapy and pharmaceutical in-dustry," by J. Modestin. ARZNEIMITTEL-FORSCHUNG.
20:877-879, July, 1970.

"The pharmacist and drug abuse education." JOURNAL OF
THE AMERICAN PHARMACEUTICAL ASSOCIATION. 10:678-679, December, 1970.

PHARMACISTS AND DRUGS
"The abuse of drugs and its prevention. The phar-

PHARMACISTS AND DRUGS (cont'd.)
   macists role," by J. C. Bloomfield. ROYAL SOCIETY
   OF HEALTH JOURNAL. 90:193-195, July-August, 1970.

"Modern pharmacy practice: new treatment for addicts,
   new control problem for pharmacist," by G. C.
   Bowles, Jr. MODERN HOSPITAL. 114:126, April,
   1970.

"The pharmacist and drug abuse education." JOURNAL
   OF THE AMERICAN PHARMACEUTICAL ASSOCIATION. 10:
   678-679, December, 1970.

"The pharmacist's role in drug abuse control," by
   E. A. Carabillo, Jr. HOSPITAL PROGRESS. 51:
   30-31, March, 1970.

"Pharmacy service in an addiction research center,"
   by C. J. Hartleib. AMERICAN JOURNAL OF HOSPITAL
   PHARMACY. 27:384-389, May, 1970.

"The role of a school of pharmacy. Drug abuse education programming for a rural state--one approach," by P. Zanowiak. JOURNAL OF THE AMERI-
   CAN PHARMACEUTICAL ASSOCIATION. 10:566-568+,
   October, 1970.

"The pharmacist's role in drug abuse control," by E.
   A. Carabillo, Jr. HOSPITAL PROGRESS. 51:30-31,
   March, 1970.

"Pharmacological actions of 1-(o-methoxyphenoxy)3-
   isopropylamino-2-propanol hydrochloride (S-D-1601),
   a new beta-blocking agent," by R. Ferrini, et al.
   ARZNEIMITTEL-FORSCHUNG. 20:1074-1079, August, 1970.

"The pharmacological basis of drug dependence," by H.
   F. Marlow. SOUTH AFRICAN MEDICAL JOURNAL. 44:610-
   615, May 23, 1970.

"Pharmacological problems of drug dependence," by Z.
   Votava. ACTIVITAS NERVOSA SUPERIOR (Praha). 12:
   136, 1970.

"Pharmacological redundancy as an adaptive mechanism
   in the central nervous system," by W. R. Martin.
   FEDERATION PROCEEDINGS. 29:13-18, January-February,
   1970.

"The pharmacologist's dilemma: when is a drug safe for

general consumption?" by P. B. Dews. PEDIATRICS.
45:3-6, January, 1970.

PHARMACOLOGY
"The pharmacological basis of drug dependence," by
H. F. Marlow. SOUTH AFRICAN MEDICAL JOURNAL.
44:610-615, May 23, 1970.

"Pharmacological problems of drug dependence," by
Z. Votava. ACTIVITAS NERVOSA SUPERIOR (Praha).
12:136, 1970.

"Pharmacological redundancy as an adaptive mechanism
in the central nervous system," by W. R. Martin.
FEDERATION PROCEEDINGS. 29:13-18, January-February, 1970.

"The pharmacologist's dilemma; when is a drug safe
for general consumption?" by P. B. Dews. PE-
DIATRICS. 45:3-6, January, 1970.

"Pharmacology of a nicotinamido-methylaminopyrazolone (Ra 101)," by E. Tubaro, et al. ARZNEI-
MITTEL-FORSCHUNG. 20:1019-1023, August, 1970.

"Pharmacology of a nicotinamido-methylaminopyrazolone
(Ra 101)," by E. Tubaro, et al. ARZNEIMITTEL-
FORSCHUNG. 20:1019-1023, August, 1970.

"Pharmacy service in an addiction research center," by
C. J. Hartleib. AMERICAN JOURNAL OF HOSPITAL PHAR-
MACY. 27:384-389, May, 1970.

PHENACETIN
"The phenacetin enigma," by W. A. Pribe. JOURNAL
OF THE AMERICAN GERIATRICS SOCIETY. 18:703-707,
September, 1970.

"The phenacetin enigma," by W. A. Pribe. JOURNAL OF
THE AMERICAN GERIATRICS SOCIETY. 18:703-707, September, 1970.

PHENMETRAZINE ABUSE
"A case of phenmetrazine addiction," by M. Slizewski.
WIADOMOSCI LEKARSKIE. 23:419-421, March 1, 1970.

"Mental disorders caused by phenmetrazine abuse,"
by B. Klosinska, et al. PSYCHIATRIA POLSKA. 4:
45-47, January-February, 1970.

PHOENIX HOUSE
"Lifeboat; Phoenix house survival therapy." MOTOR
BOATING. 126:42-43, December 3, 1970.

"Opinion: Phoenix house, a celebration of life,"
by F. Natale. MADEMOISELLE. 72:46+, December,
1970.

"The physician dependent upon drugs," by R. H. Kamp-
meier. SOUTHERN MEDICAL JOURNAL. 63:983-984, August, 1970.

"The physician, marijuana and reason," by A. S. Norris.
JOURNAL OF THE IOWA MEDICAL SOCIETY. 60:623-630,
September, 1970.

PHYSICIANS AND DRUGS
"Abuse of drugs by the public and by doctors," by
D. Dunlop. BRITISH MEDICAL BULLETIN. 26:236-
239, September, 1970.

"Dangerous doctors." BRITISH MEDICAL JOURNAL. 1:
705-706, March 21, 1970.

"Doctors at risk." MEDICAL JOURNAL OF AUSTRALIA.
1:743-744, April 11, 1970.

"Drug abuse: the doctor's role," by E. A. Wolfson.
JOURNAL OF THE MEDICAL SOCIETY OF NEW JERSEY.
67:465-471, August, 1970.

"Drug abuse in physicians." JOURNAL OF THE TENNESSEE
MEDICAL ASSOCIATION. 63:327-328, April, 1970.

"Drug dependence among physicians," by D. L. Farnsworth. NEW ENGLAND JOURNAL OF MEDICINE. 282:
392-393, February 12, 1970.

"Federal Bureau of Narcotics lists 15 don'ts as
physician safeguards." JOURNAL OF THE INDIANA
STATE MEDICAL ASSOCIATION. 63:140, February,
1970.

"Goodbye junkies. A general practitioner takes
leave of his addicts," by A. J. Hawes. LANCET.
2:258-260, August 1, 1970.

"Interns and narcotic drugs," by D. E. Miller. AMER-
ICAN JOURNAL OF HOSPITAL PHARMACY. 27:799, October, 1970.

PHYSICIANS AND DRUGS (cont'd.)

"Marijuana and the pediatrician; an attitude survey,"
by A. L. Abrams, et al. PEDIATRICS. 46:462-
464, September, 1970.

"Methadone and the private practitioner," by H. W.
Freymuth. JOURNAL OF THE MEDICAL SOCIETY OF NEW
JERSEY. 67:128-130, March, 1970.

"The physician dependent upon drugs," by R. H. Kamp-
meier. SOUTHERN MEDICAL JOURNAL. 63:983-984,
August, 1970.

"The physician, marijuana and reason," by A. S. Norris.
JOURNAL OF THE IOWA MEDICAL SOCIETY. 60:623-630,
September, 1970.

"Physicians duty to patient--to company," by D. J.
Smith. INDUSTRIAL MEDICINE AND SURGERY. 39:57-
59, September, 1970.

"The physician's role in the South Dakota drug scene,"
by D. M. Frost. SOUTH DAKOTA JOURNAL OF MEDICINE.
23:47-48, September, 1970.

"Rock doctor tells about 985 freakouts; edited by R.
Stokes," by W. Abruzzi. LIFE. 69:37, August 14,
1970.

"Secret rules no hindrance for physicians to register
young drug addicts," by R. Rooseniit. LAKARTID-
NINGEN. 67:3356-3359, July, 1970.

"3 physicians' prescriptions for narcotics criticized."
LAKARTIDNINGEN. 67:6014-6015, December 16, 1970.

"Use of amphetamine by medical students," by C. Watkins. SOUTHERN MEDICAL JOURNAL. 63:928-929,
August, 1970.

"Watch your prescribing policy, doctor addicts may
be abusing it." OHIO STATE MEDICAL JOURNAL. 66:
418, April, 1970.

"Physicians duty to patient--to company," by D. J.
Smith. INDUSTRIAL MEDICINE AND SURGERY. 39:57-
59, September, 1970.

"The physician's role in the South Dakota drug scene,"
by D. M. Frost. SOUTH DAKOTA JOURNAL OF MEDICINE.

23:47-48, September, 1970.

"Physiologic parameters of morphine dependence in man--
tolerance, early abstinence, protracted abstinence,"
by W. R. Martin, et al. PSYCHIATRY DIGEST. 31:37+,
July, 1970.

"The pill head menace. Barbiturates and tranquilizers
non-hard core addicting drugs," by H. S. Feldman.
PSYCHOSOMATICS. 11:99-103, March-April, 1970.

"Pills for Classroom Peace?", by E. T. Ladd. SATURDAY
REVIEW OF LITERATURE. 53,47:66-68, November 21,
1970.

"Place of treatment professions in society's response
to chemical abuse," by G. Edwards. BRITISH MEDICAL
JOURNAL. 2:195-199, April 25, 1970.

"Placebo as an agent in the treatment of drug abuse,"
by J. Hankiewicz. WIADOMOSCI LEKARSKIE. 23:1253-
1257, July 15, 1970.

"Planning and implementation of an effective drug abuse
education program," by C. A. Rodowskas, Jr., et al.
JOURNAL OF THE AMERICAN PHARMACEUTICAL ASSOCIATION.
10:563-565+, October, 1970.

"The political economy of junk," by S. Yurick. MONTHLY
REVIEW ✗. 22:22-31+, December, 1970.

"Polytoxitudes and communication. Some considerations,"
by J. F. Mabileau. ANNALES MEDICO-PSYCHOLOGIQUES
(Paris). 2:78-85, June, 1970.

"A Positive Approach to Drug Education," by R. L.
Mikeal and M. C. Smith. JOURNAL OF SCHOOL HEALTH.
40,8:450-452, October, 1970.

"Pot and the law; the legalization of marijuana on
a provisional basis." CHRISTIAN CENTURY. 87:1275,
October 28, 1970; Discussion. 87:1461, December 2,
1970.

"Pot boils over," by F. Poland. SCIENCE NEWS. 97:
630, June 27, 1970.

"Pot bust." NEWSWEEK. 75:92+, May 11, 1970.

"Pot facing stringent scientific examination," by B.

J. Culliton. SCIENCE NEWS. 97:102-105, January 24, 1970.

"Pot, hard drugs and the law," by G. Samuels. NEW YORK TIMES MAGAZINE. p. 4+, February 15, 1970.

"Pot in prison," by W. F. Buckley, Jr. NATIONAL REVIEW. 22:221, February 24, 1970.

"Pot, pills and people; Camp JCA, California," by M. Schlesinger. CAMPING MAGAZINE. 42:10-11+, March, 1970.

"Pot samplers may be dabbling with psychosis." TODAY's HEALTH. 48:71, August, 1970.

"Pot-smoking young executives," by S. Margetts. DUNS. 95:42-43, Fall, 1970.

PREGNANCY AND DRUGS
"Drug dependence and pregnancy: a review of the problems and their management," by R. Neuberg. JOURNAL OF OBSTETRICS AND GYNAECOLOGY OF THE BRITISH COMMONWEALTH. 77:1117-1122, December, 1970.

"LSD exposure in utero," by R. J. Warren, et al. PEDIATRICS. 45:466-469, March, 1970.

"Preliminary report on the detection and quantitation of opiates and certain other drugs of abuse as trimethysilyl derivatives by gas-liquid chromatography," by K. D. Parker, et al. JOURNAL OF FORENSIC SCIENCES. 10:17-22, January, 1970.

"Prescribing and handling drugs in hospital," by B. J. Lewis. NURSING MIRROR AND MIDWIVES JOURNAL. 131: 24-27, October 16, 1970.

PRESCRIPTIONS AND DRUGS
"Abusive prescriptions of vitamin D." PRESSE MEDICALE. 78:556, March 7, 1970.

"Drug deceptions," by S. Krippner. SCIENCE. 168: 654, May 8, 1970.

"Hazards implicit in prescribing psychoactive drugs," by H. L. Lennard, et al. SCIENCE. 169:438-441, July 31, 1970.

"Pain medications--for what reason?" by P. Jarvinen,

PRESCRIPTIONS AND DRUGS (cont'd.)
et al. SAIRAANHOITAJA. 46:383-385, May 10, 1970.

"Prescribing and handling drugs in hospital," by
B. J. Lewis. NURSING MIRROR AND MIDWIVES JOURNAL.
131:24-27, October 16, 1970.

"3 physicians' prescriptions for narcotics criticized."
LAKARTIDNINGEN. 67:6014-6015, December 16, 1970.

"Present problems with narcotics," by D. Cabanis. DEUT-
SCHES MEDIZINISCHES JOURNAL. 21:1282+, October, 1970.

"Presenting the facts. Drug abuse education." JOURNAL
OF THE AMERICAN PHARMACEUTICAL ASSOCIATION. 10:628,
November, 1970.

"Preventing drug addiction." ZAHNAERZTLICHE MITTEILUN-
GEN. 60:813-814, August, 1970.

PREVENTION AND CONTROL
"The abuse of drugs and its prevention. The pharma-
cist's role," by J. C. Bloomfield. ROYAL SOCIETY
OF HEALTH JOURNAL. 90:193-195, July-August, 1970.

"Action on amphetamines," by F. O. Wells. BRITISH
MEDICAL JOURNAL. 1:361, May 9, 1970.

"Addiction, medicine and the law." SCIENTIFIC AMER-
ICAN. 223:50, July, 1970.

"Addicts and zealots; chaotic war against drug abuse
in New York City," by M. K. Sanders. HARPER'S.
240:71-73+, June, 1970; also in READER'S DIGEST.
97:95, December, 1970.

"Adolescence and drug abuse," by J. H. McKeen. JOUR-
NAL OF THE ROYAL COLLEGE OF GENERAL PRACTITIONERS.
20:288-290, November, 1970.

"Americans abroad; the jail scene." TIME. 95:36,
April 13, 1970.

"Anti-narcotics drive 40 years old," by A. C. Vaigo.
TIMES (London) EDUCATIONAL SUPPLEMENT. 2861:16,
March 20, 1970.

"An approach to the treatment of drug abuse," by R.
I. Wang, et al. WISCONSIN MEDICAL JOURNAL. 69:
148-150, May, 1970.

PREVENTION AND CONTROL (cont'd.)
"Ban on amphetamines and barbiturates," by H. Matthew.
BRITISH MEDICAL JOURNAL. 4:801, December 26, 1970.

"Ban on barbiturates," by F. Wells. BRITISH MEDICAL
JOURNAL. 4:552, November 28, 1970.

"Blacks declare war on dope; mothers against drugs."
EBONY. 25:31-34+, June, 1970.

"Booming traffic in drugs: the government's dilemma."
U.S. NEWS AND WORLD REPORT. 69:40-41, December 7,
1970.

"Broader attack on drug abuse, to dry up the flow
of drugs." U.S. NEWS AND WORLD REPORT. 68:38,
March 23, 1970.

"Callaghan hard line likely on soft drugs," by N.
Fowler. TIMES (London). p. 6, February 7, 1970.

"The campaign against drug addiction." MEDECINE
LEGALE ET DOMMAGE CORPOREL (Paris). 3:216-219,
April-June, 1970.

"Central-stimulating amines--international control,"
by N. Retterstol. TIDSSKRIFT FOR DEN NORSKE
LAEGEFORENING. 90:2096, November 15, 1970.

"Clandestine drug laboratories," by J. W. Gunn, et
al. JOURNAL OF FORENSIC SCIENCES. 15:51-64,
January, 1970.

"The committee and the pill," by P. Diggory. LANCET.
1:86, January 10, 1970.

"Community programs and the underlying problem," by
O. H. Entwistle. COMPACT. 4,3:41-43, June, 1970.

"Comprehensive drug abuse prevention and control
act of 1970: the President's remarks at the signing ceremony at the Bureau of Narcotics and Dangerous Drugs, October 27, 1970," by R. Nixon.
COMPILATION OF PRESIDENTIAL DOCUMENTS. 6:1463,
November 2, 1970.

"Control and distribution of narcotics in the
hospital," by L. Banner, et al. HOSPITAL MAN-
AGEMENT. 110:68+, October, 1970.

PREVENTION AND CONTROL (cont'd.)
"Control of amphetamines and LSD." LANCET. 1:
708, April 4, 1970.

"Control of central stimulants: the Swedish tactics
gave the result," by S. Martens. LAKARTIDNINGEN.
67:2269-2272, May 13, 1970.

"Control of drug abuse," by S. Cohen. FEDERAL PRO-
BATION. 34:32-37, March, 1970.

"Control of drugs," by M. M. Glatt. LANCET. 1:889-
890, April 25, 1970.

"Control of psychotropic substances," by W. W. Wigle.
CANADIAN MEDICAL ASSOCIATION JOURNAL. 102:873+,
April 25, 1970.

"Control of stupefacient drugs," by B. Rolland.
ARCHIVES BELGES DE MEDECINE SOCIALE, HYGIENE,
MEDECINE DU TRAVAIL ET MEDECINE LEGALE. 28:249-
256, April, 1970.

"Control organizations for the restriction of narcotic and drug abuse," by F. Jorgensen. UGESKRIFT
FOR LAEGER. 132:2192-2194, November 12, 1970.

"The controlled dangerous substances Act of 1969,"
by M. R. Sonnenreich. BULLETIN OF THE PAREN-
TERAL DRUG ASSOCIATION. 24:14-22, January-February, 1970.

"Cooperation in drug provision." TIDSKRIFT FOR
SVERIGES SJUKSKOTERSKOR. 37:76-77, January,
1970.

"Coping with drug abuse," by S. Lecker and W. Pigott.
CANADA'S MENTAL HEALTH. 18:1+ (Suppl. 64), March-
April, 1970.

"Coping with drug abuse. I. A community social
action approach," by S. Lecker, et al. CANADIAN
JOURNAL OF PSYCHIATRIC NURSING. 11:5-9, July,
1970.

"Coping with drug abuse. II. A indigenous multidisciplinary clinic for youths," by S. Lecker.
CANADIAN JOURNAL OF PSYCHIATRIC NURSING. 11:
4-9, August, 1970.

PREVENTION AND CONTROL (cont'd.)
"Counter-measures against narcotic addiction," by
H. Kravitz. IMAGE (New York). 138:55, July, 1970.

"Criticism on the Department of Welfare. Lack of
initiative in incidents of Minamata disease and
control of drugs," by M. Hirasawa. JAPANESE JOUR-
NAL OF NURSING. 34:41-45, November, 1970.

"Current narcotics abuse from the viewpoint of
criminalistic practice," by G. Bauer. MUENCHENER
MEDIZINISCHE WOCHENSCHRIFT. 112:1562-1569, August 28, 1970.

"Dangerous doctors." BRITISH MEDICAL JOURNAL. 1:
705-706, March 21, 1970.

"Dangerous drugs at large, II," by A. Cohen. NURSING
MIRROR AND MIDWIVES JOURNAL. 131:22, October 30,
1970.

"DARE--a thinking, hoping, seeing, feeling, breathing,
speaking happening." AORN JOURNAL. 12:52-53,
September, 1970.

"Deceptions in the illicit drug market," by F. E.
Cheek, et al. SCIENCE. 167:1276, February 27,
1970.

"Declaration by the Attorneys General on the narcotics traffic; United States-Mexico joint cooperation." DEPARTMENT OF STATE BULLETIN. 63:
300, September 14, 1970.

"Department warns of penalties for drug violations
abroad: announcement, March 31, 1970." DEPART-
MENT OF STATE BULLETIN. 62:549-551, April 27,
1970.

"Determination and identification of sympathomimetic
amines in blood samples from drivers by a combination of gas chromatography and mass spectrometry," by R. Bonnichsen, et al. ZEITSCHRIFT
FUER RECHTSMEDIZIN. 67:19-26, 1970.

"Determination of drugs in biologic specimens," by
J. E. Wallace, et al. INDUSTRIAL MEDICINE AND
SURGERY. 39:412-419, October, 1970.

"The development of international control of drugs,"

PREVENTION AND CONTROL (cont'd.)
by M. M. Glatt. WHO CHRONICLE. 24:189-197, May,
1970.

"Dope stop-teen involvement," by G. E. Conroy. ARI-
ZONA MEDICINE. 27:16-17, October, 1970.

"Drug abuse; comprehensive drug abuse prevention and
control act of 1970." NEW REPUBLIC. 163:9,
October 10, 1970.

"Drug abuse in business." NATURE (London). 227:
331-332, July 25, 1970.

"Drug abuse prevention," by J. D. Swisher and R. E.
Horman. JOURNAL OF COLLEGE STUDENT PERSONNEL.
11:337-341, September, 1970.

"Drug addiction prevention program," by A. J. Friedhoff. JOURNAL OF THE AMERICAN MEDICAL ASSOCIATION.
214:1564, November 23, 1970.

"Drug education begins before kindergarten; the Glen
Cove, New York, pilot program," by R. M. Daniels.
JOURNAL OF SCHOOL HEALTH. 40:242-248, May, 1970.

"Drug explosion." ECONOMIST. 235-252+, April 4,
1970.

"Drug traffic in the middle east; a lesson for the
west?" by R. Alan. NEW LEADER. 53:16-19, September 7, 1970.

"Drug treatment and prevention." NATIONAL ASSOCIA-
TION OF SECONDARY SCHOOL PRINCIPALS BULLETIN.
54,349:95-105, November, 1970.

"Drugs: stopping the supply is not enough," by G.
Birdwood. DAILY TELEGRAPH. p. 12, April 4, 1970.

"Early steps toward preventing drug abuse; with study-
discussion program, by E. and D. Harris," by R.
E. Gould. PTA MAGAZINE. 64:6-9, March, 1970.

"Federal Bureau of Narcotics lists 15 don'ts as
physician safeguards." JOURNAL OF THE INDIANA
STATE MEDICAL ASSOCIATION. 63:140, February,
1970.

"The federal drug abuse program." PUBLIC HEALTH

PREVENTION AND CONTROL (cont'd.)
REPORTS. 85:565-568, July, 1970.

"Federal plan for narcotics and dangerous drugs,"
by F. M. Garfield. BULLETIN OF THE PARENTERAL
DRUG ASSOCIATION. 24:11-13, January-February,
1970.

"Frisking for drugs," by C. H. Rolph. NEW STATES-
MAN. 79:688, May 15, 1970.

"Getting heroin into US; how the smugglers operate;
excerpts from What everyone needs to know about
drugs." U.S. NEWS AND WORLD REPORT. 69:41-44,
December 7, 1970.

"Global headache; use of drugs spreads abroad spurring drive for international curbs," by G. Melloan
WALL STREET JOURNAL. 175:1+, March 25, 1970.

"Governor's panel explores drug abuse in Utah," by
C. L. Rampton. COMPACT. 4,3:15+, June, 1970.

"Hassle over narcotics control." SCIENCE NEWS.
97:339, April 4, 1970.

"How the schools can prevent drug abuse," by D.
C. Lewis. NATIONAL ASSOCIATION OF SECONDARY
SCHOOL PRINCIPALS BULLETIN. 54,346:43-51, May,
1970.

"International agreement on narcotic control as a
legal basis for the prevention of narcotic addiction," by M. B. Khodakov. FARMATSEVTYCHNYI
ZHURNAL (Kiev). 25:69-74, 1970.

"International control of central stimulants: five
drugs are considered as dangerous as opium. Every
state can privately sharpen the control." LAKAR-
TIDNINGEN. 67:2267-2268, May 13, 1970.

"International narcotics control," by I. G. Waddell.
AMERICAN JOURNAL OF INTERNATIONAL LAW. 64:310-
323, April, 1970.

"An international problem: Department of State joins
fight against drug smuggling," by E. L. Richardson
DEPARTMENT OF STATE NEWS LETTER. pp. 18-21, April
1970.

PREVENTION AND CONTROL (cont'd.)
"Interns and narcotic drugs," by D. E. Miller.
AMERICAN JOURNAL OF HOSPITAL PHARMACY. 27:799,
October, 1970.

"Man alive is alive, and well," by G. B. Whitman.
ALUMNAE MAGAZINE (Baltimore). 69:8-9, March,
1970.

"Marijuana; should it be controlled?" by S. Heinemann. SOUTHWESTERN MEDICINE. 51:267-268, December, 1970.

"Modern narcotic drug legislation (prepared by Criminal law education and research center study
group, New York University)." CRIMINOLOGY. 8:
156-172, August, 1970.

"Modern pharmacy practice: new treatment for addicts,
new control problem for pharmacist," by G. C.
Bowles, Jr. MODERN HOSPITAL. 114:126, April,
1970.

"Moving forward: drug-abuse bill." U.S. NEWS AND
WORLD REPORT. 68:4, February 9, 1970.

"Narcotic control and the Nalline test; the addict's
perspective," by S. E. Grupp. JOURNAL OF FORENSIC
SCIENCES. 15:34-50, January, 1970.

"Narcotics control in the hospital," by K. de Vahl.
LAKARTIDNINGEN. 67:3622-3624, August 12, 1970.

"Narcotics; the customs service; address, June 23,
1970," by M. J. Ambrose. VITAL SPEECHES. 36:
612-615, August 1, 1970.

"National drug abuse prevention program." COMPACT.
4,3:25+, June, 1970.

"The need for therapeutic and administrative partnerships," by R. S. Garber. HOSPITAL AND COMMUNITY
PSYCHIATRY. 21:349+, November, 1970.

"Nixon approves drug guidelines, gives role to
narcotics bureau," by D. Bonafede. NATIONAL
JOURNAL: INDEXED STUDIES AND SUMMARIES OF FEDERAL
GOVERNMENT ACTIONS. 2:1532-1534, July 18, 1970.

"No knock?" by W. F. Buckley, Jr. NATIONAL REVIEW.

PREVENTION AND CONTROL (cont'd.)
22:220, February 24, 1970.

"No knock drug bill." TIME. 95:11-12, February 9, 1970.

"Of plumbing and privacy; no-knock drug raids." EBONY. 25:154-155, April, 1970.

"Open season on drug-smugglers; with interview by W. B. Leithead, ed. by J. Fincher," by R. Chelminski. LIFE. 68:28-35, June 26, 1970.

"The pharmacist's role in drug abuse control," by E. A. Carabillo, Jr. HOSPITAL PROGRESS. 51:30-31, March, 1970.

"Place of treatment professions in society's response to chemical abuse," by G. Edwards. BRITISH MEDICAL JOURNAL. 2:195-199, April 25, 1970.

"Pot boils over," by F. Poland. SCIENCE NEWS. 97:630, June 27, 1970.

"Pot bust." NEWSWEEK. 75:92+, May 11, 1970.

"Pot, hard drugs and the law," by G. Samuels. NEW YORK TIMES MAGAZINE. p. 4+, February 15, 1970.

"Preventing drug addiction." ZAHNAERZTLICHE MITTEILUNGEN. 60:813-814, August, 1970.

"Prevention of toxicomania in France," by N. Simonetti. MINERVA MEDICA. 61:Suppl. 49:11-12, June 23, 1970.

"Preventive action in the battle with drugs. Project DARE, Los Angeles, California." HOSPITAL AND COMMUNITY PSYCHIATRY. 21:325-328, Winter, 1970.

"A preventive package kids can relate to." SCHOOL MANAGEMENT. 14,4:25+, April, 1970.

"The problem of drugs. Motives, prevention, and measures to be taken," by H. Baruk. ANNALES MEDICO-PSYCHOLOGIQUES (Paris). 2:136-139, June, 1970.

"The program of the Johns Hopkins Hospital drug abuse center," by L. Wurmser. ALUMNAE MAGAZINE (Baltimore). 69:10-12, March, 1970.

PREVENTION AND CONTROL (cont'd.)

"Relationship between criminal law and health protection, tasks of public health organs and institutions," by H. G. Keune. PHARMAZEUTISCHE PRAXIS; BEILAGE ZUR DIE PHARMAZIE. 5:97-101, 1970.

"The role of the Committee on Safety of Drugs," by D. Mansel-Jones. BRITISH MEDICAL BULLETIN. 26: 257-259, September, 1970.

"The role of a medical society in a drug abuse program," by C. Baron. JOURNAL OF THE KENTUCKY MEDICAN ASSOCIATION. 68:113-114, February, 1970.

"Slowdown for pep pills; new restrictions." NEWSWEEK. 76:77, August 17, 1970.

"Smugglers of misery," by W. Schulz. READER'S DIGEST. 96:49-54, April, 1970.

"Special report: 17th national AORN congress. Tells causes of teen-drug abuse; suggests ways to combat problem," by J. T. Ungerleider. HOSPITAL TOPICS. 48:101+, May, 1970.

"State action against drug abuse." COMPACT. 4,3: 28-33, June, 1970.

"State-initiated community programs," by H. Levander. COMPACT. 4,3:49+, June, 1970.

"Stop and SEARCH." LANCET. 1:1037, May 16, 1970.

"Straight and narrow; control of drugs." NATURE (London). 225:1087-1088, May 21, 1970.

"Strengthened programs of international cooperation for halting the illicit supply of drugs; address, April 2, 1970," by E. L. Richardson. DEPARTMENT OF STATE BULLETIN. 62:544-549, April 27, 1970.

"The struggle against doping and its history," by L. Prokop. JOURNAL OF SPORTS MEDICINE AND PHYSICAL FITNESS. 10:45-48, March, 1970.

"Task of the plant protection agencies," by S. Weiss. MUENCHENER MEDIZINISCHE WOCHENSCHRIFT. 112:2021-2022, October 30, 1970.

"There are people who say, well, business is business."

PREVENTION AND CONTROL (cont'd.)
FORBES. 105:19-22, April 1, 1970.

"The $30 million industry," by D. Thomas. ATLANTA
MAGAZINE. 10:44-50+, November, 1970.

"Tough bill plus research: comprehensive drug abuse
and control act of 1970." SCIENCE NEWS. 98:
332-333, October 24, 1970.

"Turning off the Tijuana grass; operation Intercept,"
by C. Kentfield. ESQUIRE. 73:8+, May, 1970.

"Uncertainty in the programs of prevention of drug
addiction in the United States," by A. Muggia.
MINERVA MEDICA. 61:Suppl. 49:10, June 23, 1970.

"Unit-dose narcotic prestock system saves effort
but maintains control," by M. R. Beahm, et al.
HOSPITAL TOPICS. 48:63+, November, 1970.

"U.S. and Mexico continue talks on control of narcotics; Department announcement with joint communique." DEPARTMENT OF STATE BULLETIN. 62:527,
April 20, 1970.

"US-Mexican discussions of marijuana, narcotics,
and dangerous drugs: declaration by Attorneys
General Mitchell and Sanchez Vargas at Puerto
Vallarta, August 21, 1970." WEEKLY COMPILATION
OF PRESIDENTIAL DOCUMENTS. 6:1092-1093, August
24, 1970.

"U.S. proposes new UN action program against illicit
narcotics," by J. E. Ingersoll. DEPARTMENT OF
STATE BULLETIN. 63:492-497, October 26, 1970.
(Statement before a meeting of the UN commission
on narcotic drugs, Geneva, September 28, 1970).

"The use and misuse of psychotropic drugs. A panel
discussion." JOURNAL OF THE IOWA MEDICAL SOCIETY.
60:98-105, February, 1970.

"War on drugs; its meaning to tourists." U.S. NEWS
AND WORLD REPORT. 69:68, September 7, 1970.

"Watch your prescribing policy, doctor addicts may
be abusing it." OHIO STATE MEDICAL JOURNAL. 66:
418, April, 1970.

PREVENTION AND CONTROL (cont'd.)
"We must declare war on drugs; ed. J. N. Bell,"
by A. Linkletter. GOOD HOUSEKEEPING. 170:94-95+,
April, 1970.

"We must fight the epidemic of drug abuse," by A.
Linkletter. READER'S DIGEST. 96:56-60, February, 1970.

"What will turn the tide against drug abuse?" by F.
X. Wamsley. MEDICAL ECONOMICS. 47:94+, December
7, 1970.

"What you can do about the drug problem," by S. Grafton. PARENTS MAGAZINE. 45:72-75+, November, 1970.

"Where prevention starts," by T. D. Bird. NORTHWEST
MEDICINE. 69:553, August, 1970.

"Prevention of toxicomania in France," by N. Simonetti.
MINERVA MEDICA. 61:Suppl. 49:11-12, June 23, 1970.

"Preventive action in the battle with drugs. Project
DARE, Los Angeles, California." HOSPITAL AND COM-
MUNITY PSYCHIATRY. 21:325-328, Winter, 1970.

"A Preventive Package Kids Can Relate To." SCHOOL MAN-
AGEMENT. 14,4:25, April, 1970.

"Price of a trip? Possibility of chromosome damage to
germ cells by LSD." TIME. 95:43, February 23, 1970.

"Princess Leda's castle in the air," by T. Burke.
ESQUIRE. 73:104-111+, March, 1970.

"Principal conclusions from the report: 'Psychology,
social-psychology and sociology of illicit drug use',"
by H. Cohen. BRITISH JOURNAL OF ADDICTION. 65:39-
44, May, 1970.

"Principles of diagnosis and treatment of addictive
drugs overdose," by J. F. Burdon. JOURNAL OF THE
ROYAL COLLEGE OF GENERAL PRACTITIONERS. 20:171-
174, September, 1970.

PRISONS AND DRUGS
"Heroin dependence and delinquency in women--a study
of heroin addicts in Holloway prison," by P. T.
d'Orban. BRITISH JOURNAL OF ADDICTION. 65:67-78,
May, 1970.

PRISONS AND DRUGS (cont'd.)
"Narcotics in prisons," by K. G. Gotestam. LAKAR-
TIDNINGEN. 67:3277-3280, July 15, 1970.

"Nonaddictive psychotropic medication for imprisoned
narcotic addicts," by H. S. Feldman, et al. JOUR-
NAL OF THE MEDICAL SOCIETY OF NEW JERSEY. 67:
278-283, June, 1970.

"Pot in prison," by W. F. Buckley, Jr. NATIONAL RE-
VIEW. 22:221, February 24, 1970.

"The role of the prison service in rehabilitation
of drug dependent," by T. G. Garner. BULLETIN ON
NARCOTICS. 22:19-23, January-March, 1970.

"Private enterprise and dope; Creative learning group,
distributor of scientific educational materials on
drug damage," by W. F. Buckley, Jr. NATIONAL REVIEW.
22:964, September 8, 1970.

"The problem of drugs. Motives, prevention and measures
to be taken," by H. Baruk. ANNALES MEDICO-PSYCHOLO-
GIQUES (Paris). 2:136-139, June, 1970.

"Problems of toxicophilia in young adults at the stage
of military obligations," by J. Paraire, et al. AN-
NALES MEDICO-PSYCHOLOGIQUES (Paris). 2:93-100, June,
1970.

"Problems regarding the introduction of a psychopharma-
ceutical agent in international markets," by P. J.
Chanas. PSYCHOSOMATICS. 11:530-531, September-
October, 1970.

"Profession, press, and television," by A. M. Campbell.
BRITISH MEDICAL JOURNAL. 3:406, August 15, 1970.

"A program for control of drug abuse in industry," by
C. H. Hine and J. A. Wright. OCCUPATIONAL HEALTH
NURSING. 18:17+, April, 1970.

"The program of the Johns Hopkins Hospital Drug Abuse
Center," by L. Wurmser. ALUMNAE MAGAZINE (Baltimore).
69:10-12, March, 1970.

"Programme on heroin." NATURE (London). 227:773-774,
August 22, 1970.

"Prohibition of marijuana," by J. Kaplan. NEW REPUBLIC.

143

163:11-12, November 21, 1970.

PROJECT DARE
"Preventive action in the battle with drugs Project
DARE. Los Angeles, California." HOSPITAL AND
COMMUNITY PSYCHIATRY. 21:325-328, Winter, 1970.

PROPOXPHENE ABUSE
"Addiction to propoxphene," by F. J. Kane, Jr., et al.
JOURNAL OF THE AMERICAN MEDICAL ASSOCIATION. 211:
300, January 12, 1970.

"Intra-arterial injection of propoxyphene into brachial artery," by H. S. Pearlman, et al. JOURNAL
OF THE AMERICAN MEDICAL ASSOCIATION. 214:2055-
2057, December 14, 1970.

PROPYLHEXEDRINE ABUSE
"Propylhexedrine (Benzedrex) psychosis," by E. D.
Anderson. NEW ZEALAND MEDICAL JOURNAL. 71:302,
May, 1970.

"Propylhexedrine (Benzedrex) psychosis," by E. D. Anderson. NEW ZEALAND MEDICAL JOURNAL. 71:302, May,
1970.

"Psychiatric drugs and trends. Drug abuse--The 1969
social concern. Part I," by E. L. Dembicki. JOUR-
NAL OF PSYCHIATRIC NURSING. 7:276+, November-December, 1969; Part II. JOURNAL OF PSYCHIATRIC NURSING.
8:49+, January-February, 1970.

"Psychiatric drugs left at home," by A. Robin, et al.
BRITISH MEDICAL JOURNAL. 1:239, January 24, 1970.

"Psychiatrist and his daughter talk frankly about marijuana; interview, edited by A. Bramson," by M. and
S. F. Yolles. SEVENTEEN. 29:134-135+, October,
1970.

"Psychoanalytic evaluation of addiction and habituation,"
by W. A. Frosch. JOURNAL OF THE AMERICAN PSYCHOANA-
LYTIC ASSOCIATION. 18:209-218, January, 1970.

"Psychodysleptic drugs. Psychological, physiological
and social complications," by J. P. Chiasson. BUL-
LETIN DES INFIRMIERES CATHOLIQUES DU CANADA. 37:
226-236, September-December, 1970.

"Psychoses due to cannabis abuse," by G. d'Elia, et al.

144

LAKARTIDNINGEN. 67:3526-3529, August 5, 1970.

"Psychotherapy of drug dependence: some theoretical considerations," by M. M. Glatt. BRITISH JOURNAL OF ADDICTION. 65:51-62, May, 1970.

"Psychotic symptoms due to cannabis abuse; a survey of newly admitted mental patients," by W. Keup. DISEASES OF THE NERVOUS SYSTEM. 31:119-126, February, 1970.

"Psychotropic agents in the generation of rebels," by M. Pestel. PRESSE MEDICALE. 78:510, February 28, 1970.

"Psychotropic drug therapy and pharmaceutical industry," by J. Modestin. ARZNEIMITTEL-FORSCHUNG. 20:877-879, July, 1970.

"Pulmonary angiothrombosis caused by 'blue velvet' addiction," by J. J. Szwed. ANNALS OF INTERNAL MEDICINE. 73:771-774, November, 1970.

"Pulmonary talc granulomatosis. A complication of drug abuse," by G. B. Hopkins, et al. AMERICAN REVIEW OF RESPIRATORY DISEASE. 101:101-104, January, 1970.

"Purposes, patterns, and protection in a campus drug using community," by E. Schaps, et al. JOURNAL OF HEALTH AND SOCIAL BEHAVIOR. 11:135-145, June, 1970.

"Pursuit of the poppy." TIME. 96:28+, September 14, 1970.

"The Pursiut of Purity: A Defensive Use of Drug Abuse in Adolescence," by W. R. Flynn. ADOLESCENCE. 5,18: 141-150, Summer, 1970.

"Putting pot in its place," by G. Tindall. GUARDIAN p. 9, January 14, 1970.

"Rarity of drug problems during political protest," by W. T. Carpenter, Jr., et al. JOURNAL OF THE AMERICAN MEDICAL ASSOCIATION. 213:1193, August 17, 1970.

"A rating scale for evaluation of the clinical course
and symptomatology in amphetamine psychosis," by
L. E. Jonsson, et al. BRITISH JOURNAL OF PSYCHIATRY.
117:661-665, December, 1970.

"Raven Progressive Matrices avoidable errors as a
measure of psychopathological ideational influences
upon reasoning ability," by J. Fracchia, et al.
PSYCHOLOGICAL REPORTS. 26:359-362, April, 1970.

"Reaction-times of methadone treated ex-heroin addicts,"
by N. B. Gordon. PSYCHOPHARMACOLOGIA. 16:337-344,
1970.

"Readers, experts examine drug problems; findings from
survey; ed. by A. Rosenthal." TODAY'S HEALTH. 48:
19-23+, September, 1970.

"Readmission rates at Lexington Hospital for 43,215
narcotic drug addicts," by J. C. Ball, et al.
PUBLIC HEALTH REPORTS. 85:610+, July, 1970.

"Recovery from drug dependence." JOURNAL OF THE AMER-
ICAN MEDICAL ASSOCIATION. 214:579, October 19, 1970.

REDUCING DRUGS ABUSE
"Motivation for addiction to amphetamine and re-
ducing drugs," by S. Robinson, et al. PSYCHIATRY
DIGEST. 31:26+, July, 1970.

"The use and abuse of reducing pills in obesity,"
by W. J. Evans. JOURNAL OF THE LOUISIANA MEDICAL
SOCIETY. 122:99-103, April, 1970.

"Regional Planning for Drug Programs," by F. Licht.
COMPACT. 4,3:12, June, 1970.

"Rehabilitation and civil commitment of addicts," by
L. H. Lentchner. JOURNAL OF REHABILITATION. 36:
28-29, November-December, 1970.

REHABILITATION AND THERAPY
"Addicts and zealots; chaotic war against drug abuse
in New York City," by M. K. Sanders. HARPER'S.
240:71-73+, June, 1970; also READER'S DIGEST.
97:95, December, 1970.

"Addicts in a therapeutic community," by C. Tarry
and R. Wilk. NURSING MIRROR. 131:132+, September 11, 1970.

REHABILITATION AND THERAPY (cont'd.)

"Architecture to help drug addicts calls for speed
and inventiveness: Manhattan rehabilitation center." ARCHITECTURAL RECORD. 147:160-161, January, 1970.

"Bridge to the turned on," by K. H. Dansky. AMER-
ICAN JOURNAL OF NURSING. 70:778-779, April,
1970.

"Caring for the 'bad trip', a review of current
status of LSD," by C. M. Martin. HAWAII MEDICAL
JOURNAL. 29:555-560, September-October, 1970.

"Case study on the attitudes of drug addicts to
treatment," by A. M. Toll. BRITISH JOURNAL OF
ADDICTION. 65:139-158, August, 1970.

"Catecholamine dependence. Pathogenesis and treatment," by F. Milazzotto, et al. CARDIOLOGA PRA-
TICA. 21:11-16, February, 1970.

"Community where drug addicts grow up; Phoenix
houses in New York City," by A. W. Birch. PTA
MAGAZINE. 65:2-5, November, 1970; also in READER'S
DIGEST. 97:92-96, December, 1970.

"Cracks in the panacea." SCIENCE NEWS. 97:366-367,
April 11, 1970.

"Curing drug addiction with former addicts help,"
by V. Brittain. TIMES (London). p. 9, May 2,
1970.

"Current trends in the treatment of drug dependence
and drug abuse," by N. B. Eddy. BULLETIN ON
NARCOTICS. 22:1-9, January-March, 1970.

"A cyclazocine typology in opiate dependence," by
R. B. Resnick, et al. AMERICAN JOURNAL OF PSY-
CHIATRY. 126:1256-1260, March, 1970.

"DARE--a thinking, hoping, seeing, feeling, breathing,
speaking happening." AORN JOURNAL. 12:52-53,
September, 1970.

"Doctor Baird of East Harlem; conductor of group
therapy sessions for narcotic addicts," by
W. F. Buckley, Jr. NATIONAL REVIEW. 22:100,
January 27, 1970.

REHABILITATION AND THERAPY (cont'd.)
"Drug abuse and social alienation." TODAY'S EDU-
CATION. 59,6:29-31, September, 1970.

"The drug abuse program at Milwaukee County Institutions. A six-month report," by R. L. Wiesen,
et al. WISCONSIN MEDICAL JOURNAL. 69:141-144,
May, 1970.

"Drug abuse rehabilitation program for youth," by C.
J. Katz, et al. ROCKY MOUNTAIN MEDICAL JOURNAL.
67:57-60, July, 1970.

"Drug addiction: an effective therapeutic approach,"
by R. C. Wolfe, et al. MEDICAL TIMES. 98:185-
193, September, 1970.

"Drug addiction--treatment or punishment?" by N.
Retterstol. TIDSSKRIFT FOR DEN NORSKE LAEGE-
FORENING. 90:2095, November 15, 1970.

"Drug crutches," by V. A. Dohner. NEW ENGLAND JOUR-
NAL OF MEDICINE. 282:876, April 9, 1970.

"Drug education and training; statement by the Pres-
ident (March 11, 1970) announcing an expanded
Federal program." WEEKLY COMPILATION OF PRESI-
DENTIAL DOCUMENTS. 6:351-353, March 16, 1970.

"Drug habit. Multiplication of preventive measures,"
C. Vaille. PRESSE MEDICALE. 78:755-757, March
28, 1970.

"Drug prevention clubs in France," by J. Ellul. IN-
TERPLAY. 3:39-41, August, 1970.

"Drug therapy II. Treatment of drug misuse," by J.
S. Holcenberg, et al. NORTHWEST MEDICINE. 69:
31-33, January, 1970.

"Drug treatment and prevention; Hope house, Inc.
Albany, N.Y.," by H. Hubbard. NATIONAL ASSOCIA-
TION OF SECONDARY SCHOOL PRINCIPALS BULLETIN. 54:
95-105, November, 1970.

"Drugs--the role of the teacher and youth leader,"
by D. A. Lane. COMMUNITY HEALTH (Bristol). 1:
327-329, May-June, 1970.

"Drugs used against addiction," by M. J. Rodman.

REHABILITATION AND THERAPY (cont'd.)
RN. 32:71-80, October, 1970.

"An effective therapeutic method for the LSD user,"
by C. Torda. PERCEPTUAL AND MOTOR SKILLS. 30:
79-88, February, 1970.

"Eighteen narcotic-addiction buildings in eighteen
months; Arthur Kill rehabilitation center. Staten
Island." AMERICAN CITY. 85:152+, June, 1970.

"European mental hygienists and drug abuse," by R.
Sarro, et al. NERVENARZT. 41:364, July, 1970.

"Evolution of a day program," by C. J. Dromberg and
J. B. Proctor. AMERICAN JOURNAL OF NURSING. 70:
2575+, December, 1970.

"An experimental clinic for narcotic abusers--the
nurse as a research coordinator," by F. Kerman.
ALUMNAE MAGAZINE (Baltimore). 69:5-7, March,
1970.

"Group therapy and group work with addicted females,"
by R. von Battegay, et al. BRITISH JOURNAL OF
ADDICTION. 65:89-98, August, 1970.

"Guidelines for program development," by D. B. Louria.
COMPACT. 4,3:13-14, June, 1970.

"Guidelines for using methadone in the outpatient
treatment of narcotic addicts," by C. B. Scrignar,
et al. JOURNAL OF THE LOUISIANA MEDICAL SOCIETY.
122:167-172, June, 1970.

"Heroin withdrawal syndrome," by C. Zelson, et al.
JOURNAL OF PEDIATRICS. 76:483-484, March, 1970.

"Hippy communities may cure drug addicts." TIMES
(London) EDUCATIONAL SUPPLEMENT. 2886:14, September 11, 1970.

"Hotline for troubled teen-agers; Los Angeles," by
J. N. Bell. READER'S DIGEST. 97:41-46, November,
1970.

"Hudegarden and its underground clinic," by O. Henriksen. UGESKRIFT FOR LAEGER. 132:2190-2191, November 12, 1970.

REHABILITATION AND THERAPY (cont'd.)
"Hypnosis and the adolescent drug abuser," by F.
Baumann. AMERICAN JOURNAL OF CLINICAL HYPNOSIS.
13:17-21, July, 1970.

"Hypnosis in living systems theory: a living systems
autopsy in a polysurgical, polymedical, polypsychiatric patient addicted to talwin," by F. T.
Kolouch. AMERICAN JOURNAL OF CLINICAL HYPNOSIS.
13:22-34, July, 1970.

"Hypothalamic-pituitary-adrenal axis in methadone-
treated heroin addicts," by P. Cushman, Jr., et
al. JOURNAL OF CLINICAL ENDOCRINOLOGY AND METAB-
OLISM. 30:24-29, January, 1970.

"In prison," by I. P. James, et al. LANCET. 1:37,
January 3, 1970.

"Instead of police raids," by K. Kettner. SCHWESTERN
REVIEW. 8:13-14, June, 1970.

"The Kilburn Square drug abuse centre," by B. M.
Garvey. BRITISH JOURNAL OF ADDICTION. 64:383-
394, January, 1970.

"The Laguna Beach experiment as a community approach
to family counseling for drug abuse; problems in
youth," by L. A. Gottschalk, et al. COMPREHENSIVE
PSYCHIATRY. 11:226-234, May, 1970.

"Leaving the drug world behind; results from the Aware
ness house project," by R. Moskowitz. AMERICAN
EDUCATION. 6:3-6, January, 1970; also in EDUCATION
DIGEST. 35:5-7, May, 1970.

"Lifeboat: Phoenix house survival therapy." MOTOR
BOATING. 126:42-43, December, 1970.

"Medical Society on care of drug addicts; forms of
care for those not yet ready to ask for care."
LAKARTIDNINGEN. 67:2872-2876, June 17, 1970.

"Menace and the malady." NATION. 211:228-229, September 21, 1970.

"Methadone and heroin addiction: rehabilitation without a cure," by J. Walsh. SCIENCE. 168:684-686,
May 8, 1970.

REHABILITATION AND THERAPY (cont'd.)
"Methadone and the private practitioner," by H. W.
Freymuth. JOURNAL OF THE MEDICAL SOCIETY OF NEW
JERSEY. 67:128-130, March, 1970.

"Methadone management of heroin addiction." BULLETIN
OF THE NEW YORK ACADEMY OF MEDICINE. 46:391-395,
June, 1970.

"The narcotic addict rehabilitation act; a change
in the federal response to the treatment of narcotic addiction," by C. B. Scrignar, et al. SOUTH-
ERN MEDICAL JOURNAL. 63:109-112, January, 1970.

"Narcotic detoxification and rehabilitation service,"
by F. D. Alley and C. Simons. HOSPITAL MANAGE-
MENT. 110-64+, October, 1970.

"The need for therapeutic and administrative partnerships," by R. S. Garber. HOSPITAL AND COMMUNITY
PSYCHIATRY. 21:349+, November, 1970.

"New hope for the hopeless. Drug addiction; its
treatment, management and the nurse's role," by
J. N. Chappel. CHART. 67:251-255, October, 1970.

"A new method for treatment of barbiturate dependence," by D. E. Smith, et al. JOURNAL OF THE
AMERICAN MEDICAL ASSOCIATION. 213:294-295, July
13, 1970.

"New York's Statutory scheme for the rehabilitation
of narcotics addicts through civil commitment,"
by M. M. D'Auria. NEW YORK STATE BAR JOURNAL.
42:436-443, August, 1970.

"Newark, narcotics, and the medical school," by E.
A. Wolfson. JOURNAL OF THE MEDICAL SOCIETY OF
NEW JERSEY. 67:207-210, May, 1970.

"Nonaddictive psychotropic medication for imprisoned
narcotic addicts," by H. S. Feldman, et al. JOUR-
NAL OF THE MEDICAL SOCIETY OF NEW JERSEY. 67:278-
283, June, 1970.

"Nursing in a narcotic-detoxification unit," by E.
H. Russaw. AMERICAN JOURNAL OF NURSING. 70:1720-
1723, August, 1970.

"Opinion; Phoenix house, a celebration of life," by

REHABILITATION AND THERAPY (cont'd.)
F. Natale. MADEMOISELLE. 72:46+, December, 1970.

"The program of the Johns Hopkins Hospital drug abuse center," by L. Wurmser. ALUMNAE MAGAZINE (Baltimore). 69:10-12, March, 1970.

"Psychotherapy of drug dependence; some theoretical considerations," by M. M. Glatt. BRITISH JOURNAL OF ADDICTION. 65:51-62, May, 1970.

"Psychotropic drug therapy and pharmaceutical industry," by J. Modestin. ARZNEIMITTEL-FORSCHUNG. 20:877-879, July, 1970.

"Reaction-times of methadone treated ex-heroin addicts," by N. B. Gordon. PSYCHOPHARMACOLOGIA. 16:337-344, 1970.

"Recovery from drug dependence." JOURNAL OF THE AMERICAN MEDICAL ASSOCIATION. 214:579, October 19, 1970.

"Regional planning for drug programs," by F. Licht. COMPACT. 4,3:12+, June, 1970.

"Rehabilitation and civil commitment of addicts," by L. H. Lentchner. JOURNAL OF REHABILITATION. 36:28-29, November-December, 1970.

"The role of a medical society in a drug abuse program," by C. Baron. JOURNAL OF THE KENTUCKY MEDICAL ASSOCIATION. 68:113-114, February, 1970.

"The role of occupational therapy in heroin detoxification," by F. W. Slobetz. AMERICAN JOURNAL OF OCCUPATIONAL THERAPY. 24:340-342, July-August, 1970.

"The role of the prison service in rehabilitation of drug dependents," by T. G. Garner. BULLETIN ON NARCOTICS. 22:19-23, January-March, 1970.

"Role of therapeutic communities." CURRENT. 120: 38-43, August, 1970.

"San Francisco tries a crash pad," by M. Alexander. SCHOOL MANAGEMENT. 14:29, April, 1970.

"Staff-patient problems in drug dependence treat-

REHABILITATION AND THERAPY (cont'd.)
　　ment clinics," by T. H. Bewley, et al. JOURNAL
　　OF PSYCHOSOMATIC RESEARCH. 14:303-306, September,
　　1970.

"The state versus the addict: uncivil commitment,"
　　by J. C. Kramer. BOSTON UNIVERSITY LAW REVIEW.
　　50:1-22, Winter, 1970.

"Survey of drug usage in dental practice. 1969. II.
　　Narcotics registry; courses taken relating to drug
　　therapy; professional society meetings attended.
　　Bureau of Economic Research and Statistics." JOUR-
　　NAL OF THE AMERICAN DENTAL ASSOCIATION. 81:1402-
　　1404, December, 1970.

"TV soliloquies help young drug users." TODAY'S
　　HEALTH. 48:64-65, April, 1970.

"Tell the 'why why trippers' the answer will come;
　　counseling and rehabilitation services," by J.
　　Marks. MADEMOISELLE. 71:188-189+, May, 1970.

"The termination of an LSD freakout through the use
　　of relaxation," by R. M. Suinn and J. Brittain.
　　JOURNAL OF CLINICAL PSYCHOLOGY. 26,1:127-128,
　　January, 1970.

"The therapeutic community and the school," by B.
　　Sugarman. INTERCHANGE. 1,2:77-96, 1970.

"The $30 million industry," by D. Thomas. ATLANTA
　　MONTHLY. 10:44-50+, November, 1970.

"Treating heroin addiction at Simmons House," by
　　G. M. Greaves and K. Ryz. NURSING TIMES. 66:49+,
　　January 8, 1970.

"Treatment of barbiturate dependence," by D. Goldman,
　　et al. JOURNAL OF THE AMERICAN MEDICAL ASSOCIATION.
　　213:2272-2273, September 28, 1970.

"Treatment of drug addiction," by P. A. Chapple, et
　　al. LANCET. 2:1134, November 28, 1970.

"The treatment of drug addiction; some comparative
　　observations," by W. N. Davis. BRITISH JOURNAL
　　OF ADDICTION. 65:227-235, November, 1970.

"Use of a freakout control center," by R. M. Casse.

REHABILITATION AND THERAPY (cont'd.)
JOURNAL OF COLLEGE STUDENT PERSONNEL. 11,6:
403-408, November, 1970.

"Use of the television monologue with adolescent
psychiatric patients," by H. A. Wilmer. AMERICAN
JOURNAL OF PSYCHIATRY. 126:1760-1766, June, 1970.

"The voluntary health agency." SCHOOL HEALTH REVIEW.
1:36, April, 1970.

"Will we ever cure them?" by M. S. Lewsley. NURSING
MIRROR AND MIDWIVES JOURNAL. 130:41+, March 17,
1970.

"Withdrawal programmes for narcotics addicts in the
USA," by K. Neudek. MUENCHENER MEDIZINISCHE
WOCHENSCHRIFT. 112:1054-1056, May 29, 1970.

"Youth and drugs," by C. E. Guernsey. JOURNAL OF
MISSISSIPPI STATE MEDICAL ASSOCIATION. 11:595-598,
November, 1970.

"Youth care and the new treatment model; the thera-
peutic society--an alternative for us?" by B.
Goransson, et al. LAKARTIDNINGEN. 67:3191-3198,
July 8, 1970.

"Relation of the A-B Distinction and Trust-Distrust
Sets to Addict Patients' Self Disclosures of Brief
Interviews," by J. I. Berzins. JOURNAL OF CON-
SULTING AND CLINICAL PSYCHOLOGY. 34,3:289-295,
June, 1970.

"Relationship between criminal law and health protection, tasks of public health organs and institutions,"
by H. G. Keune. PHARMAZEUTISCHE PRAXIS; BEILAGE ZUR
DIE PHARMAZIE. 5:97-101, 1970.

"The relationship of amphetamine-induced anorexia and
freezing under a multiple CRF-EXT operant schedule,"
by S. O. Cole. JOURNAL OF GENERAL PSYCHOLOGY. 83:
163-168, October, 1970.

"Relative activity of psychotoxic drugs on the avain
optic lobe," by N. W. Scholes, et al. EUROPEAN JOUR-
NAL OF PHARMACOLOGY. 12:289-296, 1970.

"Remarks on series of drug addicts admitted to hospital
environment," by P. Mouren, et al. MARSEILLE MEDICAL.

107:463-466, June, 1970.

"Report on drug treatment." NTRDA BULLETIN. 56:14+,
February, 1970.

"Research study on behavioral patterns in sex and drug
use on college campus," by S. Herz. ADOLESCENCE.
5:1-16, Spring, 1970.

"Rising problem of drugs on the job." TIME. 95:70,
June 29, 1970.

"The road to H: the same old opium of the masses," by
D. Rosenblatt. INTERPLAY. 3:42-45, August, 1970.

"Rock doctor tells about 985 freakouts; ed. by R.
Stokes," by W. Abruzzi. LIFE. 69:37, August 14,
1970.

"The role of brain dopamine in behavioral regulation
and the actions of psychotropic drugs," by S. H.
Snyder, et al. AMERICAN JOURNAL OF PSYCHIATRY. 127:
199-207, August, 1970.

"The role of the Committee on Safety of Drugs," by D.
Mansel-Jones. BRITISH MEDICAL BULLETIN. 26:257-
259, September, 1970.

"The role of a medical society in a drug abuse program,"
by C. Baron. JOURNAL OF THE KENTUCKY MEDICAL
ASSOCIATION. 68:113-114, February, 1970.

"The role of methylamphetamine on plasma hexosamine
level under stress," by A. K. Chatterjee, et al.
JAPANESE JOURNAL OF PHARMACOLOGY. 20:439-441,
September, 1970.

"The role of the nurse with the drug abuser and addict,"
by G. Childress. JOURNAL OF PSYCHIATRIC NURSING.
8:21+, March-April, 1970.

"The role of occupational therapy in heroin detoxification," by F. W. Slobetz. AMERICAN JOURNAL OF
OCCUPATIONAL THERAPY. 24:340-342, July-August,
1970.

"The role of the prison service in rehabilitation of
drug dependents," by T. G. Garner. BULLETIN ON
NARCOTICS. 22:19-23, January-March, 1970.

155

"The role of a school of pharmacy. Drug abuse education programming for a rural state--one approach," by P. Zanowiak. JOURNAL OF THE AMERICAN PHARMACEUTICAL ASSOCIATION. 10:566-568+, October, 1970.

"Role of therapeutic communities." CURRENT. 120: 38-43, August, 1970.

"Safe hypnotics," by A. Clift. BRITISH MEDICAL JOURNAL. 2:539, May 30, 1970.

SALICYLISM
    "Salicylism revisited. Unusual problems in diagnosis and management," by L. O. Surapathana, et al. CLINICAL PEDIATRICS. 9:658-661, November, 1970.

"Salicylism revisited. Unusual problems in diagnosis and management," by L. O. Surapathana, et al. CLINICAL PEDIATRICS. 9:658-661, November, 1970.

"San Francisco tries a crash pad," by M. Alexander. SCHOOL MANAGEMENT. 14:29, April, 1970.

"A scale to measure attitude toward smoking marijuana," by R. J. Vincent. JOURNAL OF SCHOOL HEALTH. 40: 454-456, October, 1970.

"The Scene," by B. J. Montag. AMERICAN BIOLOGY TEACHER. 32,6:337-339, September, 1970.

"The school nurse and drug abusers," by K. K. Caskey, et al. NURSING OUTLOOK. 18:27-30, December, 1970.

SCOPOLAMINE
    "Comparative effects of amphetamine, scopolamine, chlordiazepoxide, and diphenylthydantoin on operant and extinction behavior with brain stimulation and food reward," by M. E. Olds. NEURO-PHARMACOLOGY. 9:519-532, November, 1970.

"Secret rules no hindrance for physicians to register young drug addicts," by R. Rooseniit. LAKARTIDNINGEN. 67:3356-3359, July 22, 1970.

SEDATIVE ABUSE
"Sedative abuse by heroin addicts," by M. Mitcheson,
et al. LANCET. 1:606-607, March 21, 1970.

"Sedative abuse by heroin addicts," by M. Mitcheson, et
al. LANCET. 1:606-607, March 21, 1970.

"Sensitivity changes to noradrenaline in the guinea-
pig vas deferens induced by amphetamine, cocaine and
denervation," by S. de Moraes, et al. JOURNAL OF
PHARMACY AND PHARMACOLOGY. 22:717-719, September,
1970.

"The sensitivity of the brain to barbiturate during
chronic administration and withdrawal of barbitone
sodium in the rat," by I. H. Stevenson, et al.
BRITISH JOURNAL OF PHARMACOLOGY AND CHEMOTHERAPY.
39:325-333, June, 1970.

"Septic pulmonary emboli," by R. B. Jaffe, et al.
RADIOLOGY. 96:527-532, September, 1970.

"The serum hepatitis related antigen (SH) in illicit
drug users," by C. E. Cherubin, et al. AMERICAN
JOURNAL OF EPIDEMIOLOGY. 91:510-517, May, 1970.

SERVICEMEN AND DRUGS
"Another checkup on drug use by GI's." U.S. NEWS
AND WORLD REPORT. 69:33, August 31, 1970.

"Does our army fight on drugs?" by J. H. Kaplan.
LOOK. 34:72+, June 15, 1970.

"Drug abuse in the Navy," by J. A. Pursch. UNITED
STATES NAVAL INSTITUTE PROCEEDINGS. 96:52-56,
July, 1970.

"Fresh disclosures on drugs and GI's; Senate investigation into marijuana smoking." U.S. NEWS AND
WORLD REPORT. 68:32-33, April 6, 1970.

"Marijuana; the other enemy in Vietnam." U.S. NEWS
AND WORLD REPORT. 68:68-69, January 26, 1970.

"Problems of toxicophilia in young adults at the
stage of military obligations," by J. Paraire,
et al. ANNALES MEDICO-PSYCHOLOGIQUES (Paris).
2:93-100, June, 1970.

SEX AND DRUGS

"Behavioral patterns in sex and drug use on the
college campus," by S. Herz. JOURNAL OF THE
MEDICAL SOCIETY OF NEW JERSEY. 67:3-6, January,
1970.

"Love, delights and drugs. Some considerations on
the body, the erotical relations and nirvanic
ascesis under toxicomaniac influence," by P.
Bailly-Salin, et al. ANNALES MEDICO-PSYCHOLOG-
IQUES (Paris). 2:120-126, June, 1970.

"Note on sex differences in student drug usage," by
K. R. Mitchell, et al. PSYCHOLOGICAL REPORTS.
27:116, August, 1970.

"Research study on behavioral patterns in sex and
drug use on college campus," by S. Herz. ADO-
LESCENCE. 5:1-16, Spring, 1970.

"Sexual aspects of heroin addiction," by J. L.
Mathis. MEDICAL ASPECTS OF HUMAN SEXUALITY. 4,9:
98-109, September, 1970.

"Sexual Aspects of Heroin Addiction," by J. L. Mathis.
MEDICAL ASPECTS OF HUMAN SEXUALITY. 4,9:98-109,
September, 1970.

"The shot that kills." EMERGENCY MEDICINE. 2:26+,
March, 1970.

"Should the drug education bandwagon be rerouted?" by
C. H. Harrison. SCHOLASTIC TEACHER JR/SR HIGH.
18-19+, October 5, 1970.

"Simultaneous measurement technics: urinary CO2 ($C14$-
02) elimination and motor activity in mice during
metabolic experimentation with amphetamines," by A.
Benakis. EXPERIENTIA. 26:1163-1164, October 15,
1970.

"Singing is better than any dope," by H. Saal. NEWS-
WEEK. 76:124-125, October 19, 1970.

"16mm Films on Drug, Alcohol and Tobacco Abuse. Product Information Supplement No. 6." EDUCATIONAL
PRODUCT REPORT. 3,7:1-36, April, 1970.

"Skin lesions in drug addicts," by D. I. Vollum.
BRITISH MEDICAL JOURNAL. 2:647-650, June 13, 1970.

"Sleeping pills," by H. Fisher. BRITISH MEDICAL JOURNAL. 3:711, September 19, 1970.

"Slight abstinence symptoms," by U. H. Vaag. UGESKRIFT FOR LAEGER. 132:1875-1877, October, 1970.

"Slowdown for pep pills; new restrictions." NEWSWEEK. 76:77, August 17, 1970.

"Smugglers of misery," by W. Schulz. READER'S DIGEST. 96:49-54, April, 1970.

"Social and political aspects of drug use," by G. R. Edison. JOURNAL OF THE AMERICAN COLLEGE HEALTH ASSOCIATION. 18:274-277, April, 1970.

"Social and psychological correlates of drug abuse. A comparison of addict and non-addict populations from the perspective of self-theory," by H. B. Kaplan, et al. SOCIAL SCIENCE AND MEDICINE. 4: 203-225, August, 1970.

"Social pedagogy promoting development," by J. L. Jacobsen. TIDSKRIFT FOR SVERIGES SJUKSKOTERSKOR. 70:306-310, July 15, 1970.

"Social Psychology of Drug Use," by V. Nowlis. CONTEMPORARY PSYCHOLOGY. 15,2:100-102, February, 1970.

"Society and toxicomaniac appetence," by J. Carrere. ANNALES MEDICO-PSYCHOLOGIQUES (Paris). 2:85-92, June, 1970.

"Socio-medical classification of toxicomaniasis," by N. Bejerot. LAKARTIDNINGEN. 67:2413-2429, May 20, 1970.

SOLVENT ABUSE
"Centrilobular hepatic necrosis and acute renal failure in 'solvent sniffers'," by R. D. Baerg, et al. ANNALS OF INTERNAL MEDICINE. 73:713-720, November, 1970.

"Some ambiguities for research in Senate's drug bill," by J. Walsh. SCIENCE. 167:849, February 6, 1970.

"Some legal and ethical aspects of addiction," by D. F. Robb. JOURNAL OF THE ROYAL COLLEGE OF GENERAL PRACTITIONERS. 20:98-99, August, 1970.

"Some social medical aspects of addiction diseases. (Alcoholism and drug addiction)," by G. Mollhoff. OEFFENTLICHE GESUNDHEITSWESEN. 32:449-458, September, 1970.

"Some straight talk about drugs." SENIOR SCHOLASTIC. 96:4-10, March 9, 1970.

"Some thoughts on the problem of drugs," by J. West. FRIENDS' QUARTERLY. 625-628, October 16, 1970.

"Sparks fly over pot." NATION'S BUSINESS. 58:24, March, 1970.

"Special report: 17th national AORN congress. Tells causes of teen-drug abuse; suggests ways to combat problem," by J. T. Ungerleider. HOSPITAL TOPICS. 48:101+, May, 1970.

"Special supplement: drug education in the states." COMPACT. 4:21, December 8, 1970.

"A spectrophotofluorometric method for the determination of amphetamine," by C. R. Nix, et al. JOURNAL OF FORENSIC SCIENCES. 15:595-600, October, 1970.

"Speed kills: The adolescent methedrine addict," by R. R. Rodewald. PERSPECTIVES IN PSYCHIATRIC CARE. 8:160-167, July-August, 1970.

"'Speed' that kills, or worse," by J. Black. NEW YORK TIMES MAGAZINE. 14-15+, June 21, 1970; Same abr. with title, "Tempting siren called 'speed'," READER'S DIGEST. 97:153-157, October, 1970.

"A spoonful of sugar," by C. M. Wallace. NURSING MIRROR AND MIDWIVES JOURNAL. 130:32, May 8, 1970.

SPORTS AND DRUGS
"Death of a young athlete: possible role of doping. Apropos of 2 cases," by M. Yacoub, et al. MEDECINE LEGALE ET DOMMAGE CORPOREL (Paris). 3: 275-277, July-September, 1970.

"Drugs, sports and doping," by K. S. Clarke. JOURNAL OF THE MAINE MEDICAL ASSOCIATION. 61:55-58, March 8, 1970.

"High school sports flunk the saliva test," by T. Irwin. TODAY'S HEALTH. 48:44-46+, October, 1970.

SPORTS AND DRUGS (cont'd.)
"The struggle against doping and its history," by
L. Prokop. JOURNAL OF SPORTS MEDICINE AND PHY-
SICAL FITNESS. 10:45-48, March, 1970.

SPOT-REMOVER ABUSE
"Hepatorenal toxicity from sniffing spot-remover
(trichloethylene). Report of 2 cases," by H.
R. Clearfield. AMERICAN JOURNAL OF DIGESTIVE
DISEASES. 15:851-856, September, 1970.

"The spread of drug addiction in the U.K.," by P.
A. Chapple. ROYAL SOCIETY OF HEALTH JOURNAL. 90:
196-197+, July-August, 1970.

"Spurious heart disease," by C. B. Upshaw, Jr. MEDICAL
TRIAL TECHNIQUE QUARTERLY. 16:27-33, June, 1970.

"Staff-patient problems in drug dependence treatment
clinics," by T. H. Bewley, et al. JOURNAL OF PSYCHO-
SOMATIC RESEARCH. 14:303-306, September, 1970.

"Staphylococcal bacteremia in heroin addicts," by H.
O. Farhoudi, et al. MEDICAL ANNALS OF THE DISTRICT
OF COLUMBIA. 39:187-194, April, 1970.

"State Action Against Drug Abuse." COMPACT. 4,3:28-
33, June, 1970.

"State-Initiated Community Programs," by H. Levander.
COMPACT. 4,3:49, June, 1970.

"The state versus the addict: uncivil commitment," by
J. C. Kramer. BOSTON UNIVERSITY LAW REVIEW. 50:
1-22, Winter, 1970.

"Statement on The Federal Drug Abuse and Drug Dependence,
Prevention, Treatment and Rehabilitation Act of 1970
(S. 3562) by The New York Academy of Medicine." BUL-
LETIN OF THE NEW YORK ACADEMY OF MEDICINE. 46:642,
August, 1970.

"Stop and SEARCH." LANCET. 1:1037, May 16, 1970.

"Straight and narrow: control of drugs." NATURE (London).
225:1087-1088, March 21, 1970.

"Strengthened programs of international cooperation for
halting the illicit supply of drugs; address, April
2, 1970," by E. L. Richardson. DEPARTMENT OF STATE

BULLETIN. 62:544-549, April 27, 1970.

"Strengthening drug education." SCHOOL AND SOCIETY. 98:400, November, 1970.

"The struggle against doping and its history," by L. Prokop. JOURNAL OF SPORTS MEDICINE AND PHYSICAL FITNESS. 10:45-48, March, 1970.

"The Student Drug User and His Family," by J. L. Kuehn. JOURNAL OF COLLEGE STUDENT PERSONNEL. 11,6:409-413, November, 1970.

"Studies on anti-inflammatory agents. IV. On the appearance of physical dependence and analgesic activity of 2-amino-3-ethoxycarbonyl-6-benzyl-4,5,6-7-tetrahydrothieno (2,3-c)pyridine (Y-3642) by repeated administration," by M. Nakanishi, et al. JOURNAL OF THE PHARMACEUTICAL SOCIETY OF JAPAN. 90:291-295, March, 1970.

"Studies on rat brain acetylcholine and cholinesterase. II. The influence of centrally acting drugs," by S. R. Naik, et al. INDIAN JOURNAL OF MEDICAL RE-SEARCH. 58:480-486, April, 1970.

"Study indicates 'user' recognition," by R. De Alarcon, et al. AORN JOURNAL. 12:16, September, 1970.

"A study of patients with a record of drug dependence or drug abuse admitted to a private psychiatric hospital 1881-1969," by R. W. Medlicott, et al. NEW ZEALAND MEDICAL JOURNAL. 72:92-95, August, 1970.

"Subjective effects of narcotic antagonists cyclazocine and nalorphine on the Addiction Research Center inventory (ARCI)," by C. A. Haertzen. PSYCHOPHARMA-COLOGIA. 18:366-377, 1970.

"The subjective experience of addicts at the time of injection of their drug," by M. W. Riddall. JOURNAL OF PSYCHOSOMATIC RESEARCH. 14:307-312, September, 1970.

"Successful treatment of 'drinamyl' addicts and associated personality changes," by T. Kraft. CANADIAN PSYCHIATRIC ASSOCIATION JOURNAL. 15:223-227, April, 1970.

"Surgical management of infections and other complications resulting from drug abuse," by D. D. Clark. ARCHIVES OF SURGERY. 101:619-623, November, 1970.

"Surreptitious ingestion of oral anticoagulants," by T. H. Greidanus, et al. HENRY FORD HOSPITAL MEDICAL JOURNAL. 18:99-106, Summer, 1970.

"Survey of drug usage in dental practice, 1969. II. Narcotics registry; courses taken relating to drug therapy; professional society meetings attended. Bureau of Economic Research and Statistics." JOURNAL OF THE AMERICAN DENTAL ASSOCIATION. 81:1402-1404, December, 1970.

"A survey of a representative sample of addicts prescribed heroin at London clinics," by G. V. Stimson and A. C. Ogborne. BULLETIN ON NARCOTICS. 22:12-13, October-December, 1970.

"Symposium--drug action and animal behavior. 3. Comparison of the effects of amphetamines, pentobarbital, chlorpromazine and benzodiazepines on conditioned suppressive behaviors in monkeys and rats," by S. Tadokoro. FOLIA PHARMACOLOGICA JAPONICA. 66:78-79, July 20, 1970.

"Symposium on health and environment. Chronic abuse of drugs," by A. Kasanen. DUODECIM. 86:475-481, 1970.

"The syndrome of barbiturate dependence," by F. A. Whitlock. MEDICAL JOURNAL OF AUSTRALIA. 2:391-396, August 29, 1970.

"TV soliloquies help young drug users." TODAY'S HEALTH. 48:64-65, April, 1970.

"Talk about pot," by C. Adam. NEW STATESMAN. 80:674, November 20, 1970.

TALWIN ABUSE
"Hypnosis in living systems theory: a living systems autopsy in a polysurgical polymedical polypsychiatric patient addicted to talwin," by F. T. Kolouch. AMERICAN JOURNAL OF CLINICAL HYPNOSIS. 13:22-34, July, 1970.

"Task force for the alienated city," by D. Cohen and A. Latourette. GUARDIAN. p. 9, March 21, 1970.

"Task of the plant protection agencies," by S. Weiss. MUENCHENER MEDIZINISCHE WOCHENSCHRIFT. 112:2021-2022, October 30, 1970.

"Teacher evaluation of the school drug education program," by D. Pargman. SCHOOL HEALTH REVIEW. 1:14, April, 1970.

"Teenage heroin epidemic that has alarmed the U.S.," by V. Brittain. TIMES (London). p. 11, March 13, 1970.

"Teenagers take over a slum, to quit heroin," by V. Waite. DAILY TELEGRAPH. p. 17, April 10, 1970.

"Tell the 'why why trippers' the answer will come; counseling and rehabilitation services," by J. Marks. MADEMOISELLE. 71:188-189+, May, 1970.

"Ten Drug Abuse Films: What Students and Professionals Think of Them." EDUCATIONAL PRODUCT REPORT. 3,7: 16-27, April, 1970.

"The termination of an LSD freakout through the use of relaxation," by R. M. Suinn and J. Brittain. JOURNAL OF CLINICAL PSYCHOLOGY. 26,1:127-128, January, 1970.

TETANUS AND DRUGS
"Epidemiology of tetanus in narcotic addicts," by C. E. Cherubin. NEW YORK STATE JOURNAL OF MEDICINE. 70:267-271, January 15, 1970.

THEATRE AND DRUGS
"Harlem Group performs drug drama; King Heroin," by G. Lichenstein. TIMES (London) EDUCATIONAL SUPPLEMENT. 2859:9, March 6, 1970.

"The Therapeutic Community and the School," by B. Sugarman. INTERCHANGE. 1,2:77-96, 1970.

"There are people who say, Well, business is business." FORBES. 105:19-22, April 1, 1970.

"The $30 million industry Atlanta (GA.) wants to kill illicit drug traffic and the city's rehabilitation program," by D. Thomas. ATLANTA MONTHLY. 10:44-

50+, November, 1970.

"Three faces of danger from drugs," by F. Edward and L. Bruen. NEW YORK STATE BAR JOURNAL. 42:612-620, November, 1970.

"3 physicians' prescriptions for narcotics criticized." LAKARTIDNINGEN. 67:6014-6015, December 16, 1970.

"Thyroid as an adjuvant to amphetamine therapy of obesity. A controlled double-blind study," by N. M. Kaplan, et al. AMERICAN JOURNAL OF MEDICAL SCIENCES. 260:105-111, August, 1970.

"To parents: plain talk on marijuana." BUSINESS WEEK. 121, March 21, 1970.

"To youth, with love; White House conference on the drug problem," by R. L. Shayon. SATURDAY REVIEW OF LITERATURE. 53:57, November 21, 1970.

TOLUENE ABUSE
"Toluene addiction," by V. Mathies. MEDIZINISCHE KLINIK. 65:463-464, March 6, 1970.

"Toluene addiction," by V. Mathies. MEDIZINISCHE KLINIK. 65:463-464, March 6, 1970.

"Tough bill plus research: Comprehensive drug abuse and control act of 1970." SCIENCE NEWS. 98:332-333, October 24, 1970.

"Toward a rational approach to psychedelics; the controversy over popular use from a clinical viewpoint," by A. A. Weech, Jr., et al. COMPREHENSIVE PSYCHIATRY. 11:57-68, January, 1970.

"Toward a rational view of drug abuse," by G. R. Spratto. JOURNAL OF SCHOOL HEALTH. 40:192+, April, 1970.

"Toward an understanding: youth drug use and abuse," by E. A. Larson. JOURNAL OF THE LOUISIANA MEDICAL SOCIETY. 122:6-10, January, 1970.

"Towards a purpose in life...," by M. M. Glatt. HEALTH. 7:21+, Spring, 1970.

"Town deals sternly with its own; six young drug offenders sent to prison in Rupert, Idaho," by L. Wainwright. LIFE. 69:40-42+, November 6, 1970.

"Toxic derivatives of Cannabis sativa," by G. Nanas, et al. PRESSE MEDICALE. 78:1679-1684, September 19, 1970.

"Toxicological research on hashish. Apropos of some recent observations collected in the North," by T. VanKy, et al. MEDECINE LEGALE ET DOMMAGE CORPOREL (Paris). 3:245-250, July-September, 1970.

"Toxicomanogenic properties of derivatives of dextromorphan," by J. La Barre. THERAPIE. 25:565-578, May-June, 1970.

TRAFFIC SAFETY AND DRUGS
"Dagga and driving," by T. James. SOUTH AFRICAN MEDICAL JOURNAL. 44:580-581, May 16, 1970.

"Determination and identification of sympathomimetic amines in blood samples from drivers by a combination of gas chromatography and mass spectrometry, by R. Bonnichsen, et al. ZEITSCHRIFT FUER RECHTS-MEDIZIN. 67:19-26, 1970.

"Drugs, drug dependence and traffic safety," by B. Dokert. PHARMAZEUTISCHE PRAXIS; BEILAGE ZUR DIE PHARMAZIE. 1:1-6, 1970.

"Drugs, drunken driving, the delivery of medical care, the high cost of hospitalization," by S. D. Simon. RHODE ISLAND MEDICAL JOURNAL. 53:276-281+, May, 1970.

"Drunkenness, drugs, and manslaughter," by G. F. Orchard. CRIMINAL LAW REVIEW. 211-218, April, 1970.

"Visual disturbances experienced by hallucinogenic drug abusers while driving," G. E. Woody. AMERICAN JOURNAL OF PSYCHIATRY. 127:683-686, November, 1970.

"Training teachers to deal with drugs." PENNSYLVANIA SCHOOL JOURNAL. 118:258-261+, May, 1970.

TRANQUILIZERS
"The pill head menace. Barbiturates and tranquilizers: non-hard core addicting drugs," by H. S. Feldman. PSYCHOSOMATICS. 11:99-103, March-April, 1970.

"Traveling Americans warned against drug abuse." DE-
PARTMENT OF STATE NEWS LETTER. pp. 21-22, April, 1970.

"Treating heroin addiction at Simmons House," by G. M.
Greaves and K. Ryz. NURSING TIMES. 66:49+, January 8, 1970.

TREATMENT
"An approach to the treatment of drug abuse," by
R. I. Wang, et al. WISCONSIN MEDICAL JOURNAL.
69:148-150, May, 1970.

"The case of Heikki (Voluntary application for
treatment of drug addiction)." SAIRAANHOITAJA.
46:174-177, March 10, 1970.

"Case study on the attitudes of drug addicts to
treatment," by A. M. Toll. BRITISH JOURNAL OF
ADDICTION. 65:139-158, August, 1970.

"Conditioned nalorphine-induced abstinence changes:
persistence in post morphine-dependent monkeys,"
by S. R. Goldberg, et al. JOURNAL OF THE EXPER-
IMENTAL ANALYSIS OF BEHAVIOR. 14:33-46, July,
1970.

"Current drug addiction: clinical effects of agents
in use and common semiologic aspects," by P.
Deniker, et al. ANNALES MEDICO-PSYCHOLOGIQUES
(Paris). 2:7-8, June, 1970.

"Current trends in the treatment of drug dependence
and drug abuse," by N. B. Eddy. BULLETIN ON
NARCOTICS. 22:1-9, January-March, 1970.

"Diagnosis and treatment of the passively addicted
newborn," by D. Ingall and M. Zuckerstatter.
HOSPITAL PRACTICE. 5:101+, August, 1970.

"Drug addiction treatment with maintenance doses
of methadon," by M. Nimb. NORDISK MEDICIN.
83:1412, October 29, 1970.

"Drug controlled addiction," by A. Bauer. ARZNEI-
MITTEL-FORSCHUNG. 20:875-876, July, 1970.

"Drug dependence and its treatment. I.," by D. X.
Freedman. POSTGRADUATE MEDICINE. 47:110-114,
January, 1970.

TREATMENT (cont'd.)

"Drug dependence and its treatment, II," by D. X.
Freedman. POSTGRADUATE MEDICINE. 47:150-154,
February, 1970.

"Drug problem; treating preaddictive adolescents,"
by P. Caroff, et al. SOCIAL CASEWORK. 51:527-
532, November, 1970; Reply: by D. Hallowitz and
G. N. Cohen. 52:46-47, January, 1971.

"A drug to lick a drug," by F. Warshofsky. FAMILY
HEALTH. 2:22+, May, 1970.

"Drugs used against addiction," by M. J. Rodman.
RN. 32:71-80, October, 1970.

"Effect of withdrawal of corticotrophin in patients
on long-term treatment of multiple sclerosis,"
by J. H. Millar, et al. LANCET. 1:700-701,
April 4, 1970.

"Emergency care of acute drug intoxication," by E.
A. Wolfson. JOURNAL OF THE MEDICAL SOCIETY OF
NEW JERSEY. 67:820, December, 1970.

"Emergency treatment of drug abuse," by J. DeGross.
RESIDENT AND STAFF PHYSICIAN. 16:43+, February,
1970.

"Evaluation and treatment of the suspected drug
user in the emergency roon," by G. G. Dimijian,
et al. ARCHIVES OF INTERNAL MEDICINE (Chicago).
125:162-170, January, 1970.

"Heroin addiction. A comparison of two impatient
treatment methods," by M. L. LaRouche, et al.
MICHIGAN MEDICINE. 69:751-754, September, 1970.

"Hospitals in the Canadian drug scene," by L. P.
Solursh. CANADIAN HOSPITAL. 47:56-59, August,
1970.

"Hospitals responsible for alcohol and drug addicts,"
by W. Rooen. CANADIAN HOSPITAL. 47:5+, February,
1970.

"How addicts are treated." TIME. 95:20, March 16,
1970.

"How Scarborough General handles drug abuse victims,"

TREATMENT (cont'd.)
  by D. Charter. CANADIAN HOSPITAL. 47:42+,
  September, 1970.

"Management of bad trips in an evolving drug scene,"
  by R. L. Taylor, et al. JOURNAL OF THE AMERICAN
  MEDICAL ASSOCIATION. 213:422-425, July 20, 1970.

"Management of the narcotic-addicted surgical patient;
  concepts of medical and surgical care," by T. E.
  Splaver, et al. JOURNAL OF ORAL SURGERY. 28:346-
  352, May, 1970.

"New hope for the hopeless. Drug addiction; its
  treatment, management and the nurse's role," by
  J. N. Chappel. CHART. 67:251-255, October, 1970.

"A new method for treatment of barbiturate dependence," by D. E. Smith, et al. JOURNAL OF THE
  AMERICAN MEDICAL ASSOCIATION. 213:294-295, July
  13, 1970.

"Nonaddictive psychotropic medication for imprisoned
  narcotic addicts," by H. S. Feldman, et al. JOUR-
  NAL OF THE MEDICAL SOCIETY OF NEW JERSEY. 67:278-
  283, June, 1970.

"On treating drug addiction with methadone." CURRENT.
  120:35-38, August, 1970.

"An oral method of the withdrawal treatment of heroin
  dependence; a five years' study of a combination
  of diphenoxylate (Lomotil) and chlormethiazole
  (Heminevrin)," by M. M. Glatt, et al. BRITISH
  JOURNAL OF ADDICTION. 65:237-243, November, 1970.

"The personality of drug addicts and their treatment,"
  by P. Delteil, et al. ANNALES MEDICO-PSYCHOLOG-
  IQUES (Paris). 2:107-113, June, 1970.

"Place of treatment professions in society's response
  to chemical abuse," by G. Edwards. BRITISH MEDI-
  CAL JOURNAL. 2:195-199, April 25, 1970.

"Placebo as an agent in the treatment of drug abuse,"
  by J. Hankiewicz. WIADOMOSCI LEKARSKIE. 23:
  1253-1257, July 15, 1970.

"Principles of diagnosis and treatment of addictive
  drugs overdose," by J. F. Burdon. JOURNAL OF THE

TREATMENT (cont'd.)
ROYAL COLLEGE OF GENERAL PRACTITIONERS. 20:171-174, September, 1970.

"Remarks on series of drug addicts admitted to hospital environment," by P. Mouren, et al. MARSEILLE MEDICAL. 107:463-466, June, 1970.

"Report on drug treatment." NTRDA BULLETIN. 56: 14+, February, 1970.

"The sensitivity of the brain to barbiturate during chronic administration and withdrawal of barbitone sodium in the rat," by I. H. Stevenson, et al. BRITISH JOURNAL OF PHARMACOLOGY AND CHEMOTHERAPY. 39:325-333, June, 1970.

"Staff-patient problems in drug dependence treatment clinics," by T. H. Bewley, et al. JOURNAL OF PSYCHOSOMATIC RESEARCH. 14:303-306, September, 1970.

"Subjective effects of narcotic antagonists Cyclazocine and nalorphine on the Addiction Research Center Inventory (ARCI)," by C. A. Haertzen. PSYCHOPHARMACOLOGIA. 18:366-377, 1970.

"The treatment of addiction," by P. A. Chapple. BIOLOGY AND HUMAN AFFAIRS. 35,3:30-35, Summer, 1970.

"Treatment of barbiturate dependence," by D. Goldman, et al. JOURNAL OF THE AMERICAN MEDICAL ASSOCIATION. 213:2272-2273, September 28, 1970.

"Treatment of drinamyl addiction: two case studies," by T. Kraft. JOURNAL OF NERVOUS AND MENTAL DISEASE. 150:138-145, February, 1970.

"Treatment of drug addiction," by P. A. Chapple, et al. LANCET. 2:1134, November 28, 1970.

"Treatment of drug addiction: some comparative observations," by W. N. Davis. BRITISH JOURNAL OF ADDICTION. 65:227-235, November, 1970.

"Treatment of heroin dependence with opiate antagonists," by M. Fink, et al. CURRENT PSYCHIATRIC THERAPIES. 10:161-170, 1970.

TREATMENT (cont'd.)
"The use of cyclazocine in the treatment of heroin addicts," by E. S. Petursson, et al. DISEASES OF THE NERVOUS SYSTEM. 31:549-551, August, 1970.

"The Treatment of Addiction," by P. A. Chapple. BIOLOGY AND HUMAN AFFAIRS. 35,3:30-35, Summer, 1970.

"Treatment of barbiturate dependence," by D. Goldman, et al. JOURNAL OF THE AMERICAN MEDICAL ASSOCIATION. 213:2272-2273, September 28, 1970.

"Treatment of drinamyl addiction: two case studies," by T. Kraft. JOURNAL OF NERVOUS AND MENTAL DISEASE. 150:138-145, February, 1970.

"Treatment of drug addiction," by P. A. Chapple, et al. LANCET. 2:1134, November 28, 1970.

"The treatment of drug addiction: some comparative observations," by W. N. Davis. BRITISH JOURNAL OF ADDICTION. 65:227-235, November, 1970.

"Treatment of heroin dependence with opiate antagonists," by M. Fink, et al. CURRENT PSYCHIATRIC THERAPIES. 10:161-170, 1970.

TRICHLORETHYLENE ABUSE
"Trichlorethylene addiction; a discussion on the basis of observed cases," by A. Januszkiewicz-Grablas, et al. PSYCHIATRIA POLSKA. 4:395-399, July-August, 1970.

"Trichlorethylene addiction; a discussion on the basis of observed cases," by A. Januszkiewicz-Grablas, et al. PSYCHIATRIA POLSKA. 4:395-399, July-August, 1970.

"Tripping on the drug scene; some coverage of narcotics problems has been admirable, but moralizing, misinformation, and sensationalizing predominate; why not an embargo on non-news?" by M. K. Sanders. COLUMBIA JOURNALISM REVIEW. 9:35-42, Fall, 1970.

"Turning off the Tijuana grass; Operation Intercept," by C. Kentfield. ESQUIRE. 73:8+, May, 1970.

"Turning on in society," by M. Zane. NATION. 211:595-596, December 7, 1970.

"Uncertainty in the programs of prevention of drug
addiction in the United States," by A. Muggia.
MINERVA MEDICA. 61:Suppl. 49:10, June 23, 1970.

"Unchanged rate of brain serotonin synthesis during
chronic morphine treatment and failure of para-
chlorophenylalanine to attenuate withdrawal syndrome in mice," by I. Marshall, et al. NATURE
(London). 228:1206-1208, December 19, 1970.

UNION MEMBERS AND DRUG ABUSE
"Drug abuse among union members," by L. Perlis.
INDUSTRIAL MEDICINE AND SURGERY. 39:54-56,
September, 1970.

"Unit-dose narcotic prestock system saves effort but
maintains control," by M. R. Beahm, et al. HOSPITAL
TOPICS. 48:63+, November, 1970.

"U.S. and Mexico continue talks on control of narcotics;
Department announcement with joint communique." DE-
PARTMENT OF STATE BULLETIN. 62:527, April 20, 1970.

"U.S. Journal: Houston: thirty year sentence to L.
O. Johnson for giving away one marijuana cigarette,"
by C. Trillin. NEW YORKER. 46:164+, December 12,
1970.

"U.S.-Mexican discussions on marijuana, narcotics, and
dangerous drugs: declaration by Attorneys General
Mitchell and Sanchez Vargas at Puerto Vallarta,
August 21, 1970." WEEKLY COMPILATION OF PRESIDEN-
TIAL DOCUMENTS. 6:1092-1093, August 24, 1970.

"U.S. proposes new UN action program against illicit
narcotics," by J. E. Ingersoll. DEPARTMENT OF
STATE BULLETIN. 63:492-497, October 26, 1970.
Statement before a meeting of the UN commission
on narcotic drugs, Geneva, September 28, 1970.

"Unselling drugs; antidrug education and advertising,"
by D. Sanford. NEW REPUBLIC. 162:15-16, February
28, 1970.

"Unusual effect of fenfluramine," by D. V. Hawks.
BRITISH MEDICAL JOURNAL. 1:238, January 24, 1970.

"Unwanted effects of cannabis." LANCET. 2:1350,
December 26, 1970.

"Urine testing schedules in methadone maintenance treatment of heroin addiction," by A. Goldstein, et al. JOURNAL OF THE AMERICAN MEDICAL ASSOCIATION. 214:311-315, October 12, 1970.

"Use and abuse of euphoristic substances among conscripts at the Oslo sessions of 1969," by H. Jakob Stang. TIDSSKRIFT FOR DEN NORSKE LAEGEFORENING. 90:1549-1556+, August 15, 1970.

"The use and abuse of psychotropic drugs. General aspects," by D. Dunlop. PROCEEDINGS OF THE ROYAL SOCIETY OF MEDICINE. 63:1279-1282, December, 1970.

"The use and abuse of reducing pills in obesity," by W. J. Evans. JOURNAL OF THE LOUISIANA MEDICAL SOCIETY. 122:99-103, April, 1970.

"The use and abuses of drugs in psychiatry," by M. Shepherd. LANCET. 1:31-33, January 3, 1970.

"The use and misuse of psychotropic drugs. A panel discussion." JOURNAL OF THE IOWA MEDICAL SOCIETY. 60:98-105, February, 1970.

"Use of amphetamine by medical students," by C. Watkins. SOUTHERN MEDICAL JOURNAL. 63:923-929, August, 1970.

"The use of Catha edulis among Yemenite Jews," by J. P. Hes. HAREFUAH. 78:282-284, March 15, 1970.

"The use of cyclazocine in the treatment of heroin addicts," by E. S. Petursson, et al. DISEASES OF THE NERVOUS SYSTEM. 31:549-551, August, 1970.

"Use of drugs." REVUE DE L'INFIRMIERE ET DE L'ASSISTANTE SOCIALE. 20:156-157, February, 1970.

"Use of a 'Freak Out' Control Center," by R. M. Casse. JOURNAL OF COLLEGE STUDENT PERSONNEL. 11,6:403-408, November, 1970.

"Use of the television monologue with adolescent psychiatric patients," by H. A. Wilmer. AMERICAN JOURNAL OF PSYCHIATRY. 126:1760-1766, June, 1970.

"Users and nonusers of marijuana: some attitudinal and behavioral correlates," by F. W. King. JOURNAL OF THE AMERICAN COLLEGE HEALTH ASSOCIATION. 18:213-

217, February, 1970.

"Uses and abuses." ECONOMIST. 234:25, March 7, 1970.

"Using methadone to treat the heroin addict," by H. R.
Williams. CANADA'S MENTAL HEALTH. 18:4+, March-
April, 1970.

"Vacationing in jail." SENIOR SCHOLASTIC. 96:19,
May 18, 1970.

"Value of serum and urine barbiturate tests in monitoring barbiturate withdrawal," by M. S. Kleckner,
et al. JOURNAL OF THE AMERICAN MEDICAL ASSOCIATION.
213:1909, September 14, 1970.

"Ventilatory capacity in a group of opium smokers,"
by L. H. Koon, et al. SINGAPORE MEDICAL JOURNAL.
11:75-79, June, 1970.

"Video recordings," by S. H. Griffiths. NURSING TIMES.
66:1208+, September 17, 1970.

VIENNA PSYCHIATRIC-NEUROLOGICAL UNIVERSITY HOSPITAL
"Drug dependence and addiction among patients of
the Vienna Psychiatric-Neurological University
Hospital with special reference to psychotropic
drugs," by G. Hofman, et al. ARZNEIMITTEL-FOR-
SCHUNG. 20:871-873, July, 1970.

"Visual disturbances experienced by hallucinogenic
drug abusers while driving," by G. E. Woody. AMER-
ICAN JOURNAL OF PSYCHIATRY. 127:683-686, November,
1970.

"The voluntary health agency." SCHOOL HEALTH REVIEW.
1:36, April, 1970.

"WHO Expert Committee on Drug Dependence. Seventeenth
report." WORLD HEALTH ORGANIZATION TECHNICAL REPORT
SERIES. 437:1-31, 1970.

"Walk on London's wild side," by D. Moraes. NEW YORK TIMES MAGAZINE. p. 100+, September 13, 1970.

"War on drugs: its meaning to tourists." U.S. NEWS AND WORLD REPORT. 69:68, September 7, 1970.

"Watch your prescribing policy, doctor addicts may be abusing it." OHIO STATE MEDICAL JOURNAL. 66:418, April, 1970.

"Wave of LSD-taking hitting Britain," by E. Clark. OBSERVER. p. 1+, December 20, 1970.

"We must declare war on drugs; ed. by J. N. Bell," by A. Linkletter. GOOD HOUSEKEEPING. 170:94-95+, April, 1970.

"We must fight the epidemic of drug abuse!" by A. Linkletter. READER'S DIGEST. 96:56-60, February, 1970.

"Weekend junkies," by S. Yeger. NEW SOCIETY. pp. 308-309, February 19, 1970.

"What the English are doing about heroin," by M. Simons. LOOK. 34:47+, April 7, 1970.

"What legal status for marijuana?" by J. Kaplan. CURRENT. 123:44-47, November, 1970.

"What? Pot? Not Laredo. II." FORBES. 106:48, November 1, 1970.

"What price methadone addiction?" by R. F. Alsop. NEW ENGLAND JOURNAL OF MEDICINE. 282:756, March 26, 1970.

"What we have forgotten about pot, a pharmacologist's history: cannabis sativa," by S. H. Snyder. NEW YORK TIMES MAGAZINE. 26-27+, December 13, 1970.

"What will turn the tide against drug abuse?" by F. X. Wamsley. MEDICAL ECONOMICS. 47:94+, December 7, 1970.

"What you can do about the drug problem," by S. Grafton. PARENTS MAGAZINE. 45:72-75+, November, 1970.

"What you should know about the major mind-affecting drugs." GOOD HOUSEKEEPING. 171:148-149, August, 1970.

"What's Happening?" by C. M. Vry. JOURNAL OF SECONDARY EDUCATION. 45,2:95-96, February, 1970.

"What's it like to smoke marijuana." SCIENCE DIGEST. 68:18-19, October, 1970.

"When drugs become a religion," by J. Sparrow. DAILY TELEGRAPH. p. 14, February 16, 1970.

"When a holiday ends in a prison sentence," by H. Sieve. DAILY TELEGRAPH. p. 16+, October 9, 1970. (Color Suppl.).

"Where prevention starts," by T. D. Bird. NORTHWEST MEDICINE. 69:553, August, 1970.

"While doctors argue, people die," by F. Brill. TRUE. 51:62+, January, 1970.

WHITE HOUSE CONFERENCE
   "To youth with love; White House Conference on the drug problem," by R. L. Shayon. SATURDAY REVIEW OF LITERATURE. 53:57, November 21, 1970.

"White House conference on drug abuse: the President's remarks (October 14, 1970), to radio industry representatives attending the conference," by R. Nixon. WEEKLY COMPILATION OF PRESIDENTIAL DOCUMENTS. 6: 1373-1374, October 19, 1970.

"Who should evaluate drugs?" ADM; REVISTA de la ASOCIACION DENTAL MEXICANA. 27:539-549, November-December, 1970.

"Why cyclamates were banned." LANCET. 1:1091-1092, May 23, 1970.

"Why speed kills." NEWSWEEK. 76:121, November 16, 1970.

"Wild hemp of Indiana," by M. King. NATION. 211:402-403, October 26, 1970.

"Will we ever cure them?" by M. S. Lewsley. NURSING MIRROR AND MIDWIVES JOURNAL. 130:41+, March 17, 1970.

WITHDRAWAL
   "Effects of diphenylhydantoin (Dilantin) withdrawal on non-epileptics; preliminary report," by J. A.

WITHDRAWAL (cont'd.)
    Rosenblum, et al. CURRENT THERAPEUTIC RESEARCH.
    12:31-33, January, 1970.

    "Electroencephalographic study of morphine tolerance
    and withdrawal phenomena in rats," by F. Lipparini,
    et al. THERAPIE. 25:929-937, September-October,
    1970.

    "Heroin withdrawal syndrome," by C. Zelson et al.
    JOURNAL OF PEDIATRICS. 76:483-484, March, 1970.

    "In prison," by I. P. James, et al. LANCET. 1:37,
    January 3, 1970.

    "Slight abstinence symptoms," by U. H. Vaag. UGE-
    SKRIFT FOR LAEGER. 132:1875-1877, October, 1970.

    "Unchanged rate of brain serotonin synthesis during
    chronic morphine treatment and failure of para-
    chlorophenylalanine to attenuate withdrawal syn-
    drome in mice," by I. Marshall, et al. NATURE
    (London). 228:1206-1208, December 19, 1970.

"Withdrawal programmes for narcotics addicts in the
    USA," by K. Neudek. MUENCHENER MEDIZINISCHE WOCHEN-
    SCHRIFT. 112:1054-1056, May 29, 1970.

WOMEN AND DRUGS
    "Heroin dependence and delinquency in women--a study
    of heroin addicts in Holloway prison," by P. T.
    d'Orban. BRITISH JOURNAL OF ADDICTION. 65:67-
    78, May, 1970.

"Workshop on 'The Adolescent in My Practice'. The
    pediatrician's view," by C. Pincock. WOMAN PHYSICIAN.
    25:93, February, 1970.

"The young drug scene," by J. Tweedie. GUARDIAN.
    p. 9, July 6, 1970.

"The youngest addict...and ways to recognize him."
    EMERGENCY MEDICINE. 2:28+, September, 1970.

"Youngsters and drugs: making sense of what's hap-
    pening." BETTER HOMES AND GARDENS. 48:34+, October,
    1970.

YOUTH AND DRUGS

"Addiction hazards for youths," by W. Schweisheimer.
AGNES KARLL-SCHWESTER. 24:312-313, August, 1970.

"Adolescence and drug abuse," by J. H. McKeen. JOUR-
NAL OF THE ROYAL COLLEGE OF GENERAL PRACTITIONERS.
20:288-290, November, 1970.

"Adolescent drug abuse in a North London suburb,"
by A. Anumonye, et al. BRITISH JOURNAL OF AD-
DICTION. 65:25-33, May, 1970.

"Adolescents and adults: the prism of drugs," by
W. J. Cook. ILLINOIS EDUCATION. 58:293-296,
March, 1970.

"Alarm grows in U.S. as youth moves on to heroin,"
by F. Hechinger. TIMES (London) EDUCATIONAL
SUPPLETMENT. 2859:9, March 6, 1970.

"Amphetamine taking among young offenders," by
B. Lancaster, et al. BRITISH JOURNAL OF PSY-
CHIATRY. 116:349-350, March, 1970.

"Amphetamines, the teenagers' basic drug," by V.
Brittain. LONDON TIMES. p. 10, September 22,
1970.

"Blacks declare war on dope; mothers against drugs."
EBONY. 25:31-34+, June, 1970.

"Busting the boys." NEWSWEEK. 76:32, August 17,
1970.

"$C_{21}H_{23}NO_3$: a primer for parent and children," by
L. Edson. NEW YORK TIMES MAGAZINE. pp. 92-93+,
May 24, 1970.

"Can this marriage be saved?" by D. C. Disney.
LADIES HOME JOURNAL. 87:12+, December, 1970.

"Changes in the picture of drug addiction in adolescents," by R. Mader, et al. WIENER MEDI-
ZINISCHE WOCHENSCHRIFT. 120:330-333, May 2,
1970.

"Checkpoints for fighting the drug menace in camp;
education rpogram at Camp Narrin, Michigan," by
S. C. Huck and P.A. Denomme. CAMPING MAGAZINE.
42:19+, September, 1970.

YOUTH AND DRUGS (cont'd.)
"Classroom drug scene: training sessions for educators," by M. V. Gelinas. AMERICAN EDUCATION.
6:3-4, November, 1970.

"The clinician's role in the problem of drug usage
by young people," by D. H. Milman. AMERICAN
JOURNAL OF PSYCHIATRY. 126:1040, January, 1970.

"Comprehensive action model to combat drug abuse in
high school," by R. F. Petrillo. JOURNAL OF
SCHOOL PSYCHOLOGY. 8,3:226-230, 1970.

"Coping with drug abuse. II. An indigenous multidisciplinary clinic for youths," by S. Lecker.
CANADIAN JOURNAL OF PSYCHIATRIC NURSING. 11:4-
9, August, 1970.

"Counselors in the adolescent drug scene," by W.
Penner. CANADIAN COUNSELOR. 4,2:131-133, April,
1970.

"Dependency habit in delinquent adolescents," by
C. I. Backhouse, et al. BRITISH JOURNAL OF AD-
DICTION. 64:417-418, January, 1970.

"Dope about dope; publications of the Student association for the study of hallucinogens." SAT-
URDAY REVIEW OF LITERATURE. 53:80, September
19, 1970.

"Dope stop-teen involvement," by G. E. Conroy. ARI-
ZONA MEDICINE. 27:16-17, October, 1970.

"Drug abuse and the school scene; symposium." SCIENCE
TEACHER. 37:45-50, September, 1970.

"Drug abuse: implications for education," by E. B.
Luongo. NEW YORK STATE EDUCATION. 58:32-33,
November, 1970.

"Drug abuse in the schools; teacher opinion poll.
National Education Association. Research Division." TODAY'S EDUCATION. 59:7, December,
1970.

"Drug abuse in a young psychiatric population," by
M. Cohen and D. F. Klein. AMERICAN JOURNAL OF
ORTHOPSYCHIATRY. 40:448-455, April, 1970.

179

YOUTH AND DRUGS (cont'd.)

"Drug abuse; the newest and most dangerous challenge to school boards," by P. C. Barrins. AMER-
ICAN SCHOOL BOARD JOURNAL. 157:15-18, October,
1969; also in EDUCATION DIGEST. 35:24-26, January, 1970.

"Drug abuse rehabilitation program for youth," by
C. J. Katz, et al. ROCKY MOUNTAIN MEDICAL JOUR-
NAL. 67:57-60, July, 1970.

"Drug abuse. Schools find some answers," by T. J.
Miller. SCHOOL MANAGEMENT. 14,4:22-28, April,
1970.

"Drug addiction among juveniles with special con-
sideration of hashish smoking," by P. Kielholz,
et al. DEUTSCHE MEDIZINISCHE WOCHENSCHRIFT.
95:101-105, January 16, 1970.

"Drug addiction--a menace to youth in Great Britain.
A pilot epidemiological study," by D. C. Watt,
et al. ACTIVITAS NERVOSA SUPERIOR (Praha). 12:
284-287, 1970.

"Drug addiction of adolescents in Sweden," by B.
Jansson. NORDISK PSYKIATRISK TIDSSKRIFT. 24:
44-56, 1970.

"Drug addicts getting younger: with study-discussion
program, by E. Harris and D. Harris," by C.
Winick. PTA MAGAZINE. 65:6-8+, September, 1970.

"Drug education and our children." BEDSIDE NURSE.
3:13, May, 1970.

"Drug education doesn't work unless kids care," by
W. Rasberry. COMPACT. 4,3:36, June, 1970.

"Drug education in the primary grades," by R. Daniels.
JOURNAL OF THE NEW YORK STATE SCHOOL NURSE-TEACHER
ASSOCIATION. 1:37-38, July, 1970.

"Drug education in schools; by whose values?" by
M. E. Doster. DELTA KAPPA GAMMA BULLETIN. 37:
47-49, Summer, 1970.

"Drug education in the schools; panel discussion."
COMPACT. 4:41-44, October, 1970.

YOUTH AND DRUGS (cont'd.)
"Drug education in the States." COMPACT. (Special
Supplement). 4,6:21-28, December, 1970.

"Drug education; take out the glamor," by R. Carpenter. INSTRUCTOR. 80:130-133, August, 1970.

"Drug epidemic; what's a teacher to do?" by C. H.
Harrison. SCHOLASTIC TEACHER SECONDARY TEACHER
SUPPLEMENT. 4-6+, May 4, 1970.

"Drug menace; how serious? dangers in dope; teenage addicts; interview with John E. Ingersoll,
director, Federal Bureau of Narcotics." U.S. NEWS
AND WORLD REPORT. 68:38-42, May 25, 1970.

"Drug misuse in teenagers," by D. Lloyd. APPLIED
THERAPEUTICS. 12:19-25, March, 1970.

"Drug prevention clubs in France," by J. Ellul.
INTERPLAY. 3:39-41, August, 1970.

"Drug problem: treating preaddictive adolescents,"
by P. Caroff, et al. SOCIAL CASEWORK. 51:527-
532, November, 1970. Reply: by D. Hallowitz and
G. N. Cohen. 52:46-47, January, 1971.

"Drug problems and the high school principal," by
F. M. Ochberg. NATIONAL ASSOCIATION OF SECONDARY
SCHOOL PRINCIPALS BULLETIN. 54,346:52-59, May,
1970.

"Drug scene; high schools are higher now." NEWSWEEK.
75:66-67, February 16, 1970.

"Drug-taking in delinquent boys," by P. J. Noble.
BRITISH MEDICAL JOURNAL. 1:102-105, January 10,
1970.

"Drug use among the young; as teenagers see it," by
E. Herzog, et al. CHILDREN. 17:207+, November-
December, 1970.

"The drug-using adolescent as a pediatric patient,"
by I. F. Litt, et al. JOURNAL OF PEDIATRICS. 77:
195-202, August, 1970.

"Drugs, adolescents and society," by O. Jeanneret.
ZEITSCHRIFT FUR KRANKENPFLEGE. 63:9-13, January,
1970.

YOUTH AND DRUGS (cont'd.)
"Drugs and our children; a White House report; questions and answers." LADIES HOME JOURNAL. 87:112-113+, May, 1970.

"Drugs and the schools; two case studies." EDU- CATIONAL PRODUCT REPORT. 3,7:4-15, April, 1970.

"Drugs and youth," by D. P. Mogol. INDEPENDENT SCHOOL BULLETIN. 29,4:7-9, May, 1970.

"Drugs; letter to parent," by H. S. Frost. INDEPEN- DENT SCHOOL BULLETIN. 29,4:12-13, May, 1970.

"Drugs; letter to a trustee." INDEPENDENT SCHOOL BULLETIN. 29,4:10-11, May, 1970.

"Drugs--the role of the teacher and youth leader," by D. A. Lane. COMMUNITY HEALTH (Bristol). 1: 327-329, May-June, 1970.

"Drugs talk make sixth formers queasy," by T. Dev- lin. TIMES (London) EDUCATIONAL SUPPLEMENT. 2854:11, January 30, 1970.

"Drugs/teens=alcohol/parent," by T. Lawrence and J. Velleman. SCIENCE DIGEST. 68:46-48+, October, 1970.

"Drugs; what can the schools do about the problem?" by L. D. Hamilton. EDUCATION CANADA. 10,4:30- 36, December, 1970.

"Editorially speaking; youth and drug abuse," by R. Cumming. MUSIC JOURNAL. 28:4, March, 1970.

"Etiology of drug addiction of adolescents," by E. Varilo. NORDISK PSYKIATRISK TIDSSKRIFT. 24:56- 71, 1970.

"Factors influencing drug abuse in young people," by D. I. Carson, et al. TEXAS MEDICINE. 66: 50-57, January, 1970.

"Family and differential involvement with marijuana; a study of suburban teenagers," by N. Tec. JOUR- NAL OF MARRIAGE AND THE FAMILY. 32:656-664, No- vember, 1970.

"Getting the adolescent to worry about drug abuse,

182

YOUTH AND DRUGS (cont'd.)
and his parents not to," by V. R. Allen. CON-
SULTANT. 10:5+, March-April, 1970.

"Hepatitis is associated antigen in young drug a-
busers with hepatitis in Vestre hospital," by T.
Jersild, et al. NORDISK MEDICIN. 84:1537-1538,
November 26, 1970.

"Hepatitis associated antigen in young narcotic
addicts with hepatitis. Qualitative and quantitative determinations," by T. Jersild, et al.
UGESKRIFT FOR LAEGER. 132:873-874, May 7, 1970.

"Hepatitis in young drug abusers--liver pathology
and Prince antigen," by T. Jersild, et al. NOR-
DISK MEDICIN. 84:1538, November 26, 1970.

"Hepatitis in young drug users," by T. Jersild, et
al. SCANDINAVIAN JOURNAL OF GASTROENTEROLOGY
SUPPLEMENT. 7:79-83, 1970.

"Heroin addiction in adolescents," by P. Boyd. JOUR-
NAL OF PSYCHOSOMATIC RESEARCH. 14:295-301, September, 1970.

"Heroin in the schools." CHRISTIANITY TODAY. 14:
32, March 13, 1970.

"High school drug education; an interim measure,"
by M. A. LaCombe, et al. JOURNAL OF THE AMERICAN
MEDICAL ASSOCIATION. 214:1327-1328, November 16,
1970.

"A high school principal looks at drug abuse," by
R. W. Joly. COMPACT. 4,3:37-39, June, 1970.

"High school sports flunk the saliva test," by T.
Irwin. TODAY'S HEALTH. 48:44-46+, October,
1970.

"How can you tell if your child is taking drugs?" by
I. Mothner. LOOK. 34:42+, April 7, 1970.

"How I faced my son's drug arrest," by G. Astor.
LOOK. 34:87-88+, December 15, 1970.

"How Missouri high school principals deal with
student use of tobacco, alcohol, narcotics,
drugs," by R. M. Taylor and J. Rackers. SCHOOL

YOUTH AND DRUGS (cont'd.)
AND COMMUNITY. 56:7+, March, 1970.

"How the schools can prevent drug abuse," by D. C.
Lewis. NATIONAL ASSOCIATION OF SECONDARY SCHOOL
PRINCIPALS BULLETIN. 54,346:43-51, May, 1970.

"How to face up to drug abuse in your schools and
your community," by P. C. Barrins. AMERICAN
SCHOOL BOARD JOURNAL. 158:17-20+, August, 1970.

"How to talk with your teen-ager about drugs; excerpt from What you can do about drugs and your
child," by H. W. Land. READER'S DIGEST. 97:69-
72, August, 1970.

"Hyperkineticism in children." ILLINOIS MEDICAL
JOURNAL. 138:618, December, 1970.

"Hypnosis and the adolescent drug abuser," by F.
Baumann. AMERICAN JOURNAL OF CLINICAL HYPNOSIS.
13:17-21, July, 1970.

"The incidence of drug use among Halifax adolescents,"
by P. C. Whitehead. BRITISH JOURNAL OF ADDICTION.
65:159-165, August, 1970.

"Kids and heroin: the adolescent epidemic." TIME.
95:15-20+, March 16, 1970; also in READER'S DI-
GEST. 96:88-92, June, 1970.

"Knowledge and experience of young people regarding
drug abuse," by J. D. Wright. PROCEEDINGS OF THE
ROYAL SOCIETY OF MEDICINE. 63:725-729, July, 1970.

"The Laguna Beach experiment as a community approach
to family counselling for drug abuse; problems in
youth," by L. A. Gottschalk, et al. COMPREHENSIVE
PSYCHIATRY. 11:226-234, May, 1970.

"The law and drugs in the schools," by J. D. McKevitt.
COMPACT. 4,3:45-46, June, 1970.

"Leadership by local school boards," by D. H. Kurtzman. COMAPCT. 4,3:34-35, June, 1970.

"Life on two grains a day; heroin in the high schools."
LIFE. 68:24-32, February 20, 1970.

"The long-term outcome for adolescent drug users; a

184

YOUTH AND DRUGS (cont'd.)
follow-up study of 76 users and 146 nonusers,"
by L. N. Robins, et al. PROCEEDINGS OF THE AMER-
ICAN PSYCHOPATHOLOGICAL ASSOCIATION. 59:159-180,
1970.

"Marijuana and the pediatrician: an attitude survey,"
by A. L. Abrams, et al. PEDIATRICS. 46:462-464,
September, 1970.

"Marijuana in junior high school," by G. W. Wohlberg.
NEW ENGLAND JOURNAL OF MEDICINE. 282:318-319,
August 6, 1970.

"Medico-psychological contribution to the comprehen-
sion of young drug addicts," by A. Gorceix, et al.
ANNALES MEDICO-PSYCHOLOGIQUES (Paris). 2:126-132,
June, 1970.

"Narcomanism in the youth. Report from the Massa-
chusetts Medical Society," by N. Retterstol.
TIDSSKRIFT FOR DEN NORSKE LAEGEFORENING. 90:
878, May 1, 1970.

"Narcotic abuse by adolescents," by R. Langmann.
OEFFENTLICHE GESUNDHEITSWESEN. 32:43-46, January,
1970.

"Narcotic problems among youth in Randers. A 10-
month study of incidence," by E. Hansen, et al.
UGESKRIFT FOR LAEGER. 132:2187-2189, November
12, 1970.

"Narcotics; a crucial area of secondard school responsibility; fully credited courses needed,"
by R. Elliott. EDUCATION DIGEST. 36:44-47,
September, 1970.

"Narcotics; a new area of secondary school responsibility," by R. Elliott. NORTH CENTRAL ASSO-
CIATION QUARTERLY. 44:325-334, Spring, 1970;
also in EDUCATION DIGEST. 36:44-47, September,
1970.

"New skills for teachers," by J. Spillane. COMPACT.
4,3:26-27, June, 1970.

"No marijuana for adolescents," by K. Angel. NEW
YORK TIMES MAGAZINE. p. 9+, January 25, 1970.

YOUTH AND DRUGS (cont'd.)

"Observations on the current drug scene," by R. F. Aubrey. NATIONAL ASSOCIATION OF COLLEGE ADMISSIONS COUNSELORS JOURNAL. 15:24-26, November, 1970.

"Patient values on an adolescent drug unit," by E. L. Burke. AMERICAN JOURNAL OF PSYCHOTHERAPY. 24: 400-410, July, 1970.

"Patterns of drug use in school-age children," by H. B. Randall. JOURNAL OF SCHOOL HEALTH. 40:296-301, June, 1970.

"The pediatrician and the marijuana question," by V. A. Dohner, et al. PEDIATRICS. 45:1039-1040, June, 1970.

"The pediatrician and the marijuana question," by C. H. Gleason. PEDIATRICS. 45:1037, June, 1970.

"The pediatrician and the marijuana question," by Johnson, et al. PEDIATRICS. 45:1037-1038, June, 1970.

"Pep pills common in secondary schools," by C. Moorehead. TIMES (London) EDUCATIONAL SUPPLEMENT. 2895:6, November 13, 1970.

"Pep pills for youngsters; treatment of hyperactive children in Omaha." U.S. NEWS AND WORLD REPORT. 69:49, July 13, 1970.

"Pills for classroom peace?" by E. T. Ladd. SATURDAY REVIEW OF LITERATURE. 53,47:66-68+, November 21, 1970.

"A preventive package kids can relate to." SCHOOL MANAGEMENT. 14,4:25+, April, 1970.

"The pursuit of purity; a defensive use of drug abuse in adolescence," by W. R. Flynn. ADOLESCENCE. 5,18:141-150, Summer, 1970.

"The school nurse and drug abusers," by K. K. Caskey, et al. NURSING OUTLOOK. 18:27-30, December, 1970.

"Secret rules no hindrance for physicians to register young drug addicts," by R. Rooseniit.

YOUTH AND DRUGS (cont'd.)
LAKARTIDNINGEN. 67:3356-3359, July 22, 1970.

"Special report: 17th national AORN congress. Tells causes of teen-drug abuse; suggests way to combat problem," by J. T. Ungerleider. HOSPITAL TOPICS. 48:101+, May, 1970.

"Speed kills; the adolescent methedrine addict," by R. R. Rodewald. PERSPECTIVES IN PSYCHIATRIC CARE. 8:160-167, July-August, 1970.

"TV soliloquies help young drug users." TODAY'S HEALTH. 48:64-65, April, 1970.

"Teacher evaluation of the school drug education program," by D. Pargman. SCHOOL HEALTH REVIEW. 1:14, April, 1970.

"Teenage heroin epidemic that has alarmed the US," by V. Brittain. TIMES (London). p. 11, March 13, 1970.

"Teenagers take over a slum, to quit heroin," by V. Waite. DAILY TELEGRAPH. p. 17, April 10, 1970.

"Ten drug abuse films; what students and professionals think of them." EDUCATIONAL PRODUCT REPORT. 3,7:16-27, April, 1970.

"Toward an understanding; youth drug use and abuse," by E. A. Larson. JOURNAL OF THE LOUISIANA MEDICAL SOCIETY. 122:6-10, January, 1970.

"Training teachers to deal with drugs." SCHOOL JOURNAL. 118:258-261+, May, 1970.

"Use of the television monologue with adolescent psychiatric patients," by H. A. Wilmer. AMERICAN JOURNAL OF PSYCHIATRY. 126:1760-1766, June, 1970.

"Workshop on 'The adolescent in my practices,' the pediatrician's view," by C. Pincock. WOMAN PHYSICIAN. 25:93, February, 1970.

"The young drug scene," by J. Tweedie. GUARDIAN. p. 9, July 6, 1970.

YOUTH AND DRUGS (cont'd.)
"The youngest addict...and ways to recognize him."
EMERGENCY MEDICINE. 2:28, September, 1970.

"Youngsters and drugs; making sense of what's happening." BETTER HOMES AND GARDENS. 48:34+,
October, 1970.

"Youth and drugs," by C. E. Guernsey. JOURNAL OF THE
MISSISSIPPI STATE MEDICAL ASSOCIATION. 11:595-
598, November, 1970.

"Youth care and the new treatment model; the thera-
peutic society--an alternative for us?" by B.
Goransson, et al. LAKARTIDNINGEN. 67:3191-3198,
July 8, 1970.

"Youth drug witch hunt," by S. Gormely. TIMES (London). p. 4, February 23, 1970.

"Youth looks at drug use and abuse," by A. Marticelli.
JOURNAL OF THE NEW YORK STATE SCHOOL NURSE-TEACHER
ASSOCIATION. 1:39-40, June, 1970.

"Youth and drugs," by C. E. Guernsey. JOURNAL OF THE
MISSISSIPPI STATE MEDICAL ASSOCIATION. 11:595-598,
November, 1970.

"Youth care and the new treatment model: the therapeutic
society--an alternative for us?" by B. Goransson,
et al. LAKARTIDNINGEN. 67:3191-3198, July 8, 1970.

"Youth drug witch hunt," by S. Gormely. TIMES (London).
p. 4, February 23, 1970.

"Youth looks at drug use and abuse," by A. Marticelli.
JOURNAL OF THE NEW YORK STATE SCHOOL NURSE-TEACHER
ASSOCIATION. 1:39-40, June, 1970.

AUTHOR INDEX

Abelson, P.H., 43, 76, 109
Abrahams, M.J., 53, 117
Abrams, A.L., 98, 102, 129, 185
Abruzzi, W., 129, 155
Adam, C., 101, 163
Adam, K.S., 51
Adam, W.R., 21
Adler, N., 86
Alan, R., 57, 136
Albo, D., Jr., 24, 35, 65
Alexander, M., 152, 156
Allen, V.R., 71, 183
Alley, F.D., 111, 151
Alsop, R.F., 106, 175
Ambrose, M.J., 112, 138
Amo, M.F., 31, 32, 97
Anderson, E.D., 26, 38, 144
Andriole, V.T., 36, 66
Angel, K., 99, 113, 185
Anggard, E., 17, 45, 71
Angrist, B.M., 104
Anumonye, A., 12, 24, 116, 125, 178
Aronoff, L.S., 1
Astor, G., 81, 183
Aubrey, R., 186
Aubrey, R.F., 115
Auerbach, R., 88, 89
Azen, E.A., 21, 37, 115

Backhouse, C.I., 44, 179
Baerg, R.D., 29, 35, 159
Bailly-Salin, P., 96, 158
Bainborough, A.R., 35, 40
Bainbridge, J.G., 17, 84
Baldwin, M., 114
Ball, G.G., 24, 25, 70
Ball, J.C., 1, 11, 35, 95, 120, 121, 146
Banner, L., 39, 133
Barak, K., 16
Baron, C., 140, 152
Baron, C.J., 155
Barrins, P.C., 50, 82, 180, 184

Barron, S.P., 31, 87
Barták, K., 65
Bartholomew, A.A., 13, 14
Baruk, H., 68, 139, 143
Battegay, R., 85
Battig, K., 32, 39, 116
Bauer, A., 52, 167
Bauer, G., 41, 87, 135
Baumann, F., 82, 150, 184
Beahm, M.R., 141, 172
Becker, H.S., 1
Beckelhymer, H., 72
Bejerot, N., 1, 159
Bell, J.N., 81, 149
Bellizzi, J.J., 92, 94
Benakis, A., 19, 46, 158
Benforado, J.M., 54
Benion, R.E., 63, 65
Bennett, J.C., 1
Bensoussan, P.A., 69
Bentsson, U., 20, 21
Berfins, J.I., 154
Bergel, F., 1
Bergstrom, I., 56
Berzins, J.I., 41, 80
Bewley, T.H., 115, 153, 161, 170
Birch, A.W., 34, 147
Bird, T.D., 142, 176
Birdwood, G., 1, 60, 136
Bisgeier, G.P., 118
Bishop, J., 105, 106
Bittner, J.R., 31, 32, 97
Blachly, P.H., 1
Black, J., 19, 160
Black, S., 123
Blais, N., 74
Blake, J.B., 1
Blake, L., 51, 114
Bloomfield, J.C., 11, 126, 132
Bloomquist, E.R., 84
Blum, S., 98, 102
Boe, S., 60
Bonafede, D., 93, 113, 138

189

Yacoub, M., 15, 43, 109, 160
Yanagita, T., 24, 47
Yeger, S., 175
Yellen, B., 16, 48
Yolles, M., 100, 144
Yolles, S.F., 56, 100, 144
Yorke, C., 41
Yurick, S., 78, 130
Yuste Grijalba, F.J., 74

Zane, M., 171
Zanowiak, P., 64, 126, 156
Zelson, C., 77, 79, 149, 177
Zukerstatter, M., 45, 47, 84,
   167